CHILDHOOD YEARS

A Memoir

Jun'ichiro Tanizaki

Translated by
Paul McCarthy

KODANSHA INTERNATIONAL
Tokyo and New York

Jacket illustration: *Paradise under the Sea*, by Aoki Shigeru (1907), courtesy of the Ishibashi Museum of Art, Ishibashi Foundation, Kurume. The scene shows Hikohohodemi in the sea god's palace (described by Tanizaki in his section on *kagura*).

The photograph of Tanizaki's parents is reproduced with permission from Chuo Koron-sha. The one of "Tomomori with the anchor" is the property of Yoshida Chiaki.

This translation is based on the text of *Yosho jidai* in volume seventeen of Tanizaki's collected works, published by Chuo Koron-sha, 1966–68.

Publication was assisted by a grant from the Japan Foundation.

LCC 89-8213
ISBN 0-87011-924-9
ISBN 4-7700-1424-4 (in Japan)

First edition, 1988
First paperback edition, 1989

Introduction

Tanizaki Jun'ichiro (1886–1965) was without question one of the giants of twentieth-century Japanese literature. His productive career spanned the three modern imperial eras of Meiji, Taisho, and Showa, extending over half a century. Toward the end of his life, he was regarded as a prominent candidate for the Nobel prize, an award that was in fact not given to a Japanese author until three years after Tanizaki's death. Nonetheless, his reputation is secure. In the course of a career as extraordinarily prolific as it was long, he won both critical praise and wide popularity. The major awards of the Japanese literary world were his; his writings were serialized in the most widely circulated and highly respected newspapers and journals, and published by the most prestigious firms; many reached a vast audience through adaptation to the screen. A number of his principal works have appeared in translation in a variety of languages.

Tanizaki is known in Japan, first and foremost, as a novelist, and it is entirely appropriate that he was introduced to the West through translations of some of his most important fictional writings: notably, "A Portrait of Shunkin," "The Bridge of Dreams," and "A Blind Man's Tale" among others included in *Seven Japanese Tales* (translated by Howard S. Hibbett); *Naomi*, *The Secret History of the Lord of Musashi*, and *Arrowroot* (translated by Anthony H. Chambers); *Some Prefer Nettles* and *The Makioka Sisters* (translated by Edward G. Seidensticker); and *The Key* and *Diary of a Mad Old Man* (Hibbett). Other splendid works of fiction remain untranslated: *Manji* (even the interpretation of whose title presents problems—"fylfot," "swastika," "maelstrom," "whirlpool"); *The Mother of Captain Shigemoto*; and *The Cat, Shozo, and Two Women*, for example.

But there are other genres in which Tanizaki, a very catholic writer, also worked successfully: drama, literary criticism, informal essays (one splendid example of which has appeared in English: the Harper–Seidensticker translation of *In Praise of Shadows*), and autobiographical writings. In this last category, the longest and finest example is the present work, *Yosho jidai*, or *Childhood Years*. It appeared serially in the popular literary-cultural monthly *Bungei shunju* from April 1955 to March 1956, and is a memoir of childhood by the distinguished author, then entering his seventies.

From the standpoint of biographical study, there is a problem, of course, for we have no way of knowing how accurate or truthful some of Tanizaki's recollections may be. They may well tell us more about the man who writes them in his seventies than about the boy whose sensations, emotions, observations, attitudes, and actions are described. Certainly the reader will in some instances feel that little Jun'ichiro as portrayed in this memoir was an unnaturally precocious child, especially in his inner reactions to outward events. Moreover, the reader of Tanizaki's other works will not fail to experience the pleasure of recognition when he comes across certain favorite themes and motifs familiar to him from the fictional writings. These, recurring again and again in the author's works, are here seen to make their first appearance in his early life.

The central Tanizakian themes of woman as mother, as *femme fatale*, and as harlot are obviously present in *Childhood Years*. The figure of Jun'ichiro's mother, O-seki—beautiful, sensuous, nurturing yet sometimes distant—is central to the first part of the memoir, and alluded to throughout. Similar figures appear elsewhere in Tanizaki's fiction: examples that come to mind are the mother in *Haha wo kouru ki* (Longing for My Mother, 1919), Tsumura's mother in *Arrowroot* (1930), and the ambiguously overlapping mother figures in "The Bridge of Dreams" (1959). In all of these, maternal tenderness, sensuous beauty, and distance or absence—often in the radical form of death—are combined.

The *femme fatale* makes her appearance in *Childhood Years* in the form of Hanai O-ume, a Yanagibashi geisha who stabbed her lover to death with a kitchen knife. (She has an opposite number in Gozeume Kono, who was strangled and slashed by her common-law husband, then tossed over the embankment at Ochanomizu. Even though she was the victim in this crime, the popular dramatists who seized upon the incident managed to make her the true villain, responsible for driving her usually mild-mannered husband to these desperate measures by her shrewish temperament and vicious tongue.) In his fiction, Tanizaki often depicts dangerous, destructive (though seldom actually homicidal) females: the sado-masochistic heroine of "The Tattooer"; the evil Lady Nan-tzu, wife of Duke Ling of Wei, in "Unicorn"; and the redoubtable Lady Kiyo in the *The Secret History of the Lord of Musashi*, as well as many others.

Harlots too are occasionally seen in *Childhood Years*: those attractive young women in the dubious archery stalls near the Tanizaki Printers, or the imagined courtesans on whose activities Jun'ichiro and his friend model their notorious "basket game," thus earning for themselves the title of "lechers" at school. If we extend the meaning of the word "harlot" to include not only prostitutes but loose women, kept women, and café waitresses who make themselves available to their customers, there are so many in Tanizaki's fiction that one can hardly begin to list them.

Apart from these central images of women, Tanizaki displays other erotic concerns. There is in some of his works a rather ambivalent interest in homosexuality which also appears in this memoir, in the persons of the threatening young men who lie in wait for little boys in dark places, and the middle-aged men of insinuating manner who promise Jun'ichiro sweets and toys if only he will come away with them, and even, perhaps, in the imposing figure of the Imperial Army officer from a noted Kyushu family who parades about Tokyo for several hours with the terrified Jun'ichiro in his arms.

Coprophilia also is present in some of Tanizaki's fictional writings: little boys are forced to consume various revolting substances by their "queen," a formerly much-bullied, now completely dominant girl playmate, in the early story *Shonen* (Children); and the "mad old man" who is the protagonist of a very late work is only one in a long line of foot fetishists who express devotion to their mistresses in their own idiosyncratic way. In *Childhood Years*, we have the account of primary-school teachers whose care for their charges suffering from colds and runny noses takes a peculiarly direct and arresting form.

Examples could be further multiplied, but the point is that there are striking continuities between the tastes, interests, passions, and obsessions of the mature Tanizaki as revealed in his fiction and the incidents recounted in this memoir. The question, of course, is whether the autobiographical reminiscences are accurate accounts of past events which have cast their shadows forward in Tanizaki's long life, or whether the aged author reads back into his childhood the favorite literary themes of a lifetime. It is a question which by the nature of things can hardly be settled with certainty, though common sense would suggest that there are elements of both processes at work. Regarding verifiable matters of fact, accounts of the same event given by Tanizaki and his contemporaries generally agree on essential points, although they may differ as to details of time and circumstance. At any rate, the reader does not, I think, have a sense of being gulled. Tanizaki gives an impression of straightforwardness in his autobiographical writings—certainly he does not hesitate to reveal unpleasant or unflattering aspects of his own character.

His rather macabre sense of humor, which irradiates novels like *Diary of a Mad Old Man* and *The Secret History of the Lord of Musashi,* finds an outlet also in *Childhood Years,* not only in his accounts of comically embarrassing episodes but perhaps above all in startling shifts and juxtapositions: detailed reports of gruesome murder scenes interspersed among descriptions of comic farces; coprophilic details lightly inserted into lovingly elaborated depictions of Meiji costume. As in some of the novels, one can almost hear the author's cackle of glee in the background.

In the last half of the memoir, Tanizaki turns his attention more and more to cultural matters: to his memories of the Meiji Kabuki and of other, less professionalized dramatic forms; to his teachers and classmates in primary school; and to the private lessons in English conversation and classical Chinese to which he was subjected. In these last in particular, the Tanizakian sense of the ridiculous as well as an irrepressible interest in the possibly erotic side of virtually anything come to the fore. He casts a cold eye at the rigidly formalized "reading" of classical Chinese texts, without analysis or commentary, served up by an aged teacher and his young supposed daughter (actually his mistress) together with the after-aroma of the bean-paste soup they have had for breakfast. Nor is he overawed by his English conversation teachers, all of whom are young, female, and more or less attractive, and whom he suspects of following a rather different profession under cover of their pedagogical activities. Not that he is uninterested in English itself: like many Japanese, then as now, he is eager somehow to communicate with foreigners in their own tongue, and is delighted when his initial sally, "You are a pickpocket!" meets with a response demonstrating that it has been understood.

Finally, Tanizaki points out several models of literary style that he employed in his youth and suggests that no longer fashionable methods of learning to write may still have much to teach the aspiring author.

The reader may be interested to know what befell Jun'ichiro in the years immediately following the point where this memoir breaks off. In middle school he continued to be an outstanding student and to produce a variety of poems and essays for the school magazine. Their startlingly wide range of themes is evident from the titles alone: "Literature and Moralism" and "Asia, Arise!" which were essays; and "Song for a Friend," a poem dedicated to a classmate which caused some consternation at school because of an injudicious line—"Deep is the love we pledge each other, as we lie together on one bed."

Financial difficulties, however, forced Tanizaki to seek a position as live-in tutor-*cum*-houseboy with a rich family of restaurateurs. His menial duties rankled, as they always had at home in his childhood years; but he found compensation in the person of one of the housemaids, a girl three years younger than himself, who at some indeterminable point became his first mistress. The discovery of a telltale note led to the dismissal of both from the household when Jun'ichiro was twenty-one and in the second year of higher school. Forced to enter the school dormitory, he managed to make the best of his situation, forming closer friendships with his classmates and leading the pleasant, hedonistic, none-too-demanding life that young Japanese of his age and circumstances enjoyed, and continue to enjoy (for higher school then corresponded more closely to a college than to a high school now). The general picture that emerges of Jun'ichiro at this time is of a jaunty "son of Edo" reading Chikamatsu's plays covertly in lectures; delighting in such traditional townsmen's customs as morning baths followed by tofu breakfasts; keeping up with the news of the Kabuki; and, above all, ostentatiously scorning those among his classmates unfortunate enough to have come from the provinces.

In September 1908 Jun'ichiro entered Tokyo Imperial University, continuing the elite course he had followed from middle school onward. He joined the department of Japanese literature, partly out of natural interest and partly, we are told, because he thought it would be the least demanding course of study, requiring minimal time and effort. But any hopes that he would be able to continue *la dolce vita* were dashed by his impossible financial situation. It became necessary for him to return to live with his family, which suited neither party. Quarrels with his mother and father, and irritation, resentment, and guilt toward a gravely ill sister who was to die of tuberculosis in 1911, combined to precipitate what was then called "neurasthenia." Finally, just when he was due to graduate from the university, he was expelled for that most heinous of offenses, non-payment of tuition fees.

By then, however, he had different goals. He had been writing and submitting short stories and plays to a number of literary magazines. The initial response was rejection, because in these earliest pieces Tanizaki was exploring a highly colored world of aestheticist fantasy and romance. This was not at all calculated to please the editors of the literary journals, who were, almost to a man, Naturalists. This movement—compounded of elements of European-style Naturalism, with its close attention to the grubbier details of everyday life, together with a passion for self-absorbed autobiographical fiction (and, it must be added, a sensitivity to the beauties of nature)—dominated the literary world of late Meiji Japan. Its doyens were no more tolerant of rival literary creeds than are their successors today. An aestheticist like the young Tanizaki would have been as welcome among them as a biographically oriented critic would be now at a conventicle of European Deconstructionists. Reminiscing about the difficulties he faced then, Tanizaki later wrote: "Truly, the arrogance of the Naturalist School at that time was comparable to the dominance of the Proletarian literary group some years ago—they were even fiercer than our Proletarians! . . . One felt that the old saying 'If you are not a Heike, you are not a man' should be amended to 'If you are not a Naturalist, you are not a writer.' "

Nonetheless, after many frustrating rejections, Tanizaki did succeed in getting several pieces published in a small, short-lived, but highly significant magazine called *Shinshicho*, in 1910. The following year, better-known literary magazines like *Subaru* and *Chuo koron* began to carry his writings, and a laudatory article by the eminent anti-Naturalist Nagai Kafu appeared in the pages of *Mita bungaku*, associated with Keio University. The older critic praised Tanizaki's fiction in terms of what he considered to be its three outstanding characteristics: "profound, mysterious beauty arising from carnal terror"; urbanity; and perfection of style. Whatever the precise meaning of that first characteristic may be, it was clearly high praise from a powerful source. The young author was well launched.

The following years and decades were filled with literary endeavor and erotic adventure, with illnesses and recoveries, marriages and divorces. But we have followed the road that leads from the childhood years as far as we may. We must leave the young Tanizaki at the threshold of what was to be a most brilliant literary career.

This memoir, though adhering to the chronology of Tanizaki's childhood in a quite straightforward way, nonetheless has an episodic, unstructured quality which may disconcert the Western reader. Partly this is due to the fact that, like many Japanese literary works, it was first written for serialization in a magazine; partly it is because the Japanese reader does not expect a tightly organized text, with a clear-cut beginning, middle, and ending. There is a long and respected tradition of writing *zuihitsu* (literally "following the pen") informal essays, travel accounts, diaries, and commonplace books, in which the structure may be chronological, or associative, or based on seasonal reference, rather than formally logical. In this work, Tanizaki uses both chronological and associative methods appropriate to a memoir, a book of reminiscences.

No attempt has been made by the translator to tamper with Tanizaki's structure—no major transpositions of whole sections of text have been made. Occasionally, for the sake of greater English readability, sentences have been transposed, but even this has been done rarely. However, it has been found necessary to make some cuts in the text, especially of place and personal names which, though significant to Tanizaki and at least a portion of his original readership, would hardly be intelligible to the audience this translation is intended for. It would not be of consuming interest to the foreign reader to know the name of the Tanizaki family physician, who is not otherwise noteworthy or famous, for example, or the precise route taken to reach a particular shop in Shitamachi, especially when the place names and landmarks have by now been obliterated by the depradations of earthquake, war, and modernization. The reader who needs and wishes to know every such detail is directed to the original text, as reprinted in volume seventeen of the collected works of Tanizaki published by Chuo Koron-sha, 1966–68, which was the basis for this translation.

A few notes on Japanese conventions are called for. The Japanese dating system is different from, and more complex than, the Western one. Since 1868, dates have been given in terms of the reigns of the three modern emperors: Meiji (1868–1912), Taisho (1912–26), and Showa

(1926 to the present). During the Tokugawa or Edo period (1603–1868) when the Tokugawa shoguns ruled from the city of Edo (present-day Tokyo), dates were given in terms of relatively short eras, which did not neatly correspond either to the reigns of the emperors in Kyoto or to the periods of rule of the various shoguns in Edo. The potential for confusion in the pre-modern system was, and is, great. The decision was made, therefore, to convert all dates into the uniform Western system for the sake of simplicity. Occasionally this gives rise to minor inaccuracies: thus, the second decade of Meiji actually corresponds to 1878–87, but it would be given in the text as the 1880s. Similarly, the Kyoho era within the Edo period corresponds to 1716–35; it would be given as early to mid-eighteenth century. The only "raw" Japanese chronological terms with which the reader is burdened, then, are Edo and Meiji—a very light burden indeed when compared with the original text.

Again, there are differences in the traditional computing of ages in Japan and the West. A Japanese baby is regarded as one year old at the time of its birth, and gains a year at each New Year's. Usually this means a discrepancy of one or two years with the Western system. In Tanizaki's case, he would be counted as two years old on his birthday in July 1887 when he would just have become one according to the Western system. (At the following New Year's he would of course become three, though still one by our count.) Thus, one or two years should be mentally subtracted from people's ages as given in *Childhood Years* to get an idea of how old they would be in the West. It is not possible to be sure, of course, without knowing a person's precise date of birth.

Finally, regarding names: surnames precede personal names in Japan and East Asia generally. Tanizaki is the family, and Jun'ichiro the personal name. The Japanese order has been preserved throughout this translation (except on the cover and title page). A further complication is provided by the habit of taking literary and artistic names as well. Tanizaki, as it happens, did not do this, and so is almost always referred to by his family name; but some other literary figures (Nagai Kafu and Natsume Soseki, for example) are called by their literary sobriquets rather than their surnames. A further refinement occurs in the world of Kabuki where an actor assumes a succession of stage names, reflecting the point he has reached in his career. Some of the actors referred to in the text have had two or three different stage names, and Tanizaki usually provides them all so as to identify clearly the person in question. This translation provides the various names included in the original text for major actors only.

I would like to thank Professor Howard S. Hibbett of Harvard University, my dissertation director, who first aroused my interest in Tanizaki; Mrs. Tanizaki Matsuko, the author's widow, who gave her kind permission for, and generous cooperation with, this project; Mr. Stephen Shaw, my editor at Kodansha, who was from the first an enthusiastic supporter of the idea and throughout a helpful, sympathetic critic of the translation; and Mrs. Moriyasu Machiko, who conscientiously checked the entire work for accuracy.

I would like to acknowledge the generous financial assistance of the Japan Foundation, the Fulbright Program, and Surugadai University in connection with various aspects of the translation project.

This translation is dedicated to the memory of my mother, and to Mrs. Tanizaki.

Paul McCarthy
Tokyo, 1988

The author, aged four.

My earliest memories

I have two or three memories that seem to be from the time when I was four or five. But it is not an easy task to determine which of these is the very earliest. People usually begin to have fairly clear memories from about the age of five; there are some who remember things from their fourth year, but they are comparatively rare. And hardly anyone can retrieve much of his third year—apart from Yoshitsune as portrayed in the "Kumagai's Camp" scene. At any rate, though I am not absolutely certain I was four at the time, I recall that one day long ago I was riding in a rickshaw, being jounced about on my mother's lap; we came to a place in the Yanagihara section of the downtown Kanda district, a red-brick building, still unusual in late nineteenth-century Japan. We got down from the rickshaw and entered the doorway, to find Father seated at a counter with a grille in front. Mother and I bowed and greeted him from the entrance—all this I recall, vaguely to be sure, yet not as something in a dream but as reality. My memories are of the appearance of the red-brick building, the expression on my father's face, the counter with its grille, the raised threshold of the tatami room beyond, and the fact that the weather was fine. I do not remember what I or my mother or father were wearing, or what season it was. Yet, for some reason, I know that the office was in the Yanagihara section of Kanda, and that this was in the period when my father was running a lamp-lighting company. Probably my mother and my wet nurse told me these things at the time. Still, I have long puzzled over where Mother and I had been coming from that day: whether perhaps we were living with my father at Yanagihara and had just returned from a trip to some shrine, or from a visit to the main family home in Nihombashi's Kakigara-cho district. Anyway, since my memories of the place in Yanagihara are limited to this fragment of one day (like a single frame from a scene in some film) I suspect they date from my fourth year, and may well be my "very earliest." When, in preparation for writing this memoir, I asked my youngest and only surviving uncle and my late cousin about these matters, they told me that the building in Yanagihara was chiefly my father's place of business, not our residence; and that we were then living at the main house in Kakigara-cho, with Father commuting daily.

At the Kakigara-cho house we lived under the roof of my maternal uncle Tanizaki Kyuemon, who had become head of the family after the death of my grandfather, who was also named Kyuemon. Grandfather died at the age of fifty-eight, in 1888, when I was three; his wife lived till 1911, dying at seventy-three. I regret that Grandfather could not have survived even one or two years longer, so that I might have at least some vague recollections of him. It is shortly after his death that my memories begin. As a result, I have no direct knowledge of him at all; yet it sometimes seemed as if he were living hidden away in some dark corner of the house, since Grandmother and everyone else talked about "the grand old man" on various occasions—which was natural, since he had single-handedly made the Tanizakis prosperous in the course of one generation, and had remained healthy and active until only a short time before his death.

Grandfather was very fond of me, his last grandchild; and sometimes in later years I suddenly felt I could hear his voice calling my name— "Jun'ichi, Jun'ichi," as he had during my earliest years, while he was still alive. A much-enlarged photograph of him was always prominently displayed in our house, so I got to know his face well, and could call it to mind and so encounter Grandfather whenever I wished.

Long afterward, when I first got hold of the biography of the dramatist Kawatake Mokuami by his adoptive grandson and saw a photo of him, I was amazed at how very much he resembled my grandfather, in facial features, general build, and even the way he wore his kimono. But I suppose most elderly gentlemen who were around sixty in the 1890s may have had that look about them.

My parents, grandmother, and uncles and aunts—all those who surrounded me in the Tanizaki household—regarded Grandfather as a model to be emulated in every difficulty or complication that arose. According to Mother and Grandmother, everything he planned turned out wonderfully well. He himself had often said, "You just wait and see— I'll become so grand I'll be riding in a carriage one of these days!" And everyone was sure it would have been so, if only he had lived a bit longer. Grandfather had started out as head clerk of a pot and kettle maker called

Kamaroku, in Kamayabori on the bank of the Onagi River in the Fukagawa district. When the Meiji Restoration in the late 1860s threw Edo into turmoil, the master of the shop fled the city with his whole family, leaving Grandfather in charge of everything. He managed so well during this difficult time that, when peace returned, the owner showed the highest appreciation for his services. Then, taking advantage of the temporary decline in prices of land and houses during the "Ueno War," he bought for a hundred *ryo* an inn at Reiganjima in Kyobashi, called the Manazurukan. He managed the inn for only a brief period, handing it over to his second daughter's husband. Grandfather then built a house at No. 14, Kakigara-cho 2-chome, Nihombashi, where the Ginza, or Silver Mint area, had formerly been. And there he set up a print shop—the Tanizaki Printers; it was in the parlor of this traditional godown-style building, with its signboard carefully inscribed in formal characters by a well-known calligrapher, that I was born.

If as early as the 1880s my grandfather had shifted from such old-fashioned businesses as kettle maker and innkeeper to one as up-to-date as printing and publishing, it was probably the result of a conscious decision to keep abreast of the latest developments in that age of "progress and enlightenment." Walking from the print shop toward Kakigara-cho 1-chome, one passed through the rice merchants' district, with dealers' shops lining the road on either side. My grandfather had adopted a young man into the family as a husband for Hana, his eldest daughter, and the new husband, who took the name Tanizaki Kyubei, was entrusted with a rice store called the Yamaju, just across the street from the dealers' exchange. In the family, we used to refer to the main house in 2-chome as "the printer's" or simply "the main shop," and to Uncle Kyubei's place as "Yamaju" or "the rice shop." In addition, there was a branch office of the printer's in the lane behind the Icho Hachiman Shrine, still to be found on Yoroibashi Street. Grandfather had chosen to locate his printing establishments near the rice merchants' quarter because he thought it might be highly profitable to publish news of the daily fluctuations in the price of rice every evening for sale to the dealers. There were still very few newspapers then, and certainly no evening editions; and Grandfather's plan succeeded wonderfully. The "Tanizaki Daily Price List," as the sheets were known, made a lot of money for the print shop; and, in effect, Grandfather had established his own small-scale evening paper.

He also devised a plan for a lamp-lighting firm, employing a number of men to go about lighting the oil lamps that provided nighttime illumination. His staff was fairly small, so the area in question was probably only a small section of the downtown merchant and tradesmen's district commonly referred to as Shitamachi. The men were for the most part people known to my grandfather—many of them former samurai who found themselves down on their luck in the new Meiji era, men who were poor but of respectable family and character. These lamplighters were garbed in a distinctive coat, with tight-fitting trousers underneath. The coat had on its back the red globe of the sun with rays spreading from it, like the Japanese naval flag, but with the characters for "lamp-lighting" set in the middle of the globe. As evening came, the lamplighters would begin to move along the streets with their small ladders. Carefully setting them beneath each lamp, they would climb up and, opening the little glass window, light the small reserve of oil. Gas was available in a limited area of Tokyo at this time, but oil was still generally used for lamps. In the morning, the men would again set off with their ladders, this time to clean and service the lamps.

After Grandfather's death, the lamp-lighting concern was entrusted to my father, who, having failed to make a go of it, sold it to someone outside the family. The printer's, on the other hand, continued to prosper under the able hands of Uncle Kyuemon (who had taken Grandfather's name). After I became a novelist, I was often asked how it happened that someone born into a Shitamachi merchant family should have set his heart on literature. I can only surmise that Grandfather's printing and publishing business, which with its daily price lists had at least a tenuous connection with letters, may have had some influence on me. The whir and clatter of the presses daily filled my ears from my infancy; and I remember watching Uncle Kyuemon sit waiting for the latest market news each day so that he could rush his article to press. The print shop itself was in the old godown, but my uncle's office was in a Japanese-style parlor to the rear. There he would place his desk near the veranda facing the garden and, with a large flecked-lacquer box for writing paper at his side, work away at composing his articles and correcting proofs. I have no idea how well my uncle or the shop assistants could write. Since he had been sent off at a very early age to work as an apprentice in the shop of a rich Fukagawa merchant, he obviously had no chance to receive much formal education. I remember that when I was about ten the head clerk at the printer's called the younger employees together to show them a slightly difficult character which he had looked up in the dictionary. "Do you know this one, boys? It says you read it *kusamura!*" he informed them, laboriously writing out both the character and its "reading" on a sheet of paper. I imagine Uncle Kyuemon's learning was on more or less the same level; still, because of the nature of his work, he was surely more skilled in reading and writing than the average merchant of his day. And indeed I recall finding some copies of the *Bungei Club* magazine on a low cupboard in the back parlor and stealthily reading some of the stories they contained. I was captivated by this, my first exposure to adult fiction.

There is another aspect of my character that may owe something to my grandfather's blood. My grandparents first had three daughters, and then four sons in succession. Grandfather doted on his daughters but cared nothing for his sons. As a result, he kept two of the three girls at home, adopting husbands into the family for them and establishing cadet branches. Of the boys, only the eldest was kept at home to become head of the main house; the younger three were all sent away to be raised elsewhere, or even adopted by and married into other families. I've recounted how the eldest daughter Hana was married to Kyubei, who thus became an "adopted son-in-law" of the Tanizakis, and was set up in business at the Yamaju. The third daughter Seki was also provided with an adopted husband, Kuragoro, who was in fact Kyubei's younger brother. (Han, the second daughter, was the only one of the girls to be allowed to marry into another family in the normal way; but since she was provided with the Tanizaki-owned Manazurukan inn as part of her dowry, this too had something of the air of establishing yet another cadet branch about it.) Now it was this couple, Kuragoro and Seki, who were my parents; and though my siblings and I were technically only cousins to Uncle Kyubei's children, our relationship was very much closer than with ordinary cousins, since in fact the fathers on both sides were brothers and the mothers sisters.

Years later, after the Tanizaki Printers had gone bankrupt due to the second Kyuemon's profligate ways; and after my father—ever the bad businessman—had lost all the money he had inherited from Grandfather; with only Kyubei of the Yamaju still managing to prosper at the rice trade, Grandmother would say again and again: "Why did your grandfather have to dote so on the girls, and give all the boys away to strangers?

That's why the family's come to ruin—yes, that's the reason!" The three boys who had been married off used to complain about the unfairness of it too, to both Grandmother and my mother. Obviously, Grandfather was what we called in those days a "feminist"; and the roots of my own "woman-worship" would thus seem to reach very far back.

My father and Uncle Kyubei came from the Ezawa family, who ran a saké shop called the Tamagawaya at the corner of Matsuzumi-cho, where (to put it in terms of the geography of Tokyo two or three decades later than the time I am describing) the trolley used to turn off toward Hongo 3-chome after crossing Manseibashi bridge. It had apparently been a large business with as many as eleven saké warehouses, but in my time no trace of it was left. Now, of course, with the wide roads built after the destruction caused by the Great Kanto Earthquake of 1923 and the bombing raids during World War II, with the bridge itself shifted to a new site and the trolley cars following a totally different route, it is hard to say just where the original site would have been.

Uncle Kyubei's juvenile name had been Jitsunosuke, and my father's Wasuke. Even after they entered the Tanizaki family, they themselves and all their relatives continued to use these childhood names rather than their official, adult ones. As a child, I was often told things about our Tanizaki grandfather, the first Kyuemon, and so felt somehow close to him; but no one ever said a word about my other grandfather, on the Ezawa side. He and his wife both died while my father and uncle were still young, and as a result they didn't know much about them. After my grandparents' deaths, the Tamagawaya was put under the management of a guardian, who took advantage of his situation to misappropriate the shop's funds; so its fortunes inevitably began to decline. Grandfather Kyuemon, who on several occasions had lent money to the Tamagawaya, finally decided to adopt the two Ezawa boys as future husbands for his beloved daughters.

All my father could remember about his childhood at the Tamagawaya was being constantly bullied by that crook of a guardian and living wretchedly with his elder brother through those miserable days. Whenever as a child I heard the verse "Only a poor lad out collecting kegs on a snowy day—but he too is someone's son!" I thought of my father's unhappy boyhood. His position was no better than that of the apprentice in the poem—indeed, as an orphan, rather worse. He told me how he was once sent to deliver kegs of saké to a mansion in Koji-machi on a cold, snowy day: it was so cold that he could continue to walk only by letting his warm urine stream down onto his half-frozen feet.

The closeness of the bonds that united my father and his brother, after enduring such a terrible childhood together and then being adopted into the same family, was evident even to the youngest members of our family. Uncle Kyubei was always protective of his younger brother, whom he called "Wasuke-san"; and my father in turn relied on his "Jittsan" for everything. Especially after Grandfather Kyuemon's death, whenever Father failed in some business matter he would go running to Jittsan, the only person he could absolutely rely on. And Jittsan was always ready to help, without reproaches or recriminations. Yet he must have felt ashamed and embarrassed about this ne'er-do-well brother who was such a disappointment to his wife and mother-in-law. In private, Grandmother was often heard to say things like "Jitsunosuke's a fine young man, but that Wasuke's no good at all. What a mistake it was to bring *him* into the family!"

Mother was five years younger than Father, and they had been married for two or three years when I was born. When I was still a baby, Grandfather set them up in a liquor business, followed later by the lamp-lighting job in Yanagihara. But neither enterprise went well; and Grandfather died without seeing his daughter and son-in-law well established in anything. In fact, when I was five or six, Father, being without employment, was forced to give up his own house and move in for a time with Uncle Kyuemon, sharing one room at the rear of the print shop with Mother and me.

Father and Mother

It must be said, though, that failure in business was only one reason for Father moving his household back to the main family residence; another was the poor state of his health. He had a chronic stomach ailment which may, indeed, have been one of the reasons he did so poorly in his work. I myself have no recollection of him going off for the "cure" at the Shima hot springs in Joshu (present-day Gumma); but I know that he did so, and it must have been a painful period for him. For a native son of Edo who had never moved a step out of the city to leave his young wife behind and go to live in such a backward, out-of-the-way spot was doubtless like

9

receiving a sentence of "banishment to the islands" in feudal times. Admittedly, I have never visited the hot springs where Father spent his months of "exile"; but in the late nineteenth century when transportation was so difficult, it must have been dreadfully remote. Who, I wonder, could have conceived the idea of sending him to such a place? Nowadays Shima is not even particularly well known as a spa for stomach cures, but possibly it was famous for that in those days when medicine was less advanced, just as Kusatsu was. Perhaps (though this is pure conjecture on my part) the family felt that it would be better for Father to be kept away from his wife until he had recovered his health—she was, after all, a famous beauty; and it might have been that Father's excessive affection for his young bride was proving injurious to his health.

All three of Grandfather Kyuemon's daughters—O-hana, O-han, and O-seki, as they were called in the family—seem to have been known for their good looks; but it was generally agreed that O-seki was the most beautiful, followed by O-han, and then O-hana. O-hana, the mistress of the Yamaju, seemed to me as a child quite different from her sisters, with a somewhat forbidding look. Perhaps she took after her father, while her sisters resembled their mother. At any rate, attractive Shitamachi girls at that time were often made the subjects of single-sheet wood-block prints; and my mother O-seki was known as the Ozeki ("champion"—a punning reference to the second-highest rank of Sumo wrestlers) of the "illustrated books of beauties" which also circulated widely.

Much later, I saw one such print by the renowned Kunisada—a portrait of Yasuda Yukihiko's great-grandmother, who had lived only a few blocks away from us. Unfortunately, in my mother's case, though I often heard about the prints from my uncle and cousins, I never actually saw a copy. I remember hearing the story of how the son of a family called Daimo, who were wholesalers of kitchen goods, fell in love with her at first sight and came to ask for her hand. When Grandfather refused, saying "We're not giving her away as a bride—we're going to take in a husband for her!" the Daimo youth actually offered himself for adoption, with a dowry thrown in for good measure.

I've written frequently about the beauty of my mother's face, but in doing so I often wondered if it was not merely a son's partiality—after all, every man thinks his mother beautiful. And it was not only her face: the flesh of her thighs was so marvelously white and delicate that many times when we were taking a bath together, I would find myself looking at her body in amazement. It seemed to me that her skin grew whiter as I looked at it; and its whiteness was not the same as that of the women of today. Women before the turn of the century did not go out much into the light and air: they wrapped their bodies in voluminous robes and lived secluded in rooms that remained dim even at noon. No doubt that explains why their skins were so fair. My mother's skin retained its wonderful fairness until I was a young man of twenty-six or twenty-seven. Then, in the summer of 1911, she lost her eldest daughter, my sister Sono who was only sixteen. Mother had prayed for Sono's recovery throughout the long illness and would gladly have given her own life to save her daughter's. When she died, Mother seemed to age overnight: her hair began to turn white, and her complexion took on a yellowish hue.

Like most women of her day, Mother was of very small stature, barely five feet tall; her hair was jet black but a bit curly at the temples, and this was regarded as a defect.

To my knowledge, Father never left Mother by herself during their later married years, except once when he accepted his brother Jittsan's invitation to visit the shrine at Ise—and that only for two or three nights in all. When, shortly after Mother's death, someone suggested a second marriage to him, he at first laughed and ignored the advice, then answered with some exasperation, "How could I do that to my wife? We spent thirty years together."

Two years after Mother's death, Father suffered the brain hemorrhage that was to kill him. As a favor to me, since we were friends from university days, the late Dr. Sugita Naoki agreed to attend him. One day, standing at Father's bedside, he asked in a low voice, "Your father didn't by any chance ever contract syphilis, did he?" Uncle Kyuemon, who was nearby and overheard the question, immediately replied, "No, never. He's never even been to the Yoshiwara pleasure district." No wonder then that our Yamaju uncle had decided to take Father along with him to Ise, to show a bit of the world to this shy, indecisive man who had never been on a real trip in his life—if we except his visit to the Shima hot springs to take the cure. Even so, Mother was by no means pleased to see the two of them go off by themselves, even for a once-in-a-lifetime trip that was to last only two or three days.

Probably because he had not yet fully recovered his health despite the stay in Shima, Father for a time did no real work, but passed his days idly. I have no clear memories of the Shima visit, but I do vaguely recall that he went to Oiso for a change of air sometime later, and that on this occasion Mother accompanied him. Now, Oiso at that time was a country retreat for distinguished families like the Inoues, the Matsukatas, and the Saionjis: the statesman Ito Hirobumi's villa was located there, for example. Soon the townsmen of Shitamachi, not to be outdone, also began to flock to this seaside resort. It took about two and a half hours by train to get there; but, with the many villas of the rich, it was by no means an out-of-the-way country town like Shima. My parents went there several times in a short period, so they must have enjoyed the elegant atmosphere of the place. I, however, was never taken along, always being left behind in the care of my nurse. It is not hard to see why I should have been regarded as a nuisance by my young parents, intent on having a good time by the sea. Apparently I didn't make much of a fuss about being left behind, for, though I was a very spoiled child in many ways, I had been accustomed from the beginning to go to sleep cuddled in my nurse's arms. I slept with my nurse in a six-mat-sized room on the second floor of the house, which was connected by a steep ladder-staircase with the ten-mat room below in which the clerks and apprentices had their meals. I don't even know where my parents used to sleep,

Tanizaki's parents.

since there were quite a number of rooms in the family quarters behind the print shop, with several different staircases leading to the second-floor rooms, which generally did not open directly onto one another.

I have written about this period of my childhood in a passage in an early work entitled *Haha wo kouru ki* (Longing for My Mother):

> When I lived in Nihombashi, I often heard the sound of a samisen as I lay drowsing in the quilted bedclothes, cuddled to my nurse's breast. "Tempura is what I want, tempura is what I want," she would hum softly in time to the samisen's rhythm. "Doesn't it sound like that to you? Tempura is what I want, tempura is what I want. . . . Doesn't it, Jun'ichi?" And she would peer into my face as my hands pressed against her breast and my fingers played with her nipples. And indeed, as I listened, the samisen seemed to be sadly repeating those very words. The two of us would gaze at each other and listen, silently and intently, to the samisen's notes. The wooden clogs of the strolling musician echoed through the empty, frozen streets with a clear, hollow clop-clop sound as he made his way from Ningyo-cho, past our house, and on toward Komeya-cho. The sound of the samisen grew more and more distant until it seemed about to disappear. "Tempura is what I want, tempura is what I want"— that refrain, once so clear, became thin and blurred, now vanishing entirely, now brought again for a moment to our ears by the night wind. "Tempura . . . tempura is what I want. . . . What I want . . . Tempura . . . tem . . . what I . . . pura's what I . . ." Thus the sound became fragmentary, fading off into the distance. Still I strained to hear, like one who tries to follow with his eyes a spot of light that grows smaller and smaller as it moves into the depths of a tunnel. Even when the samisen seemed to break off entirely, I could still hear for a time a voice whispering in my ear: "Tempura is what I want, tempura is what I want. . . ." Is it the sound of the samisen, I wondered, or just my imagination? Thinking such thoughts, I would begin to sink softly, peacefully, into the depths of sleep.

My nurse, whom I always called "Granny," was born in the Tempo era (1830–44), and was named Miyo. She had worked as a flower and incense seller in front of the Jigen-ji Nichiren temple when it was still in Sarue, Fukagawa, before it moved to its present location in Somei.

(This was the parish temple and interment place of the Tanizaki family, and today guards the graves of Shiba Kokan and Akutagawa Ryunosuke.) One day shortly after my birth Grandfather saw her there and asked her to become my nurse. Later she served as my younger brother Seiji's nurse too; and when our family's reduced circumstances made it impossible to keep a maid any longer, she also did domestic tasks. Granny died in her sixties, when I was twelve or thirteen years old. It may be that my very earliest memories are of her rather than of my mother. Apart from the visit to the office in Yanagihara I described before, my first recollection seems to be of a day when I was about five, when Granny carried me out to the hallway to greet my mother, just back from a trip to Oiso. Father must have been with her, yet oddly I have no recollection of his face—only of Mother's.

I'd been waiting expectantly since early morning, when Granny had announced that Mother would be coming home that day. I remember how she entered from the print shop, sliding open with a clatter the narrow, latticed side door that led to the family quarters behind, and stepping down into the hallway, whose floor was a little lower than the level of the shop. Letting go of Granny's hand, I ran to her crying "Mama!" My memory of this moment is very clear, far more so than that of the visit to Yanagihara, and remains vivid in my mind to this day. It was already dark, and the figure of my mother as she stepped over the door's high threshold and down into the hallway was silhouetted against the lamplight shining from behind. I stretched out my arms and clung to her. I was so small that I could barely reach up to her waist. Her hair, though a little wispy and disordered after her hours of jostling in train and rickshaw, looked fuller and fluffier than usual, seen against the light. "Jun'ichi," she said (or rather, "Jin'ichi," in the Tokyo pronunciation of those days; or, still more accurately, "Jin'chi"), bending down and pressing her cheek against mine. If indeed I was five at the time, then Mother would have been twenty-seven.

The few years around this time would seem to have been the happiest period in my parents' thirty-odd years of married life. They particularly enjoyed the days they spent together in Oiso and often reminisced about them. There were several first-class inns in Oiso—the Toryukan, the Shosenkaku, the Gunkakuro, and the Shorinkan, among others; but it was at the Shorinkan that they always stopped. Sometimes one of Mother's sisters or nieces would come down from Tokyo for a short visit. No doubt partly they just wanted to "keep an eye on O-settchan," but another motive was to spy on the popular Kabuki actor Nakamura Fukusuke, who often stayed at the Toryukan. He was later to take the name Utaemon V, and to become the father of the present Nakamura Utaemon. Old people still talk of him and of the incredible popularity he enjoyed during the days he performed under the name Fukusuke. He far outstripped even Ebizo among contemporary Kabuki actors; and the actors and actresses who dominate the stage and screen today cannot even come close to his degree of celebrity. By the time I began to see the Kabuki regularly he was no longer very young, but, even so, his beauty and elegance as he acted the women's roles were beyond compare. One can imagine, then, how bewitchingly attractive he must have been around the time he stayed at the Toryukan, when he was only twenty-six, a year younger than my mother. Whenever he appeared on the beach, there would be a rush of guests from the various hotels. My mother too was of course one of his great fans; but the most enthusiastic of all was her elder sister O-han. One day she arrived at Oiso with a niece in tow and pleaded with my father to switch hotels: "Oh Wasuke-san, let's move to the Toryukan! What about it, Settchan? Let's go and have a look at the rooms there!"

Pressed by O-han, my mother fell in with the idea. In fact, they were more interested in catching a glimpse of Fukusuke than in examining the available guest rooms. Father too was forced to go along; but as luck would have it, all the good rooms were already taken—only ones facing in the undesirable western direction were left. On top of that, Fukusuke was out. The people at the inn said, "He's probably gone to have some sweet saké at his favorite shop." So the four of them went off to the shop in quest of the elusive Fukusuke. In the end, though, all their efforts came to nothing: they never did see him.

By now Father had taken the family to live at the main house, though not, I think, as Uncle Kyuemon's dependents: Father must have had property and an income of his own, otherwise he would hardly have been able to take his wife for prolonged stays in Oiso. Uncle Kyuemon was four years younger than Mother and still a bachelor, so Father probably felt quite at ease about asking to share the house with him. To me, the main house seemed like my own home, even though I knew that the printer's attached to it belonged to my uncle and not to us. After all, I had been born and partly raised there; and there were no other children, so I was the sole object of my grandmother's and uncle's loving attentions.

Perhaps it would be as well to try here to describe the location of the main house and print shop, and the general features of the neighborhood. Before the war, the trolley line ran from Yoroibashi, turning the corner where the Suitengu Shrine was, and then going along Ningyo-cho Avenue in the direction of Kotemma-cho. To the left, just across from a sweet saké shop which continued doing business until last year, there was a store selling illustrated pamphlets and novelettes called the Shimizuya, and a ceramics shop. If you turned the nearby corner, then walked along the right side of the street for two blocks and turned west, our house would have been the second one you came to. The former Shimizuya has now become a toy shop, and the ceramics place is a maker of sugar-and-soy-flavored foods called the Chitose, with its second floor given over to the Tamahide chicken restaurant. The printer's where I was born is no more, the site now just a vacant lot. On the corner to the west of the old printer's where a shop selling sweet bean soup now stands, there used to be a rice-cake seller that made delicious *sembei* crackers.

The actual print shop was built onto an old storehouse that had been shifted from the old Silver Mint district (the former site of our family business); and it was, I daresay, that original storehouse in which I was born. Viewed from the street, it stood to the right of a two-story plaster-walled building. Passing through the small side door facing the street, above which hung a sign saying "Tanizaki Printers," one found oneself in an earthen-floored passageway with, to the left, printing presses set upon a plank floor, and to the right, beyond a raised threshold, the business office, its floor covered with Okinawan tatami mats. Both the print shop and the business office had windows with iron grilles facing the street, and outside the windows, to left and right, were rain buckets.

The presses were at their noisiest at two or three in the afternoon: after three, the rice exchange emptied, and by four or five o'clock the print shop too grew quiet. After supper the shop assistants would change into fresh, smart-looking clothes and set off to various destinations, leaving only one or two young apprentices to look after the office. I used to wait for this hour, when I could emerge from the family quarters to play games with the apprentices or cling to the window grilles and watch the passersby on the street outside. The spaces between the iron bars were almost wide enough for me to push my face through. Pressing my cheeks against the cold metal bars, I would look up at the second-floor rooms of the Imakiyo beef restaurant opposite. West from the Imakiyo, as far as the alleyway across from the rice-cake shop, stretched a line of archery booths known as *yaba*. These were equipped with small play targets and bows and arrows; but that was just for show—in fact they were very shady establishments, like those that later proliferated in the Junikai-shita and Tamanoi districts. The women inside would call out to male passersby, and some of the men would stop and peer through the glass windows. All this could be seen from the print shop, if one craned one's neck a bit. At the age of five, I didn't find the "archery ladies" either particularly beautiful or ugly; but I did find it odd that the customers spent all their time laughing and talking with the women and never seemed to get around to drawing their bows!

Occasionally there were little incidents: one evening in summer, when it was still fairly light outside, a sexy-looking girl wearing a light yukata was turning off into the alley near the archery booths. A man approached from behind and tailed her for a short distance with his hands stretched out as if he were about to take her around the waist. I was sure he was a criminal bent on some misdeed—that the girl was about to be knocked down, tied up, and carried off. As I watched, holding my breath, the man silently drew his hands back and, with a derisive grunt and an odd smile on his face, went off in the other direction, still unnoticed by the girl.

The Kakigara-cho and Hama-cho districts

When I was about six my father changed jobs for the third time and became a dealer in rice, like my uncle Kyubei. Why a man as simple and straightforward as he would choose to become a rice dealer remains a mystery to me. Perhaps it was just that he was at loose ends, and so rather casually decided to pursue the same occupation as Jittsan, his elder brother. At any rate, he soon failed in this rice-dealing venture; yet even after that he found it impossible to break away from the world of Kakigara-cho and Kabuto-cho, though he never succeeded in becoming a real dealer. In fact, he probably would have been better off carrying on with the liquor shop or lamp-lighting company, despite the difficulties involved. Father's rice shop, called the Marukyu, was located on a back street in the rice dealers' area, in the same part of Kakigara-cho as the

Yamaju; and in the family he was known as "Marukyu-san," even long after the Marukyu shop had gone out of business, just as Uncle Kyubei was always known as "Yamaju-san."

It must have been at about this time that our family moved from the Tanizaki Printers to our own house in Hama-cho. I vaguely remember it as a small two-story structure with a low latticed door giving directly on to the street and a small six-mat parlor beyond the earthen-floored entrance hall. But I have forgotten precisely where the house was located —probably somewhere behind the old, pre-1923 earthquake Meiji Theater. We did not stay in the Hama-cho house long enough for any very significant memories to attach themselves to it, though there was the night when I nearly set the place on fire by bumping into an oil lamp that was hanging from the ceiling of the six-mat parlor, where I was engaged in playing "Benkei the Warrior" with all his seven paraphernalia strapped on my back. My parents got terribly flustered, shouting that, since it was kerosene, water wouldn't help. As the flames began to spread to the papered doors and it seemed that a real conflagration was beginning, my old nurse swiftly wrapped a large cushion in straw matting and managed to beat the fire out. Mother scolded me severely, of course: "Jun-chan—not only could you have burned the house down, you could burn *yourself* to death, playing under a kerosene lamp like that!" Still, I had not in fact been hurt in the slightest, so the thought of a fire wasn't all that horrifying to me, even if the whole house did happen to burn down.

I have no memories of my brother Seiji, who was four years younger than I, until after we moved from Hama-cho to our next house, in Minami Kayaba-cho. During our days in Hama-cho, Seiji would have been very small and so under Mother's direct care, while Granny Miyo would have served as my nurse exclusively. I was the eldest son and the only one whose childhood was passed in a period when the family was fairly well off; as a result I was by far the most spoiled and pampered of the children.

Just as Father commuted daily from the house in Hama-cho to his business in the rice dealers' area, so Mother and I were always going the short distance to the main house in Kakigara-cho to visit Grandmother and Uncle Kyuemon. Originally, to reach the living quarters there, one had to use the main entrance of the print shop, but at some point a separate, narrow rear entrance had been built to the north, near the corner where the rice-cake seller's was. (Our house half surrounded this shop from the north and west.) We would go down a narrow alley across from the Ogawa school, enter a doorway at the far end, and find ourselves facing a room where Grandmother sat before a long brazier. Mother would settle herself across from Grandmother, on the side of the brazier nearest the street entrance, and chat and gossip for hours, with me beside her. Usually I would eat my supper and have my bath there at the main house before going home to be put to bed.

Speaking of mealtimes, I recall that in those days the family did not gather together around a single large table as one would nowadays. Instead, I had my own pretty little table where Granny Miyo would serve me dinner, which I ate alone. I remember especially being given various kinds of beans—black beans, kidney beans, and so on—from a shop called the Horaiya in Yoshi-cho.

Father also usually dropped by the main house on his way home from work to take his evening bath. Sometimes when I was in the bath with him I would take fright at what I saw hanging between his legs, and cry out. Then Father would cover himself with a hand towel, saying "There—it's gone!"

There were two storehouses at the main house. The first, with a kind of guest parlor on the first floor, I have described earlier as a relic of the days when the family business was in the Silver Mint district. The second was built in Grandfather's time and was actually used for storage. It was located in the farthest reaches of the property: to get to it, one had to pass through the little room where Grandmother sat all day before the brazier; then through a room with a formal alcove, which my uncle used as a study; then along a passage which led ultimately to a separate two-story building. There was usually no one about the storehouse except when something was being put into it, or taken out. For the most part, the place was perfectly quiet. I liked to sneak off there by myself and sit on the cold stone steps where no voices broke the silence and even the noise of the print shop was reduced to a dull and distant hum. I would press my face against the gleaming black double-doors, which were covered with wire netting and closed by a large padlock, and try to peer into the dark interior through the crack between them. I didn't know just what was hidden within, but there was a faint, elegant fragrance like aloes and musk mingled with the inevitable smell of damp and mold.

The area in front of the storehouse doors was floored with wood, and just beyond was the entrance to a small annex. It had been built for some purpose or other well after the main house, and its two stories fronted on a small garden. When I was a boy, it was uninhabited and always a place of solitude and silence. I would creep in and with stealthy footsteps explore the second-floor parlor and the six-mat room below, where an icon of the Virgin Mary stood on a low cupboard. I have forgotten who it was that told me about Grandfather's conversion: how in his old age he had become a Christian, keeping it all a secret from Grandmother. (It was, I think, Mother who told me that his final illness was stomach cancer, and that the famous Dr. Baelz had come to the house to examine him.)

According to one of my uncles, and other relatives, Grandfather became a member of the Russian Orthodox Church at Nikolai-do in Kanda; and a priest of that church came to visit him on his deathbed. At that point, a religious argument ensued between the Orthodox priest and a Nichiren Buddhist monk who had also been summoned. After Grandfather's death, the family debated whether the funeral should be held at Nikolai-do or at a Nichiren temple. In the end, the latter won; and Grandfather was interred in the Jigen-ji cemetery as a Nichiren believer. I of course knew nothing of such complications, being just a child; indeed, I did not even know what the Nikolai-do group was. Yet when I looked at the image of the Virgin holding the infant Christ, there was a solemnness different from my emotions when I stood before the family Buddhist altar, as Grandmother and the others recited the sutras morning and evening. Gazing with inexpressible reverence into the Virgin Mother's eyes, so full of tenderness and mercy, I felt I never wanted to leave her side. I understood something of my grandfather's feelings as he prayed before this image of the Western goddess. There was a certain strangeness about it all, yet I sensed that someday I too might well do as he had done.

Even at the busiest, noisiest time of the day, the sound of the printing presses did not penetrate as far as this annex. Its garden was very small and, though there must have been a neighboring house just beyond the high spiked wall, I could not imagine what kind of people might live there, for there was never the slightest sound from that direction. If, however, one went up to the second floor and looked out of the small windows that faced away from the garden, one could sometimes hear a voice chanting parts of a No drama from our neighbors on that side.

The garden connected this annex with the main house, and one could reach the veranda outside my uncle's study by following a series of stepping-stones that meandered through the garden. Every year in December a man would come to cover the trees and shrubs with straw to keep the frost off; he would also spread a carpet of pine needles over everything. I used to enjoy watching this yearly transformation. I also enjoyed running through the wintry garden barefoot, over the pine-needled path from the main house to the annex.

When the weather was fine, Granny often carried me piggyback to various temple fairs and markets—to the Seisho-ko, which was closest to our house in Hama-cho; to the Suitengu in Ningyo-cho; to the O-Kannon, and the Kobo Daishi Temple in Royanohara; and sometimes as far as the Nishi-gashi Jizo beyond Nihombashi Avenue. Of them all I felt most at home at the O-Kannon, since it was right in our neighborhood. I have no idea what it looks like now; but it used to be set back a bit from the street, and numerous toy shops lined both sides of the flagstoned path that led to the Main Hall—like a smaller version of the celebrated Nakamise arcade in front of the Asakusa Kannon Temple. Whenever we went there, I wheedled Granny for some toy or souvenir to take home with me. Once I discovered a splendid toy saber, but Granny was not about to give in easily to my demands for such an expensive present.

"Jun-chan, you'd better have your Mama buy that for you next time. Granny'll get you something else—something real nice!"

"No, no, no, no, no!" I exploded.

"Now don't act like a baby, Jun-chan. Granny doesn't have the money to buy something as expensive as that...."

"No, no, no, no, no!" As I went on screaming, a cat darted from the interior of the shop, sprang at my face, and scratched me on the cheek with its claws. It didn't hurt much, but it left an ugly red mark near my eye, and I cried and screamed even more violently than before. The old lady who ran the toy shop, seeing all this, felt sorry for me and finally sold Granny the saber at a much-reduced price.

There was another quite frightening incident at the O-Kannon. The temple had set up large dolls representing Inuzuka Shino and Inukai Gempachi (two heroes of Bakin's nineteenth-century novel the *Hakken-den*) on the great tiled roof of the Main Hall, which was meant to represent the roof of the Horyukaku in the novel. Granny and I had paid the entrance fee and were making our way up the long staircase to the roof when suddenly the crowd, which had been climbing slowly in the direction of the exhibit, turned and began to push and shove its way down. Granny and I had no idea what had happened, but we found ourselves jostled along by the crowd down the steps, out of the temple, and all the way to the street outside. It was only later that we learned the reason: some people at the head of the line thought that the dolls had suddenly begun to move by themselves, and panicked.

In which section of the Hama-cho embankment was it, I wonder, that Hanai O-ume had her geisha's teahouse, the Suigetsu? When I wrote the tale *O-tsuya koroshi* (The Murder of O-tsuya) I used the area in front of the Hosokawa mansion, on the Sumida River, as the scene of Shinsuke's murder of Santa because that part òf the embankment road, backed by the long earthen wall of the Hosokawa residence, had remained in my memory as a place that was peculiarly lonely and eerie, especially at night. It was in the early summer of 1887 that O-ume killed her lover, a geisha's attendant named Minekichi. He had asked her to meet him near the wall of that same mansion on a night of drizzling rain, and there she stabbed him to death with his own kitchen knife.

Our family moved to the area some years after the notorious incident, but Mother must have known O-ume's face from having seen her when she was in Yanagibashi or at the Suigetsu. After she achieved notoriety through the murder, Mother commented, "She was a very stylish geisha, with a rather dark complexion. But there was always something a bit weird about her. . . . I suppose that's what they must mean when they talk about 'a real woman'!"

The photograph that Mother had given me with the words "This is the famous O-ume!" I kept with the greatest care until the Kanto Earthquake of 1923, when it was lost. And, just looking at the picture, I felt I could understand what Mother meant by her comments on O-ume. She had been twenty-four at the time of the incident. After serving a fifteen-year sentence, she started a small restaurant specializing in sweet bean soup in Asakusa, then worked as a variety-hall entertainer and the like. Once, having heard that she was appearing in a film, I went on purpose just to see her—it must have been near the Opera House. But she did not look at all like the face in the photograph I had at home, though that may have been due in part to the fogginess of the early twentieth-century cinema. Afterward, in the 1910s and '20s, I saw plays about O-ume with various famous artists in the role. However, leaving aside the merits of the acting as such, I never once came across anyone who communicated even a trace of the stylish femininity so characteristic of the Yanagibashi geisha. No doubt it was an unreasonable expectation. At any rate, I regarded that single photograph as more precious than the finest performances of the greatest actors and actresses of the land.

Tanizaki Kyuemon II

We usually referred to the uncle who had succeeded to Grandfather's name and status as "the printer's uncle"; but his childhood name had been Shoshichi, so my grandmother and parents called him simply "Sho-chan." Speaking of ways of referring to family members, I would like to note that Shitamachi families of those days never used "Okusan" (Madam) for the wife of the house, nor "Botchan" and "Ojoosan" (Young Master and Mistress) for the children. Those terms, now standard everywhere, were originally from the more aristocratic uplands of Yamanote. In the Meiji era, we in the Shitamachi lowlands called the wife "Okamisan," and the children of the house by name; this was the case even with the servants. Thus, I was "Jun-chan" to everybody—hardly ever "Botchan." The shift in pronunciation of the terms for father and mother (from "Otottsan" and "Okkasan" to "Otoosan" and "Okaasan") is also a result of the Yamanote influence. The same is true of the terms for brother and sister; when we wished to add the polite "o-" prefix, we said "Oaniisama" and "Oaneesama," not "Oniisan" and "Oneesan."

I remember how my friend at the Tokyo First Middle School, Hosaka Koji (currently head of the Ginza Merchants' Association—the "Lord of the Ginza," as it were), used to say, "When I have a wife, I hope people will call her 'Okamisan'—certainly *not* 'Okusan'!" Actually, until just after the turn of the century, all Shitamachi people rather made fun of Yamanote speech and manners, regarding them as a bit crude and rustic-sounding. No doubt "Ko-chan" shared that view when we were still in middle school; but afterward Yamanote modes of speech gradually threatened to overwhelm Shitamachi, and even the very distinction between the two areas of the city, each with its own ways, tended to be lost. These days, I am sure that even the conservative Mr. Hosaka can no longer insist on his wife being addressed as "Okamisan"—though I regret to say that I neglected the opportunity to confirm this when, last

New Year's, for the first time in many years, I met my old friend, who is now endowed with a magnificent head of hair of the purest white.

But to return to Uncle Kyuemon: judging from some photographs preserved by a cousin of mine, it must have been when I was around five, before our family moved to Hama-cho, that he married. I remember how the shop eaves were hung with paper lanterns and candlesticks glittered in the business office the night the bridal chest was brought in; how I sat on a crimson carpet, dressed in a formal, crested kimono and a *haori* coat of black twilled silk, waiting for the bride to arrive with her entourage. I suppose my uncle had followed the usual practice of people in Kakigara-cho by having both the ceremony and wedding supper at some restaurant like the Hyakuseki (Shinto weddings were not common at the time.) But I cannot be sure, for all I clearly remember is waiting at home for the bridal party's arrival.

I recall how frightened I was when, urged by Mother to "go and see the new bride" on the following morning, I slid open the door of the room where the newlyweds sat: the six-mat parlor with the image of the Virgin Mary, which became the young couple's bedroom from that night on. As I opened the door, the bride, seated facing in my direction, looked straight at me. Given my bashfulness and awkwardness, I am sure I gave her a rather cross look, at the same time staring good and hard in an attempt to find out just what sort of person she might be. She was quite good-looking, if in a rather standard sort of way. She smiled and spoke to me, but I continued to stand there looking ill at ease. Then my uncle, seated beside her, burst out laughing and made some friendly remark to me. That, however, made me even more uneasy, and I turned tail and fled in the direction of the main house, where Mother was.

Uncle Kyuemon was only twenty-three at the time, and his bride Kiku was a year younger; but they say he had been married once before, to a girl from a family in Ta-cho, Kanda, who ran both a fan shop and a mandarin orange wholesalers' business. On the wedding night itself, my uncle discovered that his bride had had a relationship with another man and in a rage carried all his bedding out of the bridal chamber and up to the second floor. It seems that the girl had not been born and raised in the Ta-cho family, but had been taken in when her mother entered it by remarriage. It turned out there were many rumors about her: that she had a passion for actors; that she was too close to her stepfather in Ta-cho, and so on. However, she was a brilliant samisen player; and, after

24

the abrogation of the marriage contract was announced, she is said to have given the Tanizaki household a virtually non-stop ten-day free concert out of pure spite, before finally agreeing to depart!

My guess is that Uncle Kyuemon, who had an eye for beautiful women, had been so taken with her good looks that he had been willing to ignore the rumors about her, at least up to a point. Even when it came to his second marriage, he was bent on finding a beauty: if, while out walking in the city, he came across a girl he thought attractive enough, he would have someone follow her and make inquiries. So of course his new bride, Kiku, was pretty; still, looking back now, I would say she was only slightly above average in looks—certainly not a raving beauty.

Kiku was the "daughter" of Sakurai Kameji, president of the Tokyo Bay Steamship Company at the Shogen embankment in Kyobashi. Mr. Sakurai had acted as guardian of the late company president's widow, and had eventually married her and become president himself. Thus Kiku too, like my uncle's first wife, was not her "father's" child. Nor was she the actual daughter of her "mother's" previous husband—she was in fact a niece or cousin of the president's wife, and had been adopted into the family with the permission of her real father, who was captain of a ship plying the Tokyo–Chiba route. I only visited the Sakurai family house once with my mother—I remember looking out over the bay at Shinagawa from their parlor, so the house was probably very near the steamship company's offices on the Shogen embankment. During our visit, Mr. Sakurai brought out a long telescope for me to survey the bay with, and showed me intricate clocks and music boxes, heavy, richly ornamented photograph albums, and other unusual objects calculated to delight a boy's heart and stir his imagination.

Now Kiku, though like Uncle Kyuemon's first wife in family background, was quite unlike her in being a chaste wife. Yet this marriage too did not last long. The trouble began when my uncle started to learn *gidayu* chant and met a Yanagibashi geisha called O-sumi at his teacher's house in Hama-cho. For reasons that will become clear, I have much sharper memories of O-sumi than of Kiku: frankly speaking, O-sumi had a far more individualized sort of beauty than Kiku. She had a slightly dark complexion and the distinctive smartness of the Yanagibashi geisha. In fact she closely resembled her sister-geisha O-ume, the one who had killed her lover, the attendant Minekichi. Were there perhaps a great many beauties of that same type in Yanagibashi then?

Could it be that the Shitamachi connoisseurs of those days would accept no other type?

Grandfather Kyuemon in his day is said to have kept a mistress at a house in Kakigara-cho 1-chome, without Grandmother's knowing anything about it. Now Uncle Kyuemon did something even bolder, first bringing O-sumi to live on the embankment near the O-Kannon Temple, only a stone's throw away, and then introducing her into the main house to share it with his wife. Kiku endured all this with admirable calm and patience, and so for a time the three of them—husband, wife, and mistress—slept side by side. Since Grandmother was still living, Uncle Kyuemon no doubt lacked the courage actually to reject his legal wife. But one day, after this strange situation had gone on for some time, a message came from the Sakurais, asking Kiku to "come home for a while." Off she went, as if nothing were the matter; but she never returned. My uncle sent people to fetch her back two or three times, but the Sakurais would have none of it. He and Kiku had lived together barely three years—if only they had had even one child during that time, perhaps the marriage could have been saved. We heard later that she remarried into a family in Shiba, but what her life was like after that I do not know. Our last contact with her was one evening in Ningyo-cho Avenue during the Suitengu Shrine fair, when Mother heard a voice call her and turned to find it was Kiku. The two of them stood for a long time in the light of the small hanging lanterns, talking of the past, and crying.

Finally I must mention Kiku's set of court dolls. I have forgotten if it was the night she arrived at our house, or the first Girl's Day Festival following the wedding. At any rate, the bride's full set of court dolls arrived one day from the Sakurais. I remember it particularly because the display was so lavish. Mounted on a large base covered with oilcoth, the set was carried to our house by several men from the Sakurais and transferred to the hands of our shop clerks who carried it into the family quarters. I still remember how the elegant dolls representing the imperial couple and the rest of the court were arranged within the model of the palace, with its massive, imposing roof. I had never seen such a gorgeous set before.

However, it has always been the custom in both eastern and western Japan for families who care about such things to avoid displaying a dolls' set that includes a *roofed* palace. The palace itself is not unlucky, but showing its roof is: the family that does so will be ruined. In such cases, then, the roof is always left off. Could it be that both the Sakurais and the Tanizakis were ignorant of this taboo? Or that they decided to disregard it as a foolish superstition? Whichever it was, the threatened punishment did indeed fall upon the Tanizaki household; for, some ten years later, Uncle Kyuemon faced utter ruin.

Our first house in Minami Kayaba-cho

We lived at the house in Hama-cho for only a few months, moving to No. 45, Minami Kayaba-cho, sometime before the autumn of 1891. A glance at a recent (February 1953) map of Chuo Ward reveals that a number of wide roads now crisscross the area that was formerly Minami Kayaba-cho, so it is hard to determine just where either our first or our second house was. It would be easier if I could investigate the area on foot, but that is quite impossible, given my present physical state; so I shall have to rely on a comparison of maps, old and new, for this section of my memoirs. Even the name "Minami (South) Kayaba-cho" has disappeared, replaced by mere "Kayaba-cho," which is divided into both *chome* ("blocks") and *banchi* ("lots"). We had only *banchi*, and their numbering was completely different from today's. Even the positions of the bridges in the area have shifted, so it is difficult to fix any landmarks at all. The patterns of change have sometimes been complex: I remember being told as a child that there had originally been a ferry-crossing where Yoroibashi bridge then was; now the bridge is gone again, torn down because of dilapidation and replaced with the new Kayababashi bridge further downstream. Thus in a sense we have come full circle, back to what things were like in the old days, before I was born.

Coming from the direction of Koami-cho, at the point where the old Yoroibashi bridge crossed the river, you saw the Kabuto-cho stock exchange on the right. The first road to the left was called Kayaba-cho "Front Street," while the next, parallel to it, was "Back Street." Going south along Front Street for one or two blocks, you came to a shop on the right-hand corner called Namikawa, which made and sold bicycles and baby carriages. Turning right and going straight until you emerged on Back Street, you found a seller of bags and pouches called Katsumi on the northeast corner; our house was the second one to the east of the opposite, southeast corner.

We were no more than a block or so from the former site of the Hie and Tenmangu shrines and the Yakushi Temple, now all transferred elsewhere; and right next door to us was the Homero Western-style restaurant which pioneered the so-called "Eurasian box-lunch," combining various Western foods with steamed rice, all served in special chinaware containers. The "Eurasian box-lunch" was a clever idea, the Kabuto-cho business district being so near; and the Homero did very well for many years, though whether or not it is still in business today I do not know.

Next door to Katsumi was the Ashidas' house, quite large and surrounded by a stone wall. They had a son about my own age and were from the Kansai area, around Kyoto and Osaka. One day when Mrs. Ashida came to call and was chatting with Mother, I heard her use a typical Kansai expression. To my young ears, though, it sounded like rather rough male Tokyo speech; and I thought it very odd that so genteel a lady should be using such language.

Our house was not so grand as the Ashidas' but it was better than the one we had had in Hama-cho. It looked like a solid, middle-class merchant's residence. This sort of house has disappeared in Tokyo but can still be seen in Kyoto, lining Hanami-koji Street, for example. It was built like a Gion teahouse, with the entire front covered with a wooden grille and a small latticed entrance off to one side; the only thing it lacked was the teahouse's characteristic half-curtain hanging over the entrance. Shitamachi people always built their houses and shops in this style— the rice dealers' offices in Kakigara-cho would be another example. It would not have occurred to them to have a gate or more formal entrance attached.

Passing through the narrow entrance, then, one found oneself in an earthen-floored corridor that ran all the way to the back, with on one side the raised threshold of a tatami room and on the other a place for cooking, a draining board, and so on. In all these details it resembled a Kyoto teahouse—or, for that matter, a traditional Kyoto townsman's dwelling, for even today in the older sections of that city there are many such houses. They may be inconvenient, as is often said, but they remind me of the old days, and I love them for it.

It is not clear to me whether the Kayaba-cho place was rented or belonged to us; but even if it was only rented, the cost cannot have been small for a house so well situated on the broad street leading to Reigan-jima. On the first floor there was a family parlor and, on the second, one for use when guests came. Father would sometimes invite customers home for a dinner party and then Mother would dress in her finest kimono and join the guests in the upstairs parlor. The food itself would probably have been ordered in from a good restaurant like the Kusatsu-tei in the grounds of the nearby Yakushi Temple.

When we were living in Kakigara-cho and Hama-cho, I found the precincts of the Suitengu Shrine and the O-Kannon Temple made fine playgrounds, but the Yakushi Temple in our new neighborhood was even better—an ideal place for a child. During the seventeenth and eighteenth centuries, when such celebrated figures as the Confucianist Ogyu Sorai and the haiku poet Enomoto Kikaku lived nearby, the area was apparently a very tranquil place, covered with reeds. Even around the turn of the present century it was still a quiet, slow-moving part of the city. The temple grounds were the size of a small park, and included many chapels and sanctuaries: the Tenmangu in the south corner, dedicated to Sugawara no Michizane, deified as the god of learning; the Okina Inari, sacred to the god of rice and other grains, whose messenger is the fox; the Sengen Shrine, associated with the cult of Mt. Fuji; the Kagura-do, where sacred dances were performed; the Hie Shrine; the Yakushi Hall, enshrining the Buddha of Healing; the Emma Chapel, with its image of the King of the Underworld; and the Founder's Hall. There were numerous entrances to the precincts: the main pilgrims' way leading from the potted tree and plant shops of Sakamoto-cho, now Kabuto-cho; the smaller street running parallel to the pilgrims' way; the entrance from the street running through "Back" Kayaba-cho; the entrance in front of the Homero restaurant; and the one from Kitajima-cho with its old official residences. Within the temple grounds there were, in addition to the numerous shrines and halls, the Western-style restaurants Yayoi-ken and Kusatsutei (even older than the Homero); the Marukin, specializ-ing in mud fish; the Miyamatsutei, a traditional vaudeville theater; and the Kagawa teahouse. On sunny days there would always be street ven-dors selling candy, cakes, and rice-flour pastries, with children crowded around. The vendors not only sold ready-made confections, but would mold a variety of shapes and objects, skillfully modeling and coloring them before their delighted young audience's eyes. Like the other children, I would stand for hours watching them at work and sometimes order a "pot of stew" for myself. The confectioner would smear some oil on his fingertips to keep them from sticking, form the white dough into the shape of a pot, and set it on a small wooden tray. Then he would fashion pieces of "fish cake" of various kinds from appropriately colored steamed-rice dough and put them in the pot, which was even supplied with a natural-looking rim made of red-colored dough. Finally molasses would be poured over the entire concoction, which was then ready to be devoured: the only thing I used to leave was the wooden tray! The sellers of glutenous-rice candy too would blow their wares up like bubble gum into various fantastic shapes, though none of these was as pleasing to me as the rice-dough "pot of stew." I also enjoyed "cannonballs" and pretzel-like *karinto*, both made with crystallized brown sugar. Looking back, I realize how crude and even insanitary most of these snacks were—yet at the time no one seemed to mind.

The small sanctuary of the Sengen Shrine was built on top of a little hill shaped to resemble Mt. Fuji, and we children amused ourselves by running up and down this miniature sacred mountain. The shrine festival was held on the last day of May and the first of June; and on those two days, snakes made from plaited straw were entwined on cryptomeria branches and sold to the pilgrims who came to pay their respects to "Mt. Fuji" during the festival.

All my attention, however, was focused on the chapel of Emma, King of the Underworld, next to the Yakushi Hall. This fearsome judge of the dead seemed always to be casting his baleful gaze in my direction. And Granny of course was a ready source of timely warnings: "Jun-chan, King Emma will pull your little tongue out if he catches you telling lies," she would explain; or "Now then—if you don't do as I say, I'll have to tell King Emma. . . . And you know what *that* means—out'll come your tongue!" She gave me these warnings so often that, though skeptical at first, I gradually came to feel there must be something in them. According to Granny, the King Emma enshrined in Yotsuya was especially fierce: one day he ate in one gulp a naughty boy who often disobeyed his mother and father. A little strip of the lad's clothing could still be seen dangling from between King Emma's lips in the chapel there. "It's true, Jun-chan—if you don't believe me, I'll take you there next time and show you, from right up close!" Again my suspicions that all this was just designed to frighten me and keep me in line were quelled by frequent and insistent repetition. It must really have happened, I thought, and tried from then on to avoid going near the Emma Chapel. But the attractions of danger made me venture into the chapel every time I played in the temple grounds, to see whether King Emma really would turn his angry gaze upon me.

After I started grade school, I began paying frequent visits to the shrine of Tenjin-sama (the deified Lord Sugawara no Michizane), who was supposed to confer on children the gift of good handwriting. When a writing brush wore out, we would take it to Tenjin-sama's shrine and place it between the legs of one of the Korean lion-dogs that guarded the deity. There was always quite a bundle of these used children's brushes piled up around the carved stone feet.

The Nobi Earthquake of October 28, 1891, occurred after our move to Minami Kayaba-cho: I remember how strong the tremors were even in Tokyo itself. No doubt the whole of the Kanto area felt some of the effects of this, the strongest earthquake during the forty-odd years of the Meiji era. It occurred shortly after 6:30 A.M. when we were still asleep. Mother, who feared and hated earthquakes, leaped from her bed and fled outdoors, dragging me along. I don't remember the details of what happened—where Father and Granny were, and whether Mother tried to warn them or simply rushed to get me to safety. Father was the type who liked to appear calm and cool in an emergency, so it is quite possible that he stayed in bed, with some remark like "You don't expect me to go rushing out for a little quake like this, do you?"

Mother was terrified of thunder as well as earthquakes: I suppose most of the city-bred women of that time were more timid about such things than is the case nowadays. For them, such timidity was a part of being a woman—both a virtue one needed to possess inwardly, and a posture one had to adopt before the world. Father often reproached her about it, though: "It's no good you being so scared of things—that's why the boy is such a crybaby!" And indeed it does seem that my dislike of thunder and even small earthquakes was due to Mother. I overcame my fear of thunder in my early teens; but the terror of earthquakes has persisted even into my seventies, so strong is the influence of one's mother in early childhood. The reason her attitude toward earthquakes influenced me so profoundly is that I happened to be alone with her on the two occasions when I experienced really powerful quakes: in October of 1891, as I have described, when I was six; and in June of 1894, when I was nine.

But how great, in fact, were the effects on Tokyo of the 1891 earthquake? I have the impression that they were far less than those resulting from the one that occurred three years later; that the effects of the earlier one could be called minor. At any rate, what upset me was not so much the earthquake itself as the fact that Mother was so obviously frightened. After escaping from the house, she hurried in the direction of the Kamejima River, with me following behind. She was of course still in her nightgown, and barefooted. Coming to the house of our family physician, two or three houses from the riverbank and to the left, Mother stopped and stood on the front step. Meanwhile the tremors had ceased and Granny had managed to catch up with us. But Mother's naked feet, small and white in the dawn, the soles muddy from the road, did not stop trembling. . . .

Up to about the time we were living at our first house in Minami Kayaba-cho, the married women of Shitamachi maintained the custom of blackening their teeth. Several times I watched Mother place a long, narrow brass plate across the rim of a small basin of the same material, and a small jar on top of that, and begin to color her teeth with black dye. Occasionally she would spit a blackish liquid into the basin. The dye gave off a strong, peculiar odor which filled the room during the blackening process. It was not a very pleasant smell, but it has been so long since I experienced it that I think of it now with a certain nostalgia.

Granny used to say in later years that I suckled at my mother's breasts till I was six or so; and my memories bear this out: we were still living in the first house in Minami Kayaba-cho, and Seiji had already been born. After Mother had finished giving the breast to Seiji, I would sit on her lap, press at her breasts, and have my turn. "My, my—look at that! And him so big!" Granny would laugh as she watched us; and Mother would look a bit embarrassed as she continued to let me drink. It was not so much the taste of the milk that I craved as its sweet smell and the gentle warmth of Mother's breast.

The old-timers used to recall how unprecedentedly hot the year 1886 was; and I had been born in midsummer of that year, on the twenty-fourth of July, in a dim, airless storehouse. As I sat on Mother's lap, taking in the sweet odor of her milk, I would picture to myself how it had been then—how Mother would have lifted up the diapered infant that was myself six years before and languidly have wiped the beads of perspiration from her breasts.

Even after the move to Minami Kayaba-cho, I still went almost daily to visit the main house with Mother and Granny. The distance was no more than it had been when we were in Hama-cho—some five or six blocks. We passed from "Back" to "Front" Kayaba-cho via the Katsumi side street; crossed Yoroibashi bridge and turned left toward Koami-cho; then turned right and passed through the rice dealers' district. It took only fifteen minutes, even for Granny and me. There were as yet no streetcars or automobiles about, but Granny always warned me to be careful not to be hit by a rickshaw as I crossed the wide road beyond Yoroibashi bridge to get to the pavement on the other side.

The bridge was at that time raised somewhat higher than the surface of the road, and sloped down to meet it; and the rickshaws that sped down the slope often found it impossible to make sudden stops, so it could be quite dangerous. Yoroibashi was one of the not-so-numerous steel bridges then in Tokyo, while Shin Ohashi and Eitaibashi bridges were still made of wood. I used to stand in the middle of it and watch the flow of the Nihombashi River. As I pressed my face against the iron railings and gazed down at the surface of the water, it seemed as if it were the bridge and not the river that was moving.

Crossing the bridge from Kayaba-cho, one could see the fantastic Shibusawa mansion rising like a fairy-tale palace on the banks of Kabuto-cho, further upstream. There, where the Nissho Building now stands, the Gothic-style mansion with its Venetian galleries and pillars stood facing the river, its walls rising from the stony cliff of the small promontory on which it had been built. Whose idea was it, I wonder, to construct such an exotically traditional Western-style residence right in the middle of late nineteenth-century Tokyo? I never tired of gazing at its romantic outlines with a kind of rapture. Across the river on the Koami-cho embankment were lined the white walls of innumerable storehouses. Though the Edobashi and Nihombashi bridges stood just beyond the promontory, this little section of Shitamachi had a foreign air, like some scenic lithograph of Europe. Yet it did not clash with the river and surrounding buildings—in fact, the various old-fashioned barges and lighters that moved up and down the stream past the "palace" were strangely in harmony with it, like gondolas moving on a Venetian canal....

Uncle Kyuemon at the main house took advantage of his wife Kiku's flight to her family to pay ever more attention to his geisha-mistress O-sumi. But now that he had taken her into the house and established her as his unofficial wife, Grandmother felt free to order her about just as she wished. My mother and my Yamaju aunt no doubt also behaved like typically strict sisters-in-law. It all must have made my uncle feel very awkward.

I usually still had my evening bath at the main house, just as when we lived in Hama-cho; and one day when I was soaking in the hot water with Uncle Kyuemon, the back door of the bathroom opened and O-sumi appeared, panting heavily as she carried in a bucket full of water. She hauled it with difficulty to the scrubbing area and said, gasping for breath, "It's . . . too much for me. . . . It's so . . . heavy!" The bucket was not exceptionally large or heavy—the kitchenmaid used it daily without any problem; but to O-sumi, with her slim, delicate arms, carrying water from the well behind the bathroom must have been a very hard task indeed. My uncle looked sorry for her but forced himself to laugh and make a joke. O-sumi for her part spoke boldly, as she never did before her mother- or sisters-in-law—after all, there was no one to observe her but me, who was too young to count. Even so, I sensed something in O-sumi, despite her air of diligence as she performed household tasks, her kimono sleeves tied back for work. In the way she held herself and the movements of her hands and feet, I was aware of a sensuous charm that I had never found in my mother or my aunts. Now for the first time I realized the difference between a geisha and an ordinary woman. Several times I had the chance to watch Uncle Kyuemon and O-sumi talking to one another in the bath, and I guessed that these were almost the only occasions when they could speak together in a completely natural way, without worrying about anyone else. I also realized how very fond my uncle was of her, despite the constraints imposed by his concern for appearances; and I felt somehow sorry for him, impertinent as that may sound given my age. When I was twenty-eight I wrote a play called *Koi wo shiru koro* (Coming to Love); I was not conscious of doing so at the time, but I suspect that I was drawing on my memories of O-sumi and those conversations in the bath as I wrote that play.

I have said that O-sumi was a Yanagibashi geisha; my very first visit to that celebrated pleasure district was in 1890, on or around the tenth of June. It was the third anniversary of Grandfather's death, and the family had hired a fleet of rickshaws to take us first to the temple in Sarue for the memorial service and then on to a banquet at the Kamesei in Yanagibashi. At that time Uncle Kyuemon was still acting the serious young man, taking good care of his wife Kiku and working hard to maintain the prosperity that was my grandfather's legacy. As a result, the Tanizakis were as well off as ever—indeed, the printing business may have been at its highest peak. I remember leaving Yanagibashi after the banquet and returning to Kakigara-cho by rickshaw. As I sat on my mother's lap in one of the lead rickshaws, I looked back from time to time at the long line of vehicles extending to the next corner and into the side street beyond, all filled with our friends and acquaintances, various foremen, carpenters, and tradesmen, drunk as lords and threatening to fall from their rickshaws at any moment; then Mother and I looked at each other, and smiled: "Look! They just keep coming and coming. . . ."

Yanagibashi bridge.

The Sakamoto Primary School

Before entering primary school I went for a time to the Kogishi Kindergarten in Reiganjima, Kyobashi Ward. I forget why I was sent there, or for how long a period; though not, I suppose, for very long. The kindergarten was very close to our house since we were just across the Kamejima River from Kyobashi Ward: all you had to do was cross the Reiganbashi bridge and there you were. Also, just to the left after the bridge, two or three houses down from the point where the Kamejima

River flowed into the Nihombashi, was the Manazurukan inn which Mother's second eldest sister O-han ran. O-han had a daughter just my age, as well as an older boy and girl; and it may be that it was O-han who told Mother about the kindergarten. To get there from our house, you did not turn left after crossing the bridge but went straight on, so I hardly ever visited the Manazurukan on the way. On one or two occasions, though, when we had forgotten to bring our box-lunches with us, Granny and I dropped in for something to eat. I'm not sure whether I saw my cousins there that day; but I do remember being extremely well fed by my aunt and her housekeeper.

What sorts of things were taught in kindergartens of that period? All I remember is singing a congratulatory song on the Emperor's Birthday, and making three-dimensional rectangles and triangles with those little bamboo skewers used in cooking. The words of the birthday song went:

> Today is the morning of November the third:
> Our Rising Sun flag shines
> In the bright morning light—
> See how it waves on each and every gate!

At some point during my primary-school years this was changed to the more familiar:

> Today, this happy day,
> Our sovereign lord was born....

One evening (though whether I was then in kindergarten or primary school I cannot be sure), a fire broke out in Reiganjima, and my two girl cousins from the Manazurukan came to stay with us. It turned out not to be a major fire and was quickly brought under control, so they were able to return to the inn almost immediately. The older of the girls was ten and the other only six or seven; but watching them come for refuge wearing kerchiefs over their heads like adults and with their long kimono sleeves asway, I found myself feeling not only sympathy but a kind of sensuous attraction to them. "If only they'd stay, at least for tonight...," I thought to myself.

I entered the Sakamoto Primary School at No. 28, Sakamoto-cho, Nihombashi, in September 1892, at the beginning of the second term of the school year. Since my birthday fell in the latter half of the year, I could in theory have waited until April 1893 to go to school; or at least that would be the rule in today's educational system. But such a rule either did not yet exist or was not strictly enforced, because there were many other "late-born" children in the first year of primary school in those days, including some as young as six.

The reason I was entering in September rather than earlier in the year was that I had shown strong resistance to the whole idea of going to school. I have already mentioned how I was spoiled rotten as a child— the proverbial "unsatisfactory eldest son"—and I absolutely refused to go to school in April, no matter how hard my parents tried to persuade me. Mother and Granny attempted to shame me by repeating the old adage about being "a tyrant at home and a weakling abroad"; and indeed it was true—I was an obstreperous and mischievous brat at home but a timid crybaby whenever I stepped outside.

Which reminds me: there used to be vendors who would wander about the streets calling out "Any pests . . . any pests?" They were selling Iwami Ginzan's Rat Poison; but when Granny, with her usual skill in child psychology, pointedly called my attention to them ("Listen to that, Jun-chan—they're out looking for *pests*!"), I was convinced that the unseen owners of the voices really *had* come to get bad children and take them away.

Anyway, I was a trial to my family but shy, timid, and usually utterly mute before strangers. I would not even walk the few blocks from our house in Kayaba-cho to the main house by myself, without Granny in attendance. And if I lost sight of her in the street even for a moment, I would instantly start howling. In kindergarten too Granny had to come into the classroom with me and sit beside my chair the whole time— otherwise the tears would flow. But now primary school would have to be a different story: "It's not going to be like kindergarten—you've got to get that into your head, Jun-chan. Granny can go with you to school for the first few days, but she *can't* come into the classroom! If you try anything like that, the teacher will be very angry, and scold you in front of everyone." Of course, the more my parents preached at me like this, the less inclined I was to start school. Thus, I objected and delayed day by day until finally the second term had arrived.

In addition, I had never dreamed I would be sent anywhere other than the Arima Primary School behind the Suitengu Shrine. I was most at home in the area where it was located, ever since my earlier days in the Kakigara-cho house. If you entered Nakanohashi Street from Ningyo-cho Avenue, you came to the Yukosha factory, specializing in the manufacture of Western-type paper, whose huge brick chimney constantly spouted clouds of black smoke. An unbearably foul smell hung over the whole area—the result, it seemed, of the reprocessing of rags and wastepaper. Whenever I caught a whiff of that odor, I thought with sympathy of the poor students at the Arima school next door, and was resigned to sharing their fate in the near future. Yet when I actually started going to the Sakamoto school, I realized that it was much closer to us in Minami Kayaba-cho than the Arima school was. The Sakamoto school, by the way, still stands on its original site with its name unchanged even though Sakamoto-cho itself has disappeared, swallowed up by neighboring Kabuto-cho. Even now, anyone who lives in Nihombashi Ward will recognize the school's name. To get to it from our house, I would cut through the Yakushi Temple precincts or through the old official residences area; cross the road leading from Yoroibashi to Sakurabashi bridge, to the west; go straight along the street with numerous gardening shops to the north and Sakamoto Park to the south; come to the front of the Ohara Inari Shrine, with its large gingko tree; and then go south along the road that ran along the bank of the Momiji River. The Sakamoto school was next to the fire station, with Shimbabashi bridge, leading to Nihombashi Avenue, directly in front of the main gate. South of the school was the Mitsui Bussan Company, and if you turned the corner to the north you came upon a bank's assembly hall.

On registration day, Father himself took me to school and completed the necessary forms and procedures. Why, I wonder, did I finally agree to go in September despite my aversion to schools? I suppose it was probably that I myself was becoming uneasy about not knowing the basics of reading, writing, and arithmetic. The principal was a Mr. Kishi, and the teacher in charge of first-grade boys was Mr. Inaba Seikichi. I have nothing in particular to record concerning the principal or his successor. Mr. Inaba, on the other hand, had a profound influence on me in later years: there has probably been no teacher or mentor in my whole life who influenced me more than he. But that was some years after the period I am now describing, when, during my first year in the upper level at the school, Mr. Inaba once again became my chief instructor. In the first grade of the lower level, I had Mr. Inaba for only seven months, from the second through the third terms. From the second grade on, my teacher was Mr. Nogawa Gin'ei.

There was no question of my being anything like Mr. Inaba's star pupil during that first year—on the contrary, from the very first I daily created endless problems for him. I insisted that Granny should always stay beside me as she had in kindergarten; but since the teacher could not allow nursemaids actually inside the classroom, poor Granny was forced to station herself in the hallway outside, so her face would always be visible to me through the corridor window. One day it started to rain while I was having a class, and Granny rushed home to get an umbrella for us. When I happened to glance through the window and find her gone, I immediately burst into tears. Ignoring Mr. Inaba's attempts to restrain me, I broke away from him and rushed out into the hall, screaming at the top of my lungs. I ran as fast as I could out of the building and all the way home through the rain, drawing my coat up over my head for protection. I soon became notorious throughout the school, for even among the first-graders there was no other crybaby quite on my scale.

Another thing that set me apart was the quality and extravagance of my clothes. But perhaps it would be as well to say a word first about how the average student, and teacher, dressed in those distant days. The teachers usually wore Western-style suits; but one sometimes saw Japanese dress too. They wore their Western clothes very badly: they might have stiffly starched collars and cuffs, but as likely as not there would be a gap between their vests and their trousers revealing an expanse of white shirt. Many of the teachers dispensed with suspenders or leather belts and wore instead a narrow waistband of blue, white, or purple crepe de Chine; and some wore traditional sandals instead of shoes. Mr. Inaba was more careful in his dress than many, but he, too, often combined a suit with sandals. (I remember he lived in Tamachi, Shiba, preferring to walk all the way to school each morning rather than take the horse-drawn trolley available from Shimbashi.) He liked Japanese clothing, and in later years wore it more and more often. He wore a *hakama* divided skirt very correctly over a silk kimono; but I never saw him in a formal *haori* coat. Whenever he appeared in Japanese dress, he had sandals on his bare feet, which were rather larger than average—perhaps ten or ten and a half inches long. In fact, the little toe of each foot projected beyond the sandal's rim and onto the road surface. (Even these "little" toes were long—about the size of a man's index finger.)

The students all wore Japanese dress. The boys' kimonos had to be narrow-sleeved, though *haori* coats could be worn over them. In

Shitamachi schools at any rate, *hakama* skirts were not part of the students' outfit. The girls wore nothing over their kimonos while the boys had a kind of apron to protect their clothes from dirt. Japan was not as sanitary a place then as it is now, and there were often many children with discharges from the ears and runny noses. (There were actually some teachers who would suck up the mucous running from their pupils' noses!) The boys' kimonos were for the most part made of cotton, either solid dark blue or with a splashed pattern, with sons of richer families wearing silk, including especially thin silk in the summer. The cleats attached to the soles of the boys' sandals made a characteristic metallic sound as they walked along. The narrow waistbands that held the kimonos together were usually of crepe de Chine, but some of the boys wore real *mousseline de soie*, dyed black so as not to be quite so conspicuous. I remember one day as I was being carried along on Granny's back, wearing a broad sash of *mousseline de soie*, a street thief sneaked up from behind and, with a single slash of his razor-sharp knife, cut through my sash and made off with it. (It must have been white, and so very conspicuous.) At any rate, I was always dressed in a stylish, rather showy manner, like a child actor in the Kabuki theater; and I stood out from most of the other children at the Sakamoto school for this reason as well.

Mother loved to dress me up, and almost anything could be made an occasion for a display of my finery. "Today let's make you look really nice," she'd say, opening a chest of drawers and taking out some carefully wrapped garment. As the cool silk of the singlet touched my skin, my whole body would start to tingle. Mother had me stand up straight and added to the singlet the various under- and overgarments in layer after layer of fine silk. Finally she adjusted the collar of the kimono so that it was snug and neat, tied the tasseled cords, and wound the long, pale green silk sash several times around my waist. The sash, kimono, and other garments were made to fit a child; but otherwise, in cut, pattern, and material, they were exactly what a well-dressed adult would wear when he went to pay a visit. It all made me very happy; and Mother seemed happier still, turning me this way and that as she gazed at me.

The first public holiday after my entrance into the Sakamoto Primary School was the Emperor's Birthday in November, and Mother prepared specially fine clothes for it long in advance. I cannot recall precisely what I wore that day, but I imagine the under-kimono was of figured silk and the coat of black, finely woven silk, embellished with our family crest. The kimono's sleeves would have been full-cut for the occasion, and a Sendaihira *hakama* skirt and *geta* clogs with white deerskin thongs would have completed my costume. Granny was probably carrying handsome hemp-soled sandals for me to change into once inside the school. When we entered the school yard, a great crowd of friends and classmates gathered to admire the splendor of my clothes. Some of them made a game of counting the layers of my under-kimonos, all of which were visible at the neckline: "One for Virtue, two for Fortune, three means Happy, four means Poor, five's for Money, six for Treasure, seven for Colic. . . ."

Everything went splendidly until it was time for the ceremony to begin. As the students were formed into ranks and told to enter the hall, I began to insist that Granny should come in with me. Not only Mr. Inaba but the other teachers one after another came out into the corridor and tried to persuade me to go in with the other students. The more they scolded, the tighter I held on to the balcony railing. Finally someone grabbed me by the arm and dragged me into the hall by force; naturally, this made me howl even louder. I then managed to break away from the teacher's grip and run out of the place.

The scene I had fled was presumably the lecture hall on the second floor, at the front, where the portrait of the Emperor was enshrined. Above the main entrance of the school hung a formal plaque with the school's name written in impressive and unusual characters by Sanjo Sanetomi; it was just below this plaque that the lecture hall was located. On the day of the ceremony it was filled with ranks of students, all standing politely at attention; but unlike my classroom, it had no corridor window through which I could keep Granny's reassuring face in sight. That was why I made such a fuss.

The result was that I stood in the corridor clinging to Granny all through the ceremony until the other pupils filed out. Still, dressed in my festive garb, I did receive the special lotus-seed cake filled with sweet bean paste and crowned with the imperial chrysanthemum crest, together with all the other students. Naturally, I was severely scolded for my cowardice by Mother and Granny after I got home. But this made no difference: I am sure that at the New Year's Day celebration in the following year, on National Foundation Day in February, and at the end-of-school ceremony in March, I raised the same kind of rumpus, making trouble for the teachers and turning myself again into the school joke. When the new school year began in April, I found that I had been resoundingly failed and so had to repeat the entire first year.

Mr. Nogawa

The new teacher in my (second) first-grade class was Mr. Nogawa Gin'ei. He was a native of Okayama in southern Honshu and spoke with the local accent. Father commented on his rather unusual name: "Is it really 'Gin'ei'? Not 'An'ei'? . . . Sounds like a masseur or something!" In the old days, people liked to use unusual characters in personal names, and it is no wonder that the average person (to say nothing of my father, who had very little formal education) could not recognize a difficult one like the "Gin" of "Gin'ei." Even today probably most people would not know it. In the upper level of primary school I began to attend a private academy teaching classical Chinese, and encountered passages like "With great officers of the higher grade, Confucius spoke *gently and courteously*" (*Analects*, Book X) and "The disciple Min was standing by his side, looking *gentle and courteous*" (*Analects*, Book XI) in which the character "Gin" occurs. Even the "Jun" of my own name was probably unintelligible to most people in the Meiji period; I suppose it was taken from the line in the Confucian *Great Learning*: "Wealth *adorns* a house, while Virtue *adorns* a man." I cannot be sure, though, since I neglected to ask my parents just who named me, and why.

Mr. Inaba had graduated from the Ochanomizu Teachers' College, but it is unclear whether Mr. Nogawa had had regular training to qualify as a primary-school teacher. He was an accomplished painter in the Japanese style and that was probably his real specialty, with training in the Chinese classics as a second subject. At any rate, he was, at around the age of thirty, a more knowledgeable and experienced teacher than his younger colleague who had only just left the Ochanomizu college. Mr. Nogawa was good at dealing with students; and that was no doubt part of the reason why, after he became my teacher, I stopped being such a crybaby and was willing to go to school by myself without Granny in attendance. School ceased to be frightening, and I did well in all my subjects, from Japanese to arithmetic. Mr. Nogawa is supposed to have told Mr. Inaba that "the boy's no dunce. Of course, he's been badly spoiled, but he's sharp and is getting very good marks. Just wait and see—he'll be top of the class soon." And indeed in March of the following year I turned out to have been the best student in the first-grade class, and so was promoted at last to the second grade.

At the ceremony to mark the school year's end, I acted as the representative of the first-grade boys and accepted the certificates of completion of the year's work on everyone's behalf. I also received a special certificate and prize for being the best student. Thus I returned home in triumph—in marked contrast to the previous year. Mother was overjoyed and promptly took me on the rounds of the main house and the rice shop to show my prizes to Grandmother, Uncle Kyuemon, and my Yamaju aunt.

Thanks to Mr. Nogawa, I came to realize that I was more talented than the average student, and so was freed from a sense of inferiority. I no longer just clung to Granny's skirts all day: not that I began suddenly to range all over town by myself, but I was able to go farther afield on my own, and often went to markets and fairs in other neighborhoods. Before I set off, Mother would warn me against going "anywhere dangerous. . . . And don't talk to strangers, even if they talk to you."

If I asked for a little spending money, I'd usually get a two-sen copper coin; there were one-sen and half-sen pieces as well. (Old Edo coins, issued in the 1830s, also circulated in early Meiji, with a value of something less than a sen.) It was only under the most exceptional circumstances that I received a five-sen nickel or a ten-sen silver coin.

It was not uncommon at the time for children to be abducted by strangers—one often heard stories of such kidnappings. Once in Hamacho I actually witnessed an abduction: a strange man came up to a child about my own age in broad daylight, gagged him, tied him on his back, and ran off. Of course I may be wrong—it might not have been a kidnapping at all; but I myself was later approached on two occasions by suspicious characters. Both times it was on the day of the Suitengu fair: I had visited the main house on my way home from school; from there I went to Ningyo-cho and had gone a block or two past the corner where the Shimizuya bookshop was, in the direction of the Miharado store. The street was lined on one side with vendors' stalls, and its narrow breadth was crowded with passersby. Suddenly someone slipped up to me and, bringing his lips close to my ear so no one else could hear, said in a soft, honeyed voice, "Hi, little man. Come along with me. I'll take you somewhere really nice: there'll be lots of good things for you to eat, and presents too—whatever you want."

I recognized at once that it was precisely this that Mother had so often warned me about; but I was not in the least afraid because I was sure the fellow could do nothing to me in such a crowded spot. If by any chance he did try to drag me off by force, I would scream and the people nearby would help me. No matter what he said to me, then, I resolved not to answer, and not to look at him either. I simply turned and went back the way I had come, without a backward glance. When I reached the main house and told Mother what had happened, she said "I'm sure it was a kidnapper. If it ever happens again, you must do exactly the same thing!"

The second time, I was coming back from a visit to the Suitengu Shrine and had almost arrived at the main house, when I heard someone call "Sonny!" from behind me. His soft, insinuating tone and the words he used were very similar to what I had heard before—perhaps it was the same man. If so, it meant he was making a point of following me about. But since I was only a stone's throw from the family printer's, I felt even less anxious this time.

Usually kidnappers would take children and then demand a ransom for them; or, if the children were exceptionally good-looking, carry them off to some distant province and sell them there. Assuming that the man was after me in particular, I wonder what his motive might have been. Around this time I often used to visit the typesetters at our print shop; and I remember how one day one of the young men said to me quite seriously as he went about his work, "You're going to be a fine-looking guy, Jun-chan. Just wait ten years, and you'll have so many girls in love with you you won't know what to do with them all!" I was too young to be pleased at his remark, or even really to understand its meaning. But his words stuck in some corner of my mind, to be recalled on several occasions somewhat later. In fact, I was never made much of by girls when I was child, but I was often pursued by older youths. A pederastic taste for handsome little boys was on the increase in Tokyo toward the end of the century, perhaps due to the strong influence of Kyushu politicians from the former Satsuma domains, a traditional hotbed of such practices.

Another episode occurred when I was repeating the first grade under

Mr. Nogawa, on either National Foundation Day or the Emperor's Birthday (almost certainly the former, I think), when I was nine years old. After the ceremony at school, Granny came to get me and took me in the direction of Nihombashi so I could see how lively things were on that festive day. I was of course dressed in my best formal kimono and *haori* coat and must have looked rather fetching. As we were crossing Shimbabashi bridge, there appeared a tall, well-built military officer dressed in a glittering uniform (perhaps a lieutenant or captain) who seemed to be on his way back from some official celebration. "Well, my fine lad," he called to me, "I think I'll just pick you up and carry you off—shall I?" And indeed he did just that, turning back toward Nihombashi with me in his arms, and Granny following along after him in bewilderment. Holding me lightly in one arm, he told her "not to worry— I'll give him right back," and walked on, crossing Nihombashi Avenue and arriving at Gofukubashi. What could Granny do against this tall, imposing officer with splendid sideburns, whose slightly ruddy face confirmed the evidence of his breath, sweet with the smell of saké. I was too stunned and frightened even to cry out as I was borne victoriously along. Obviously this resplendent officer was not a common kidnapper of the sort I had already encountered twice before, but I could not imagine where he was taking me, or why. As Granny continued to dither anxiously, the officer told her again not to worry and withdrew from a pocket his name-card which he handed to her. He also tried to soothe me with kind and gentle remarks, but I was too scared to do anything but nod and mumble in reply. All I wanted was to get away from him as fast as possible.

We crossed Gofukubashi bridge, cut across Mitsubishigahara (the present-day Marunouchi high-rise district), and came to the moat around the imperial palace; then, near the police box at Babasakimon, he put me down briefly in order to urinate by the side of the road. Still, Granny and I didn't dare run away, for fear he would come after us. But the policeman on duty approached Granny and quietly asked her if the officer was a friend of ours. To us, that policeman was like a guardian angel straight from heaven! When the officer had finished his business at the roadside, he confronted the policeman and an exchange of words began. As the argument became more and more heated, Granny and I took advantage of the chance to run off.

In all we had spent about two hours being led around town by this officer. When we finally got home, Granny apologized to Mother over and over for her irresponsibility and the anxiety she had caused. "This is the gentleman's name," she said, bringing out his card. It remained for a long time in a tea-chest drawer in our house but then somehow was lost. As a result I don't know the officer's precise identity; but his name was certainly Nozu Shizutake, and he was in the Imperial Army. Father said that with that name, and being in the army, he must have been related to the famous General Nozu himself.

Childhood friends

They say that the Tokyoite has no true hometown, and certainly this applies in my case. Due to the Great Kanto Earthquake of 1923 and the bombings of World War II, to such repeated and violent changes, almost all my friends from primary-school days have scattered. There are only two or three of whom I have any news—where they are now, what they are doing. When you think about it, it is surprising that I know anything at all, even of them. The Sakamoto school suffered several major fires, with the result that most of the records from my years there have been lost. Some time ago I asked that a friend be allowed to look at the list of graduates for that period, only to be told that there was no longer any such list at the school.

According to the revised *History of Nihombashi Ward*, published by the ward office in October 1937, the Sakamoto Primary School was founded by "citizens from twenty-five subdistricts, including Kabuto-cho, who met and began collecting funds to build a primary school. A building occupying some two thousand square yards of land at No. 28, Sakamoto-cho, which had formerly been a residence and meeting hall of the Kumamoto fiefdom under the Shogunate, was granted for the purpose by the city government...." It was "the first public primary school established in Nihombashi Ward after the promulgation of the new school regulations," and "the number of students enrolled was thirty-six." The school had been in existence for twenty years when I entered it in 1892, and had been enlarged and rebuilt several times.

It was a Shitamachi school and, though there were a goodly number of children of the middle class, there were almost none from political, scholarly, aristocratic, or official families. One day, however, the news spread throughout the school that the well-known seismologist Dr. Omori Fusakichi, who was an alumnus, would be visiting. We all assembled on the playground and listened to an improving talk by the distinguished visitor, who either had just received a doctorate in recognition of his contributions to seismology, or was recently returned from a period of scholarly research in Europe or America. The only other reasonably well known alumnus was Horino Yoshichi, who wrote children's fiction for the *Boys' World* magazine and used the pen name Kyo no Warabei. Mr. Horino was himself the owner of the Bunrokudo publishing house, which had its shop on the east side of Higashi Naka Avenue in Kuremasa-cho, Nihombashi. Though he contributed to the *Boys' World*, he did not have to depend on writing for his livelihood like the ordinary man of letters. The family business was traditionally that of rouge seller, and the old shop was well known locally from the Edo period on; but Yoshichi, the present heir, had devoted himself mainly to *senryu* comic verse, adopting a pen name and mixing with the aesthetes of the Kenyusha Society as an equal. According to Kimura Shoshu's *History of Children's Literature*, "the whole area around Higashi Naka Avenue . . . was filled with long-established antique and curio shops and preserved an extraordinarily old-fashioned atmosphere. In contrast, the Bunrokudo, the only bookseller in the area, presented a very up-to-date, fashionable appearance with its handsomest books carefully displayed in a wide bay window. . . . Warabei himself wrote and published such works as *Five Great Tales of Japan* and *A Classified Collection of Current Comedy*, and gradually gained a reputation in the publishing business. But in fact all this was merely a hobby or pastime for the young man: to borrow his own words, 'You're only young once; so I say, enjoy yourself and have a good time!' And evidently his account books just sat and gathered dust. . . ."

Mr. Horino came occasionally to take part in school festivities and give talks to the students. He looked very much the young master of an old merchant family in his silk *haori* coat and fine kimono—an impressive figure, but with nothing of the man of letters about him. Yet he *was* a writer; and since I already felt a strong fascination for that world, I would look forward to his visit all day if I heard in the morning that Kyo no Warabei was due to appear. Sometimes I even went to the Bunrokudo and loitered about in front, hoping to catch a glimpse of him from close up.

I must not forget to mention another famous alumnus—the late Takahashi Eijiro, better known by his Kabuki stage name of Ichikawa Sadanji II. At the time I am describing, the elder Sadanji was still alive, and his heir was known by the juvenile stage name Botan ("Peony"). The family apparently was living in Shintomi-cho, Kyobashi, and the Bunkai school in Tsukiji would have been closer than ours; so I really cannot say why he was sent to Sakamoto. At any rate, he was six years older than I, and so would have been in the advanced grades when I was in the lower: in fact, we never met during our primary-school days. I knew, though, that there was a school tradition to the effect that the son of Sadanji had been a pupil at Sakamoto and had often gone home in tears because the other students, from local merchant and tradesmen's families, were always taunting him as "an actor's brat." Many years later, when I got to know Sadanji II, I asked him about this; but he flatly denied it: "That's absolute rubbish! Who? Me? Go home crying? Ha!"

Finally, the late Ishiwata Shotaro, who served as minister of finance and head of the Imperial Household Agency, also graduated from Sakamoto and, like me, studied under Mr. Inaba. But he was several years my junior, and we never met.

Since I had to repeat the first year of primary school, I actually had two different sets of first-grade classmates. I remember very little about the original group, since we were together only for one term during which I behaved, and was treated, as the class crybaby. In the next group, however, I was able for the first time to make lots of friends. But the only one with whom I have been able to maintain contact over the past sixty-odd years is Sasanuma Gennosuke, the son of the proprietor of the Kairakuen, the oldest Chinese restaurant in Tokyo, which continued to flourish from its opening in 1884 right up to the Pacific War. Yet there are others whom I still remember well even though we have lost touch— their names, and faces, and certain incidents from those early years.

There was, for instance, Kojima, the son of a ferryman who lived on a riverboat moored near the Yoroibashi bridge. Readers may remember the passage in my early story *Shonen* (Children): ". . . so as not to be discovered by my friends Kokichi from the wigmaker's shop and Tekko, the ferryman's son . . ."; or one from *Haha wo kouru ki*: "What had become of Tekko, the ferryman's son from Yoroibashi? Were he, and Shinko from the fish-cake shop, and Kojiro from the clog seller's, and the others still good friends? And did they still put on plays every day on the second floor of Kakiuchi the tobacconist's? . . ." Well, Kojima was the model for "Tekko, the ferryman's son" in these stories. He lived in a boat moored to the unloading dock in "Front" Kayaba-cho, beneath the bridge. Each morning he would cross a wooden plank, climb up the embankment, and set off for school. Once or twice Kojima invited me to his "house"—it was, undeniably, a boat, but it was designed to be almost perfectly stable on the water. The roof was made of rush matting, and a small stove and pots and pans were set out on the stern where Mrs. Kojima did her cooking. At Tekko's invitation, I went in beneath the matting and found a sitting room carpeted with thick, bordered mats and containing a long *hibachi* brazier, tea chests, and other pieces of furniture, just as in an ordinary house. The only difference was that when a river steamer passed under the bridge, the boat's hull would rock a bit and the liquid in the teacups shift ever so slightly.

There were real-life children corresponding to "Kokichi from the wigmaker's" and "Shinko from the fish-cake shop" as well. The wigmaker's was located in one part of a gardening shop on the right-hand side of Yoroibashi Street, going toward Sakamoto Park. The name of the family was Yukiuchi, and this was the source of the "Ko" of "Kokichi" (using an alternate pronunciation of the first character in the name) and of the "uchi" of "Kakiuchi" in the story *Shonen*. I used to go with Tekko and the others to put on plays in the Yukiuchis' second-floor parlor. One day Tekko played the part of a masterful swordsman who could cut men down as if they were grass. He acted the part with consummate skill, his child's face turning red with rage. (By contrast, I remember nothing about Shinko apart from his name and the fact that the fish-cake shop was in the same general neighborhood.)

Then there was the Shibagakis' box-lunch shop: the eldest son Tokutaro was my classmate, and the second son, my brother Seiji's. When Seiji paid me a visit in August 1954, he told me that the Shibagakis' second son had come to see him at his office at Waseda University one day, the first time they had met in decades. So perhaps Tokutaro too is still living—though unfortunately Seiji forgot to ask about him.

The classmate who lived nearest our house was Maruyama Kin'ichiro, the son of a thread seller at No. 28 or 29, where one came out into "Back" Kayaba-cho after cutting through the Yakushi Temple grounds. He is said to have died many years ago.

The section of present-day Kayaba-cho 2-chome, to the south of the trolley line that runs from Chiyodabashi toward Reiganbashi, is an area where a number of official residences from the Edo period stood. According to the *History of Nihombashi Ward*, "during the early eighteenth century the area changed from samurai family residences to lodgings for the constabulary." When I was a child, there were still a number of people who had served in the old constabulary living in the section extending from Hatchobori to Kamejima and Kitajima-cho.

Before the Meiji Restoration these constables were held in some dread by the common people and referred to as "the Masters of Hatchobori"; but by my time they had no special power and lived like ordinary citizens. Still, they preserved a certain aura from the old days: they were of samurai origin, after all, and had served the Shogunate. So the area they inhabited was still informally called "the official residences district." I had a classmate named Wakita whose father had been a constable and who lived in that area. Though in the same class, he was two years younger than I, having started school at the age of six. (Whether that was generally allowed at the time or whether he was given special consideration as the son of a former samurai, I do not know.) I often went to play at Wakita's house because it too was very close. It had a long clapboard wall which clearly set it apart from the usual Shitamachi houses, and an imposing front gate which was not normally in use. To get in, I used to stand outside the wall and call my friend's name; he would then come out and open the narrow service door used by the greengrocer and fishmonger. It was a rather large and impressive building, rectangular in shape and of one story but with many rooms and with the floors raised high above the ground. Clearly people of the rank of constable were not to be trifled with in the old days. Wakita's father died shortly after I came to know the family, but while he was still with them he spent a great deal of time in the room at the rear of the house. In the last days of the Shogunate he must often have brought suspected criminals here for preliminary investigation. Though the back room lacked the traditional interlocking swastika pattern that one would have expected to find on its sliding doors, it did face onto a garden that looked very like the white-graveled ones where prisoners were questioned. The back room's veranda was joined to the garden by a short flight of steps reminiscent of the "Kumagai's Camp" scene and *The Tale of Sanemori*. The bottom of the garden was given over to vegetable plots.

My aunt O-han's husband, the owner of the Manazurukan inn, had once lived next door to the Wakita family, so Aunt O-han was a ready source of information on them. According to her, the father was originally from Ise and had had extremely close ties to the rich Mitsui family when he served as a constable. Apparently there was a reason why the Mitsuis would never abandon the Wakitas in any circumstances whatsoever.

My classmate was the fourth son and the youngest child; above him were three brothers and two sisters. The mother was said to be from a Koji-machi merchant family; but she had entered a samurai family by marriage and was naturally referred to by the upper-class terms "Oku-san" or "Goshinsan" rather than the townsman's "Okamisan." The youngest son was called by his personal name alone, without any honorific suffix, not only by his elder brothers but by his sisters as well. In fact, the Wakitas' whole way of speaking and behaving, and the general atmosphere of the household, set them apart from their more plebeian neighbors. They were somehow more refined than we were; and the self-conscious overrefinement in speech and butter-wouldn't-melt-in-her-mouth manner of Mrs. Wakita provided fuel for some rather harsh comments on the part of my aunt. She had a few things to say about Mr. Wakita as well—he was from Ise and had the extreme thriftiness, not to say stinginess, of people from that region: "When you go to the bathroom there, you find strips of newspaper instead of regular toilet paper!" My friend himself seems to have had some affinity for his father's native place because years later he married into a rich family in the Ise area. I have heard that he is still alive and well, but somehow we have lost contact.

The Little Kingdom

I must not neglect to mention that it was a child nicknamed "Nossan" who made the strongest impression on all of us in the class. His real name was Shinoda Gentaro; the "Nossan" was a contraction of "Shinoda-san." Everyone called him that with a mixture of affection, respect, and fear. Nossan was the son of a barber, and became the model for the central character in my story *Chiisana okoku* (The Little Kingdom); readers who know that piece need only recall "Numakura" to get an idea of what Nossan was like. The story is set in a rural primary school in one of the prefectures near Tokyo, and Numakura is described as a newcomer to the school, the son of a worker who has recently come to be employed in the local textile mill. In these and several other respects, there are many inventions and exaggerations; but the portrait of Numakura's Stalin-like assumption of power and exercise of strict control over his numerous classmates is drawn from life, from my memories of Nossan.

Thus when I reread the following passage from *Chiisana okoku* in which the teacher Kaishima goes to the playground at noon one day, childhood scenes from the Sakamoto school playground come to mind, as if they had happened only yesterday:

> Kaishima found his pupils had divided into two groups and were playing at war. That in itself was not unusual, but there was something exceedingly strange in the way they were divided up. Of the fifty pupils, forty were in one group and only ten in the other. The first was led by Nishimura, the pharmacist's son, who directed his troops with great earnestness as he sat astride two lads who served as his horse. The leader of the second, much smaller group was, to Kaishima's surprise, Numakura Shokichi, the new boy. This usually quiet boy too was on horseback; and with loud shouts and eyes blazing he commanded his troops to attack, himself taking the lead in charging into the massed enemy ranks. At once the larger force began to give way, breaking formation and finally fleeing wildly in all directions. It was true that the members of Numakura's small army were all extremely strong boys, heroes of the playground; even so, the Nishimura forces' display of cowardice in their rout was amazing. They seemed especially terrified of Numakura himself: no sooner did he come charging at them on his horse than they wavered and collapsed, not daring to put up a real fight at all.

The only part of this passage that is truly fictional is the statement that Nossan/Numakura was a new boy at school. The numbers involved (forty on one side, ten on the other) may be a bit exaggerated; but the relative ratio at least is accurate. The story continues:

> And yet Numakura himself did not use any violence, but only broke through the enemy lines time after time from several directions, shouting commands to his troops and invectives at the enemy: "Right—let's do it again! This time we'll do it with *seven* men. Seven'll be enough for us!" And sending three of his soldiers over

to the enemy side, he joined battle again; and again Nishimura's army was soundly defeated. The third time, the seven were reduced to five; even so, Numakura's small troop prevailed after a fierce struggle. . . .

Numakura was a boy richly endowed with courage, magnanimity, and the spirit of chivalry; and these qualities gradually made him the ruler among his classmates. He was not perhaps physically the strongest in the class—Nishimura probably would have won if it came to a wrestling match. . . . But Numakura was incredibly tough in a fight. Quite apart from physical strength, his bold, commanding spirit and air of indomitable authority made short work of any resistance on the part of his opponents. Even top students like Nakamura and Suzuki who had not easily given in when Nishimura was boss of the class became the most faithful of Numakura's followers, constantly flattering and humoring him so as to remain in favor. . . . Thus there was in fact no one who opposed Numakura in any way. Everyone was only too pleased to do his bidding. Occasionally his commands were clearly egotistical, but for the most part he ruled justly. His only concern was that his authority be established; once that was accomplished, he almost never abused it. If one of his followers was found bullying weaker children or doing anything mean-spirited, he could expect extremely harsh treatment. As a result, weaklings like the Arita boy were most grateful of all for Numakura's reign.

I have forgotten who the former class boss, Nishimura, was based on; but the reader may safely attribute the actions of Numakura described in the story to the real-life Nossan—Shinoda Gentaro. In *Chiisana okoku* Numakura gradually comes to have more power than the teacher, Kaishima:

He compiled his own class list and kept a close watch on his classmates' daily behavior, giving marks according to his own system. "Present," "Absent," "Tardy," "Went home early"—with the same authority as a teacher, he noted all this daily in his record book. . . . Students who missed lessons were made to give the reason, and Numakura would dispatch "private detectives" to check whether it was true. . . . The regular class leader appointed by Mr. Kaishima was shunted aside to make way for the strong, mischievous boy appointed "supervisor" by Numakura.... Other officers were installed as aides to President Numakura.... Subordinates emerged to carry out the higher officials' orders....

Nossan really did do most of this, as I recall. Under his influence the pupils carefully observed the school rules and preserved the strictest silence during lessons: "Everyone prayed in fear and trembling that there would be no untoward incidents." The real-life Mr. Nogawa was as amazed at all this as was Mr. Kaishima in the story, who comments on the changed atmosphere of the class: "How is it you've all become so well behaved lately? You're so nice and quiet, I'm really impressed. No, not just impressed—astonished!" Mr. Nogawa did say something very like this to the class. And the children in *Chiisana okoku*, who were expecting just such words of praise from their teacher, "broke into happy laughter as they heard him express his amazement." We, good little subjects of Nossan's kingdom, did likewise.

> "When you're good like this, you make me feel very proud of you. Even the teachers of the other classes have noticed . . . the principal too! He said just the other day that you're so quiet and well behaved you're a model for the rest of the school. So you should all be aware of what a fine reputation you have and do your best to keep it, not only for the time being but always. Be careful you don't just make a good start and then give up halfway along, all right?"

This speech of Mr. Kaishima's in the story was taken directly from Mr. Nogawa's talk to us. But the "Presidents' " reactions were different: the fictional Numakura just grinned; but Nossan in fact turned back to the class triumphantly and gave us a complacent smile. Numakura is described as "a stocky, heavyset boy, dark-complexioned and with a rather melancholy look in his eyes; round-shouldered and square-faced with traces of a scalp infection visible here and there on his very large, round head." Nossan was certainly stocky and thickset, but his scalp seemed healthy enough. His complexion was dark and his face square in shape, but there was nothing especially melancholy about his eyes. On the other hand, he was not a particularly lively-looking lad either; rather, he gave an impression of heaviness.

In *Chiisana okoku* Numakura even established a system of decorations for his followers.

He ordered his officials to devise appropriate names for the various medals (made of lead, and bought at a neighborhood toy store) and awarded them to people according to their degree of meritorious service. A special official was put in charge of this new department.... Then someone suggested appointing a Secretary of the Treasury to issue currency. Uchimura, the son of a liquor dealer, was promptly entrusted with this important post, and from then on spent the hours after school holed up on the second floor of his house together with two private secretaries, busily printing bills in denominations ranging from fifty to a hundred thousand yen. These were then taken to the President's office where they were stamped with his official "Numakura" seal, thus becoming legal tender. All of the citizen-pupils were paid wages by the President, the amount depending on their rank within the system.

The Secretary of the Treasury in Nossan's kingdom was, I think, Sasanuma "Gen-chan," the son of the wealthy owner of the Kairakuen Chinese restaurant. Every day a few of us would gather in his room with printing type and ink-pads to create the currency, using various sizes of paper depending on the denomination. It says in *Chiisana okoku* that "as the pupils began to accumulate wealth, they started buying and selling goods, using the Numakura currency. Numakura himself could buy whatever he liked from his followers since he had an unlimited supply of funds. For example, the Arita boy greatly prized an air gun his father had bought him in Tokyo; but when Numakura said he'd give him five hundred thousand yen for it, it was truly an offer he couldn't refuse."

In Nossan's kingdom too such things took place; President Shinoda could on occasion be fully as dictatorial as President Numakura. But there were things described in *Chiisana okoku* that had no counterpart in our regime, being purely fictional—for example, "the pupils got together and held market fairs in parks or wooded areas in the suburbs"; or, "anyone who received spending money from his parents was required to convert it into goods and then bring them to the market to trade"; or again, "the pupils were absolutely forbidden to use any money other than that issued by President Numakura"; "Numakura's currency took the place of ordinary money in all the children's daily purchases"; and "the items sold at the children's market were of an astonishing variety."

Finally, though Mr. Kaishima in the story is so hard-pressed for money that he breaks down and asks Numakura for some of the kingdom's currency, nothing like that ever happened with the real Mr. Nogawa.

I am not sure what finally became of President Nossan: by the time our class graduated from primary school he was no longer enrolled, as I recall. Did he leave school to help out in his father's barbershop? His kingdom existed only among a group of children aged around ten or eleven; but even so, to have been able to master and control all the pupils in a given class showed a strength of character that the ordinary tough guy or "leader of the pack" does not possess. Yet, because he was the son of a barber, it may be that he was forced to drop out of school and resign himself to following his father's trade. In later years, Sakamoto graduates would often talk about him when they got together: "That Nossan was really something, wasn't he? I wouldn't be surprised if he suddenly turned up somewhere, really famous—you know, a hero or something. . . ." But in fact nothing was ever heard of him again; he seems to have been lost in the hurly-burly of life. He could well still be alive, though, somewhere. . . .

The Sino-Japanese War

The Sino-Japanese War began with the sea battle off Pung-do island in July 1894. By then we had moved from the house at No. 45, Minami Kayaba-cho, and begun to live in the back of the Marukyu shop, behind the rice dealers' area. Father's rice dealership was not doing well, and it became necessary to economize by living on the premises rather than maintaining a separate establishment. Our financial situation had become precarious, though as a child I did not realize it at the time. We still had a head clerk and assistants in the shop, and Granny and a maid in the kitchen. Moreover, the rooms behind the shop were large enough to accommodate my parents and us two children without our feeling especially cramped.

But we did not stay long even there; within a year or so, Father's business was truly failing and we retreated to what became our second house in Minami Kayaba-cho—No. 56, at the end of the alley where the Meitoku Inari Shrine stood. The most memorable event during our stay in the rice dealers' area had been the earthquake of the summer of 1894, far greater in intensity than the Nobi quake of 1891. It was said to have been the greatest earthquake to strike Tokyo in the entire Meiji period of over forty years. It occurred on June 20, about a month before the outbreak of the war. The Chinese army had already landed at Inchon and our envoy, Otori Keisuke, had set out for Seoul—the Korean peninsula was in a state of extraordinary tension. The earthquake struck at around two o'clock in the afternoon when the exchange was very crowded, with groups of rice dealers filling the streets and the shops and offices that lined them. I had just come back from school and was having a dish of sweet bean paste and shaved ice in the kitchen. As soon as I felt the quake, I dashed outside. The streets in the back section of the rice dealers' area, where our shop was, were much narrower than those in other parts; and I was terrified of being crushed if the houses on either side collapsed. I ran for my life to the wide road that separated 1-chome and 2-chome and stood right in the middle of the intersection where one turned off on the way to the Tanizaki Printers.

Only then did I notice my mother: had she been with me all along, or had she only now caught up with me? I found her hugging me tightly as we stood there together. The first violent up-and-down movement had ceased, but the ground was still undulating in great, slow waves. From where we stood huddling together, the surface of Ningyo-cho Avenue about one block away seemed to rise and sink, over and over again. My face was pressed against my mother. Her kimono had come open at the neck, and the whiteness of her breasts blocked the fearful scene before me. Suddenly I became aware that I had a writing brush gripped tightly in my right hand. (I had, I know, been eating an ice when the earthquake came and, throwing it down, had dashed out of the house. How, then, did this brush come to be in my hand? Why had I picked it up, and when? . . .) As we stood in the middle of the intersection, holding on to one another as we swayed back and forth, I began to move the brush, tracing lines in black ink upon my mother's breasts.

The Marukyu shop and the printer's were each about the same distance from the intersection where we stood; but when the earthquake stopped, Mother did not try to return home. Instead she went straight to see Grandmother at the print shop, pulling me along after her. The memory of that morning on October 28 three years earlier, when we fled barefoot along the streets of Kayaba-cho until we reached our doctor's front door, came vividly to mind. When we arrived at the print shop, Mother sat on the raised threshold of the tatami room and rinsed her muddy feet with water. Grandmother had been crouching beneath a trap-door in the kitchen ceiling while the house was shaken with tremors; but by the time we arrived, she had returned to her usual place by the long brazier and managed to seem quite calm. Then suddenly an after-shock began, and all three of us rushed pell-mell into the kitchen. "We're just lucky it was only an aftershock—I was afraid it was the start of a really big one this time!" said Grandmother, who went on to tell us about the great earthquake of 1855, which struck one October night. Grand-mother had been born in 1839 so she would have been seventeen at the time. The earthquake came at around 10 P.M. when she was already in bed. Enjoying the sound sleep of the young and healthy, she was com-pletely unaware of the quake itself. She awoke suddenly when the house collapsed around her: the bedside lamp had gone out, but her head was protected by a trapdoor which had fallen from above, covering her. She was able to crawl out from the wreckage uninjured, and found the other family members frantically searching for her. Of the surrounding houses not one was left standing.

It was about the time of this 1894 earthquake that the Tonghak reb-els were wreaking havoc in Korea, and Kim Okkyun, the pro-Japanese political leader, was assassinated at a hotel in Shanghai. The incident remains very clear in my memory, probably because everyone was talk-ing about it, with the newspapers playing it up as a probable presage of war.

I even remember seeing a representation of Kim's assassination at the annual chrysanthemum-doll display at Dangozaka in the fall of that year. Since the war officially lasted only from August 1894, when the imperial declaration of war was issued, to the following April, it was by today's standards a very minor and relaxed affair. I could not understand why we were fighting, though, and one day I asked Father. "All right, I'll ex-plain it nice and simply so you can understand. Come over here," he said, seating me next to the small table where he was having supper. Between sips of his evening cup of saké, he gave a rather long speech —alas, it was too involved for me really to comprehend. It seemed very strange to me that the Japanese army should be mobilized because of a rebellion in Korea, and that they should be dispatched to the penin-sula to fight another army from China.

The Shimizuya bookshop in the meantime was busily stocking three-leaf colored prints depicting scenes from the war. These were mostly by three artists: Mizuno Toshikata, Ogata Gekko, and Kobayashi Kiyochika. Hung at the front of the bookshop for all to see, they were immensely popular with us boys, who would stand gazing at them almost daily, our eyes shining with pleasure, though we were rarely able to buy them. Even today I can recall some of the scenes described: the heroic death of Shirokami Genjiro, the bugler who won fame in the battle of Songhwon; Harada Jukichi breaching the gate at Hyonmumun; T'ing Ju-ch'ang, Admiral of the Northern Seas, taking poison on board the battleship *Chenyuan*; Ito Hirobumi and Mutsu Munemitsu at the negotiating table with Li Hung-chang. Of the three artists, I especially liked Mizuno Toshikata: after studying his prints carefully outside the Shimizuya, I would rush home to make my own versions of them. Observing how Uncle Kyuemon, the master of the Tanizaki Printers, was able to buy each new three-leaf set as it appeared, I was consumed with envy.

I am not sure whether it was in 1894 or early 1895 that Father's business dealings took a sharp turn for the worse, forcing him to close the Marukyu shop, which he had been barely managing to sustain. At any rate, even I was able to sense that there had been a major change in our family's fortunes. The Yamaju shop was growing even more prosperous; and the print shop too was carrying on the family business that had been bequeathed by the former generation, though not with the same degree of success, due to Uncle Kyuemon's prodigal ways. Yet our branch of the family was no longer able to manage independently. From now on we would have to depend on our relatives' kindness, and become accustomed to the uncomfortable status of hangers-on. It was not that anyone told me this directly: it was something that even a child could sense.

At a time when the Marukyu business was still surviving, though just barely, Mother gave birth to a third son, providing Seiji with a younger brother. Immediately after the birth, however, the infant was sent off to be raised by foster parents in the village of Nakayama in Chiba Prefecture, a place best known for the Hokkekyo-ji temple located there. This was the first time Mother had given up one of her children to strangers; later, when two girls were born, each of them was sent away as well. But of the three who were sent off, never to return, this infant son must have been the hardest to part with, since it was Mother's first experience of such sorrow. In later years she told me how when the foster parents came from Nakayama, put the baby in their rickshaw, and began to drive off, she ran after them for many blocks, crying in her pain at parting. Was it really necessary, I wonder, to give up her child at the cost of such suffering? Was it done because it was considered more economical to pay foster parents to raise a child in the country than to bring him up in the midst of a luxury-loving city family? And if it was for reasons of economy, did the idea proceed from Father, or from Mother? Was she finally persuaded by Father's arguments that the Tanizakis had for generations had the custom of sending children to be raised by foster parents—hadn't Grandfather Kyuemon even sent three of his four sons off?

Despite our straitened circumstances, we continued to enjoy seasonal outings thanks to our uncles at the print shop and the Yamaju: digging for shellfish at the Battery at low tide; watching the fireworks from a boat on the Sumida; occasional trips to the Kabuki theater to see Danjuro and Kikugoro. So there was no real cause for complaint; but somehow there were no more family outings with only us children and our parents; we were always being "taken places" by our other relatives. From earlier, more prosperous days, I remember especially our excursions to the Kannon Temple in Asakusa where we enjoyed looking at the "Panorama," the Ryounkaku "Cloud-defying Pavilion," and the "Flower Garden" amusement park. Our parents would buy us toys in the shopping arcade; then we would have supper at the Mambai restaurant nearby, where departing guests were seen off by attendants carrying little collapsible lanterns. Turning back, I would see how the Okuyama district behind the temple, so lively in the daytime, had now become dark and deserted. (When I went to Asakusa with Granny alone by horse-drawn trolley, we used to have supper at the more ordinary Ujinosato restaurant; while when I went with my parents by rickshaw, it was usually Mambai or Ichinao where we ate.)

I also have quite a few memories of going to eat somewhere with Father alone. He knew a good many rather well-known restaurants, whose cuisine appealed to epicurean Tokyoites, and used to enjoy going out to dine. One spring when the cherry trees were in full bloom, Father took me for a walk along the Mukojima embankment as far as the Sanya ferry: "Seeing we've come this far," he said, "I'd like to go to the Jubako." So, crossing the river, we made our way to the restaurant. It was the first time I had heard of this establishment, which moved to Atami in

Shizuoka Prefecture about twenty years ago. The current proprietor, Mr. Otani, a primary-school classmate of Kubota Mantaro, the well-known writer, represents the fifth generation of his family in the business. His father must have been in charge when I visited the old Sanya Jubako with Father that day.

We also went several times to the Tenkin tempura restaurant on the Ginza: I remember that the young employees were still wearing their hair in the traditional topknot even then. They used to serve a dish of salted squid innards to accompany the saké. Father said it was "no dish for children"; but I insisted on tasting just a little with the tip of my tongue and discovered a wholly new and exceedingly complex kind of sensation.

As described in my early story *Himitsu* (The Secret), I once visited Fuyuki on the way back from a trip to the Fukagawa Hachiman Shrine. "Let's cross the river and have some of those famous noodles at the rice market at Fuyuki," Father said. And so we boarded one of the small boats that plied back and forth across the narrow, low-banked river, propelled by two or three pushes of the boatman's pole. How different the atmosphere was from the canals in the heart of Tokyo.

Then there was the time we had breakfast at the Sasanoyuki after viewing the morning glories at Iriya. "The tofu's great, but the rice is no good," was Father's comment on that restaurant.

In Negishi there was a restaurant called the Okano, which had a splendid garden. I remember going there two or three times—perhaps after viewing the chrysanthemum displays at Dangozaka, in which case Mother may very well have been with us. The Okano had originally specialized in sweet bean soup, though other foods were also available. The rooms were large, designed to accommodate many parties of customers; and the Konohana garden, as it was called, was wonderful, with landscaped hills and pools fed by waterfalls, with springs and artfully placed stones and rocks. I felt as if I had been drawn into a dream world, a nobleman's private garden of the sort I had seen only on the stage and in historical prints.

Our second house in Minami Kayaba-cho

Starting with my first house in Shin-Koume, Honjo, when I was not quite thirty, I have changed lodgings almost thirty times, including moves within Tokyo and nearby prefectures as well as in Kyoto, Osaka, and west-central Japan in general. I wonder if this was not due to my father's influence, since he made at least ten moves that I know of. True, this does not compare with my own extraordinary record; but I at least had the excuse of earthquakes and war and other external forces to contend with; Father shifted back and forth within Nihombashi and Kanda wards in downtown Tokyo for purely private reasons.

Among all these moves, we stayed longest in our second Minami Kayaba-cho house, which thus became the locus of most of my childhood memories. This was at No. 56, only a short distance from the first house at No. 45. At No. 54 stood the small Meitoku Inari Shrine, with its stage for sacred *kagura* dances. Just next to the shrine was an alley leading to the official residences district: our house was in the middle of that alley, on the eastern side. In those days retired people, married men's mistresses, shop clerks, workmen, idlers, gamblers, and others of modest means were the sort of persons who lived in such narrow lanes. Among the various dwellings, ours was better than most, standing independently and built in such a way that the interior was shielded from the curious gaze of passersby. There was another alleyway which came to a dead end just behind the house, where a rather dashing-looking family engaged in the building trade lived. Since we were driven to live in this sort of area due to Father's failure in business, the place was of course rented. Our monthly rent, according to my brother, was eight and a half yen; but that seems a bit steep for that kind of house at the time. Perhaps the rent was gradually raised to that level over a number of years. There was a small, low doorway next to the storehouse facing the alley. Entering, one passed along an irregular path of stepping-stones with the walls of the storehouse on one's left and a wooden-boarded wall to the right. Very soon one came to another low lattice door, beyond which was an earthen-floored entranceway with a raised threshold supporting a pair of sliding doors that were partly glazed. Opening them, one found oneself in a six-mat-sized parlor. There was no proper entrance hall; there were in fact only three rooms—the parlor, an eight-mat room on the first floor of the two-story storehouse, and a small maid's room of three- or four-and-a-half mats. Yet, despite its modest size, it had a small garden with some evergreen shrubs onto which both the parlor and the eight-mat room looked and from which one could reach the kitchen entrance to the rear. In the parlor was a long brazier, on the left side of which Father would sit, facing the garden, while Mother's place was on the right, where the tea chest sat against the wall. At night our parents would move to the room in the storehouse, so Seiji and I could sleep in the parlor. Granny slept in the maid's room. And so the five of us lived together in this rented house—five, that is to say, up to the birth of Sono, the first daughter.

One afternoon very soon after moving to this house (within twenty days or so) when Father was relaxing at home doing nothing in particular, five or six tough-looking characters came barging in, tucked up the skirts of their kimonos, and settled down in a row opposite my father, who was in his usual place near the brazier. Mother fled to the storehouse as soon as she saw them; and Granny too, after bringing out tea and the tobacco tray, hid herself in her own tiny room. But, even though I was a bit afraid, I stayed to watch what would happen, guessing that as a child I would be safe. The fellow who seemed to be the boss began saying something in a rough, threatening voice, tapping the bowl of his pipe against the brazier for emphasis. Meanwhile Father sat there with furrowed brow and an utterly downcast look. Even the gang boss seemed taken aback by his evident misery; and, after some abusive remarks lasting perhaps fifteen to twenty minutes, he and his underlings slouched off as suddenly as they had come. My guess is that Father had left some rather large debts when he closed his business in Kakigara-cho and that his former colleagues had dispatched the hoodlums out of spite. What could have been a very nasty episode was brought to a fairly simple conclusion precisely because my father's misery and helplessness were so obvious.

After the gangsters had gone, Mother emerged from the safety of the storehouse and commented, half disgusted and half amused, on Father's state: "I've never seen such a hangdog look—and you a man too! What a pathetic creature you are! Why, you looked as if you were going to burst into tears at any moment. Of course, that's why that ruffian left so soon. . . . 'Try looking at yourself in a mirror, fella!'. . . . That's what he said when he went out, wasn't it?"

Meanwhile, in the kitchen, Granny was brushing away tears of chagrin and softly railing against "those brutes."

Father had not been putting on an act; his shame and misery simply showed so clearly in his face that even the gangsters had been affected. I became used to seeing that same tearful expression on Father's face over the succeeding years whenever some crisis arose; that hopeless, "Try looking at yourself in a mirror" sort of look which Mother had so scathingly described.

Around this time, I was still going to the print shop every day to take my evening bath, but the trip to and fro was a bit spooky since there were as yet only a few street lamps, even in the crowded Shitamachi area. There were several places in particular that I was afraid of when I made the return trip after dark, and I would run past these points at top speed. In dim, shadowy spots where passersby were few, young men (students, from their look) would sometimes lie in wait for unwary, good-looking little boys. Ever since my "abduction" by the army officer, I had been cautious when it came to older youths and men. In addition, beginning with the Sino-Japanese War in the 1890s, pederastic tastes and practices had begun to flourish, with typical Satsuma dialect expressions like *nise-san* ("elder brother") and *yoka chigo* ("handsome laddie") coming into use even in Tokyo. At any rate, the young delinquents who liked to pursue still younger boys wore a distinctive garb, easily recognizable even in the dark and at some distance. Before the war, silk was often worn by boys as well as girls, but by this time boys generally wore a variety of cotton kimonos in keeping with the new martial spirit of the nation. The prowlers almost always had cotton *haori*, either black and crested or with a splashed pattern, with ridiculously long tie-strings made of strands of thick white wool. These were tied together at the very tips and then brought back to rest on the nape of the neck. When the youths lay in wait for little boys in some dark corner, they would cover their heads with the coat as if it were a hood, with the tie-strings visible on top, their whiteness making them stand out all the more clearly against the dead-black background.

Looking back on it now, I would judge that there were few who had any real criminal intent; most of them doubtless just enjoyed giving the timid little boys a good scare. In any event, I often found my way home blocked by such youths and was forced to flee into a side street and then race home as fast as my legs would carry me. Usually my pursuers would not in fact try very hard to catch up with me, but contented themselves with whistles and catcalls directed at my fleeing form.

The streets became much darker after one left Kakigara-cho, crossing the bridge to enter Minami Kayaba-cho. The reason was that in "Front" Kayaba-cho there were many warehouses, and "Back" Kayaba-cho too had relatively few ordinary shops. Fortunately, there was a power station belonging to the Tokyo Electric Light Company at No. 50, "Back" Kayaba-cho, on the right side of the street a little before one came to the Meitoku Inari Shrine. The power station was faintly lit, and I always felt relieved when I reached it. Still, though there were lights within the building, only one lamppost stood outside. In front was a large ditch; throughout the night the machinery inside the station rumbled away, emitting big puffs of white steam in the direction of the ditch. My house was only about half a block from it, but to get there I had to pass through one more terrifying spot. It was the corner where one turned off into a side alley beside the shrine. The shrine's sanctuary was set well back from the road; and before it there loomed a high, roofed-over stage for the sacred *kagura* dances, which gave a rather eerie effect. A festival was observed on the eighth of each month, and then the precincts were lively with dances and rude comic farces held into the evening. But ordinarily it was very quiet even in the daytime, with no worshipers at all. The sanctuary itself was quite small and unpretentious, and there was no resident priest. Only occasionally—a few times a month—a priest would come, a man with long hair, wearing a white kimono and high clogs, to say a few prayers and then disappear. The floor of the *kagura* stage was raised very high, so that a man could actually pass beneath it. Thus, the shadows were especially deep around the shrine; and I used to hurry past with my eyes shut, wondering if there were not some dangerous characters lurking in the darkness of the stage, or if perhaps a monstrous apparition might not emerge from the sanctuary beyond. Sometimes I would hear a faint noise in the darkness, or a white "something" would gleam softly from the depths of the sanctuary. Then I would feel goose bumps spread over the back of my neck and the hair all over my body stand on end as I caught glimpses of all sorts of things that were not there.

Even at home it was quite lonely after nightfall. More and more ordinary families had electricity by then; but in our household, conservative in this as in everything else, we continued to depend on oil lamps until we moved to Kanda. After the family went to bed, the only light was a single paper lantern in our parents' bedroom. The oil lamps had to be cleaned every evening, and it was my job to do this: a task whose disagreeableness I remember to this day. These lamps were very simple affairs with flat, narrow wicks made of cotton which absorbed the oil and were then set alight. (Even "air lamps" were not yet in use.) To clean them you would remove the glass chimney and blow on it until it steamed over. Then you wrapped cloth around a cotton core to make a ball, attached it to the end of a bamboo stick, and used this tool to polish the inside of the chimney. The chimneys were for the most part shaped like saké bottles, with a narrow neck and a lower portion that bulged outward. This "belly" was very hard to clean—it had to be rubbed and polished with the bamboo tool over and over again. Next you had to take a pair of scissors and try to trim the wick straight across, making it as even as possible. If you cut too much off the left side of the wick, you would have to trim down the right side; and sometimes you would repeat the same mistake again and again on alternate sides. It really was more time-consuming than one might expect. (If the wick was improperly cut, the flame would elongate and give off smoke and soot, eventually causing the chimney to shatter.) Finally, you had to fill the glass reservoir with oil and wipe the outside clean with a cloth. I have always been clumsy with my hands, and by the time I had performed all these tasks my hands and arms, my kimono sleeves and skirt—in short, my whole person—would be covered with oil. And because of the mishap with the oil lamp in the house in Hama-cho some years earlier, I tended to be if anything too careful in my handling of the lamps, thus making my task all the harder.

Often Father and Mother stayed out late; and Granny, Seiji, and I were left alone in the house. Sometimes our parents would be visiting the Kakigara-cho house and stay on talking till late at night. At other times, I suppose, Father might have gone to bed early in the room in the storehouse, while Mother went to the public baths. In those days most people in the Shitamachi area used them: only quite wealthy families had baths of their own. Among my relatives, for example, only the Tanizaki Printers' household had bathing facilities; at the Yamaju house (which was one of the most prosperous in Komeya-cho), the entire family from my uncle on down, and the apprentices as well of course, went to the local bathhouse. (Incidentally, the term used was *yuya*, rather than the word *sento* more common nowadays.)

Father liked to have a cup of saké in the morning and then go off for a bath, so naturally he preferred the public baths which were open all day. But Mother also started going there regularly after we moved to No. 56, leaving me as the only one who continued for a time to take his evening bath at the print shop. Mother always waited until about ten o'clock before leaving for the bathhouse, which was near the official residences area. The reason was that she and Father took so long over supper, which they ate together as a rule. After Father had had a flask of saké, he would begin to feel good and start to display his singing skills, leaning a little forward at the table with his eyes shut. Apparently he would often sing popular songs when he went to a geisha party; and in my judgment these light *dodoitsu* and *hauta* were better rendered than Uncle Kyuemon's more serious and dramatic *gidayu* numbers. Of course Father had no more than a superficial knowledge of music and knew by heart the words of only a few well-known songs. When he felt impelled by the power of saké to sing something, it was almost always "Stray Locks of Hair" or "The Hidden Paths of Love." After he had run through this limited repertoire, he would sing snatches of *gidayu, kiyomoto, tokiwazu, nagauta,* or whatever. I remember thinking as I sat listening to him how much fun it would be to grow up and be able to sing songs like that.

Sometimes when Father was really letting himself go, Mother would intervene: "If you keep on this way you'll bother the neighbors, you know...." These were the people involved in the building trade who lived just behind us: at Father's back as he sat singing in the parlor was a window, and beyond that a clapboard wall, and then a narrow lane of perhaps three feet separating us from our neighbors. Occasionally, large groups of young men would gather there to practice traditional Edo workmen's songs; their spirited efforts were clearly audible from across the alley.

After Father had sung his fill, he would lie down and drop off to sleep, snoring loudly.

"You'll catch cold, lying there like that!" Mother would say, covering him with a comforter. Finally, pulling at his arms and legs, she would lift him up and with great difficulty trundle him off to bed in the storehouse. That accomplished, she could set off for the bathhouse, sometimes taking Granny along with her.

"You can get under the covers now, Jun'ichi; but be sure not to fall asleep till Mama comes back to say goodnight." And off she would go. When Granny went, she usually finished her bath quickly and came right back; but Mother enjoyed a long, leisurely bath that took over an hour. I found it impossible to get to sleep, waiting for Mother to return and with the ceiling lamp still burning. As the hour grew later, the rumbling from the power station seemed to come closer and closer, like the gradual approach of distant thunder through the night.

"Why isn't Mama back yet? What's taking her so long anyway?" I strained to hear the clip-clop of her *geta* winding their way along the narrow alley. At this hour there were few passersby: only occasionally would someone cut through from "Back" Kayaba-cho or the official residences district, their clogs echoing clearly along the pavement. As I lay there listening for each noise and counting one after another, there came a sound, at first faint and distant, then gradually growing clearer and clearer—the familiar, longed-for sound of Mother's *geta*. No matter how far off and faint they may be, a child always knows his mother's footsteps.

"Are you still awake, Jun'ichi?" she would say when she entered the parlor, peering at me as I lay wide-awake among the bedclothes. Mother's cheeks glowed red in the lamplight, all the more so because she had spent the past hour soaking and scrubbing herself with a bran-bag.

I rarely had to get up to go to the toilet during the night; but when it was absolutely necessary I did so with fear and trembling. The water closet was at the end of the veranda which led from the parlor past the storehouse. The only illumination was the lantern by my parents' pillow, which shed a faint light from within the storehouse through the paper screens onto the veranda; all else was utter darkness. I was especially afraid while washing my hands in the basin afterward. In those days there were no sinks inside the house, so I had to use a stone basin in the garden. The veranda was equipped with heavy wooden rain-doors that were kept closed at night, but there was a panel set into them which could be opened so that I could reach out into the garden for the water ladle attached to the basin. All at once the thick darkness of the garden would rush in upon me.

The terror I felt then was not so much a fear of attack by robbers as it was of ghosts and spirits, of foxes and badgers with preternatural powers. My mother and grandmother had often told me how a badger kept appearing at the foot of the Ogibashi bridge in Fukagawa, playing tricks on the unwary residents. I was particularly terrified by the stories of badgers that transformed themselves into giant monsters. I had actually heard on two or three occasions the sound of badgers drumming on their bellies, as they are fabled to do: "There it is—do you hear it, Jun'ichi?" the adults would say when the strange sound came to us as if from a great distance. Thus I believed, even if not wholly, that foxes and badgers and suchlike could in fact inveigle and deceive human beings; I believed it, and was afraid.

Once, late at night, Mother came rushing out of the toilet screaming for Father to come quickly. Her voice woke me and I listened, still half-asleep, to them whispering together on the veranda. It seemed that when Mother entered the water closet she found a strange man trying to crawl up into the room from the pit beneath—reason enough to flee screaming. But when my father went to look, there was no trace of anyone. Mother kept trying to explain what had happened: a hand had suddenly emerged from below, she said. And there was more; but whenever she got to what seemed a crucial part, she lowered her voice so I could not hear. At any rate, the strange creature apparently had fled on hearing my mother's screams. My parents seemed to think he was not just a common thief or burglar. At last they went back to their room, the house became quiet again, and I fell uneasily asleep.

The next day when I got back from school, still upset by what had happened the previous night, I asked Seiji about it. He said nothing, but took a slate and stylus from his satchel and rapidly drew a picture for me, which he then almost immediately erased. It showed a hand emerging from the hole in the floor of the water closet. Each of the five fingers was dramatically sketched in. Still, I could not understand why a hand should suddenly appear from such a place and then as suddenly disappear completely. Now, of course, I realize it must have been the

Jun'ichiro (11) and his brother Seiji (7).

69

act of a pervert. The incident happened when I was at least eleven or twelve, since Seiji too was already attending primary school at the time.

The Kairakuen

It was with Sasanuma Gennosuke, the son of the owner of the Kairakuen Chinese restaurant, that I was to maintain the closest ties over the years; and I would now like to say something about him and about our friendship.

In an essay entitled "My Friend Tanizaki," inserted in the volume of my writings in Kadokawa's *Anthology of Showa Literature*, Sasanuma states: "I still remember how I felt the first time I saw Tanizaki. . . . It was on our first or second day in primary school, and Tanizaki was drawing a picture of a warrior on his slate. . . . He was eight years old and I was seven. . . . He erased that picture and then went on to draw a young woman. He often drew one or the other."

Indeed I do remember sitting at a desk in the classroom during recess drawing pictures of samurai warriors on my slate. I don't remember any pictures of young women; but if Sasanuma says I drew them, why, I suppose I must have. Soon, during the Sino-Japanese War, I developed a passion for war scenes: I enjoyed making carefully detailed drawings of the different types of battleships and of military uniforms of the various ranks.

Actually, the very first time we were together in a class would seem to have been at the Kogishi Kindergarten in Reiganjima, one or two years before we entered the Sakamoto Primary School. But we were not aware of this at the time—it was only later, at the Sakamoto school, that we discovered the fact. Sasanuma says he got to know me on the first or second day; unfortunately, my own memories of our relationship do not go back so far. Let me recount my earliest one of him: it was on a day when Mr. Nogawa's place was being taken by Mr. Kuroda, the gym teacher. After carefully scanning the class, Mr. Kuroda pointed at Sasanuma and made him come and stand in front of the teacher's desk. Then he pointed at me: "You too." With the two of us lined up at the front of the classroom, Mr. Kuroda descended from the podium and made both of us take off our *haori* coats. Holding them high before the other pupils, one in each hand, he made a short speech: "You all see that I have here Sasanuma's coat, and Tanizaki's. Now observe: as I hold them, Sasanuma's feels light, while Tanizaki's feels heavy. The lighter one is made of silk and is expensive. The heavier one is cotton and is cheap. But this cheaper cotton one actually wears better than the expensive silk! So I urge all of you to use *cotton* kimonos, even if they are a bit heavy. When you get home, please tell your mothers that Teacher said so."

When he had finished this little homily, he returned our *haori* to us and let us sit down.

This must have happened in the second or third grade since I began to wear cotton rather than silk only after the onset of the war. Doubtless most children were already using cotton by then; the silk-wearers must have been a distinct minority. It happened that Sasanuma, as the only son of a prosperous restaurateur, was one of the few, and exceptionally well dressed to boot, and thus caught the teacher's eye. But as for me, even though I had been the object of Mr. Kuroda's praise, tears welled up when he handed back my coat. The onrush of tears took me by surprise, and I couldn't have said myself just why I felt so miserable. Probably it was the sudden realization of the change in my situation: I, who had been raised in such comfortable circumstances up to one or two years before, was now the son of a poor family. My wearing cotton was in part due to changes in society at large; but, even aside from that, I was simply no longer in a position to wear silk. The desire to return to the days when I had been coddled and sheltered, as it were, under my nurse's parasol was always dormant somewhere within me, and now suddenly it burst out in the form of these unexpected tears.

When I went home and told Mother what had happened, she was rather bitter toward Mr. Kuroda: "There was no call for him to single you out from all the others and compare your clothes with the Sasanuma boy's. It's outrageous!"

Nonetheless, that day's embarrassing incident was the beginning of the friendship between Sasanuma and myself; from then on I was always going over to his house. The family ran the only Chinese restaurant in the city, located at No. 29, Kamejima-cho 1-chome, Nihombashi, the second shop from the corner of Jizobashi bridge. Later on, the channel through which water from the Kamejima River flowed under the bridge was made into a culvert and the bridge itself vanished, as did the medical clinic that had been located on the corner lot, and so finally the Kairakuen came to occupy that more conspicuous site. The restaurant prospered for some sixty years, from 1884, when Sasanuma's father Gengo became the owner, up to March 1944, when, along with all the other expensive restaurants in Tokyo, it was forced to close in accordance with the austerity policies of the wartime government. It never reopened, yet I am sure there are many who will remember the name Kairakuen. Since I had very close ties with the family, I shall devote a little space to the history of this famous restaurant.

In the food and drink section of Ishii Kendo's *Meiji Origins* there is a chapter on "The Chinese Restaurants of Tokyo" which starts by quoting an article from the *Progress News* of October 30, 1883:

> Plans are currently being made for the construction in Kamejima-cho of a large restaurant to be called the Kairakuen, which will specialize in Chinese cuisine. It will be jointly owned by a group of stockholders and begin with a capital of thirty thousand yen. The menu is expected to include such Chinese delicacies as pig's ichor, boiled mutton-paste rolls, and mouse tempura—which begins to sound like the list of dishes in Act III of *Coxinga*!

Ishii's book then goes on to remark:

> This was the only Chinese restaurant in Tokyo at the time. . . . In fact, until about 1915 there were very few Chinese restaurants in the city, although from 1922 or so onward each ward had several, even if only small ones.

This account is largely corroborated by the *History of Nihombashi Ward* as well. Sasanuma himself says that the restaurant was started in 1883 by a group of mainly Nagasaki natives, with millionaires like Shibusawa Eiichi, Okura Kihachiro, and Asano Soichiro becoming the principal stockholders; and the restaurant was at first open on a members-only basis. Sasanuma's father was appointed general manager and then, one year later, acquired the restaurant for himself, opening it to the general public. It seems that business was quite bad at first, and Sasanuma's mother had to make quiet trips to the pawnshop to keep things going. But by the time I got to know the family they had been in business for some ten years and were growing richer day by day. When I went to visit the Sasanumas, turning into the street that led to Jizobashi bridge, the pungent odors characteristic of Chinese cooking would begin to invade my nostrils from two or three blocks away. These exotic and almost unbearably wonderful smells, still very rarely met with in Tokyo, stimulated my boyish appetite for rich foods and made me envy my friend, who could enjoy such culinary delights every day. The odors of Chinese food clung to Sasanuma, to his hands and clothing, even when he came to school. And when the cooks at the Kairakuen went to the red-light district in Suzaki, the girls guessed at once what kind of work they did, for the same reason. We pupils at the Sakamoto school used to exchange the contents of our box-lunches with Sasanuma whenever we had the chance, at the regular lunch hour or on picnics and sports days. Usually his lunch included things like pork meatballs, pork ribs in sweet sauce, *wansai* omelets, and Chinese-style tempura. But Sasanuma had these rich foods every day and was tired of them, so he was happy to exchange them for simple Japanese fare like salted salmon, boiled fish, and devil's-tongue. Naturally, we all looked forward to these culinary swapping sessions.

There must have been several reasons for the Kairakuen's extraordinary success among the fine restaurants of Tokyo, but it seems to me that the greatest was the talents and efforts of Sasanuma's mother, To. All too often in this world there are people of great merit who go unrecognized, and surely Sasanuma To was one of these. She was by no means the sort of shrewd lady-manager type one encounters so frequently nowadays. Admittedly, she had the full-bodied, portly figure of such a woman; but she seemed above all a gentle person, with a strong Tochigi accent and a country air about her. She never had a harsh word for the employees, but simply sat all day at the brazier quietly smoking her long, old-fashioned pipe. Yet most people sensed something in her that made them feel great respect for her. One could tell at a glance that she was a compassionate person, one who could not remain indifferent to another's suffering. It showed in the warm, sincere expression on her face, which would disarm even the most wicked and cold-hearted of men.

Sasanuma Gengo himself experienced many hardships and disappointments, failing at various ventures before he took on the ownership of the Kairakuen. He was even said to have attempted suicide by leaping from a bridge in Senju when he was forty. If he was able to succeed with the Kairakuen and lead a happy, prosperous life in his later years, I am sure it was very largely due to the unobtrusive virtues and talents of his saintly wife.

Another undeniable reason for the restaurant's success was the fact that its unique cuisine appealed enormously to the tastes of contemporary Tokyoites. Since it had been established by people from Nagasaki, the food offered was in fact not so much purely Chinese as mixed Chinese-Japanese, Nagasaki cooking. The rooms were Japanese-style tatami ones, precisely like those in an expensive Japanese restaurant. In the center of each room was a round *shippoku* table, imported from Nagasaki and bright red in color, around which the customers sat on thick cushions laid on the tatami. Later, when the fashion for pure Chinese food began, the Kairakuen followed the other restaurants' lead by adding Chinese-style rooms and hiring a Chinese cook to make real Chinese dishes. Even so, the old customers preferred to eat sitting on tatami around the Nagasaki tables, and continued to order the hybrid, rather than the more authentically Chinese, dishes.

During the Meiji period there were frequent epidemics of cholera, sometimes so severe that it was difficult to dispose of the bodies. Whenever conditions got especially bad, the number of customers at the Japanese restaurants would fall dramatically while the Kairakuen's business prospered.

In addition to the health factor, another advantage the restaurant enjoyed lay in its policy of not admitting geisha to entertain guests, as Japanese restaurants did. In those days there were few halls large enough to accommodate the two or three hundred persons who might be attending a political meeting; thus the large hall at the Kairakuen was reserved virtually every day for political banquets during the sessions of the National Diet. Since geisha were not admitted, the management took care to hire very good-looking waitresses, and this became one of its attractions (as was also true of the Koyokan in Shiba Park). There were even rumors that the Kairakuen girls sometimes served as mistresses to high officials and powerful politicians, but I can say with confidence that such rumors were totally groundless.

Even today, though, I can recall the features of several of the girls, so beautiful were they. Probably the best known was O-ito, the head waitress. She was a true child of the Nihombashi area, an admirer of the novelist Ozaki Koyo, and, if I recall correctly, the daughter of a pawnbroker in Kamejima-cho. She was not only a graceful beauty of the sort the artist Kiyokata loved to depict, but also a woman of real intelligence. Since Sasanuma's mother was so benevolent and easygoing a person, it was in a sense necessary to have as head waitress a girl like O-ito, who could be sharp when necessary. Between the two of them, they were able to manage the employees very well, far better than either could have done alone. However, there was some gossip about O-ito's personal life: that she was involved in a questionable relationship with a certain high police official; that she was in love with a distant relation of the Sasanumas, who served as live-in student-houseboy; and similar stories.

Over the years there were many and various waitresses at the Kairakuen, but all of them worked hard and most were able to better themselves. One seldom heard tales of girls who had "gone wrong," or ended up as some man's mistress. My favorite waitress, for example, married a very talented artisan and is leading a happy married life to this day, though she could doubtless have had an easier, if less respectable, sort of life had she wished it.

To tell the truth, there were two of the girls there around that time that I myself was thinking of marrying. I met the first one while my mother was still alive, when I was writing the early short stories *Kirin* (Unicorn) and *Hokan* (The Jester) for the revived *Shinshicho* journal. Having won Sasanuma's approval, I brought my mother to the restaurant one day to take a quiet look at the young woman. That done, I made my proposal of marriage through Sasanuma, only to be flatly turned down.

The second time was just after my divorce from my first wife, Chiyoko: I had had my eye on a particular girl at the Kairakuen for quite a while, so I traveled from my home in Okamoto in the Osaka-Kobe area, passing along the Japan Sea coast and finally going on to Tokyo to discuss the matter with Sasanuma's wife. To my surprise, her response was that the young woman in question had only the other day gone off and married someone else. Since I had reason to assume that Mrs. Sasanuma was not unaware of my interest in the girl, I was more than a little disappointed and resentful that she had not let me know beforehand what the girl was about to do. Probably the reason was that Mrs. Sasanuma, having no confidence whatever in my moral character and fearing the worst if the girl should marry a man like me, had mentally crossed me off her list from the very start.

Incidentally, the first girl, the one who had rejected me herself, went on to marry somebody else but then was divorced. I have heard rumors that she is living alone somewhere in the suburbs of Tokyo; she must be in her sixties by now, and I find myself hoping somehow that her remaining years will be happy ones.

Gen-chan

My friend Sasanuma was an only son and was named Gennosuke. After he entered the Municipal Middle School in Tsukiji he acquired the nickname "Porky" because he was as fat as the proverbial pig. Not only his middle-school classmates but also his friends from primary school and eventually even his wife called him "Porky" in preference to his real name. When I first knew him at the Sakamoto school, however, he was still "Gen-chan." As I noted earlier, the term "Botchan" (Young Master) was not used by Shitamachi families, so he was "Gen-chan" to everyone, including the Kairakuen employees. What set the Sasanumas apart in my eyes, though, was the fact that Gen-chan also added the affectionate or polite suffixes "-chan" or "-san" to the employees' names rather than addressing them more abruptly by their names alone. There was really nothing so strange about this since it was, after all, a restaurant and not just the family home; but to me it seemed odd at first to hear Gen-chan call O-ito, the head waitress, "Ito-chan."

When it came to our grades in school, I usually ranked first and Gen-chan second. (Later, two other pupils overtook us, so I fell to third place and Gen-chan to fourth.) But though his grades on average were lower than mine, in certain subjects he did so outstandingly well that the teachers were amazed. He had impressive powers of reasoning and usually got perfect marks in arithmetic; but he had little talent for Japanese language and literature, composition, and the like. His only strength in these areas was grammatical analysis.

On several occasions I was really impressed by Gen-chan's analytical mind. One day, two or three of us had gathered at his house and were browsing through *Boys' World* or one of the other children's magazines when we came across the following riddle:

> When Yoshitsune and Benkei were approaching the Ataka Barrier, they came upon a young girl at play, with her baby brother on her back. Benkei asked the girl how many children there were in her

family. She answered, "Five from my father, and five from my mother; that's eight in all." Benkei could not make head or tail of this, but Yoshitsune understood at once. What is the solution?

"Why, that's easy as pie," said Gen-chan as the rest of us scratched our heads. "The girl's mother had three kids from an earlier marriage, and so did her father. Then they had two more together. So the total is eight children, but the father and mother each had five!"

Even after this explanation, it took the rest of us a few minutes to get the point. Obviously Gen-chan was a Yoshitsune, and we were all Benkeis.

Then there was the time we discovered in some magazine or other the poem "Gathering mushrooms—like poem cards, right under your nose!" Once again, as the rest of us were discussing what on earth it could mean, Gen-chan came up with the answer: "When you play the poem-card game, you always shout 'Here it is, here it is' when you find the card you were looking for 'right under your nose,' and then grab for it. And it's the same with picking mushrooms: 'Here one is,' you say, and grab the mushroom growing right in front of you."

We were all amazed at how sharp he was; and even though, as I said before, he did not have a natural talent for literature, in this case his acuteness won the day.

There is another incident I would like to relate, though it is unconnected with Gen-chan's skill in reasoning. Usually it was I who went to visit him at the Kairakuen, but occasionally he would come to my house to invite me over. Since our house was so small, he did not come in but would stand outside the front door and call my name; I'd tell Mother I was going to Gen-chan's, and then rush off. Mother felt badly about my always imposing on the Sasanumas and used to say things like "Well, I suppose it's all right, but it seems you're always visiting the Sasanumas and being given things.... We really ought to have Gen-chan in at least for tea and cakes sometime.... But this place is just so small, there's no room to entertain anyone...."

Then one day when he called on me, Mother said I should invite him in. "Tell him your mother just wants to meet him and thank him for all his hospitality." Mother went to the front door herself and virtually dragged Gen-chan, who was trying politely to decline, into the six-mat parlor, where she ensconced him on a thick cushion.

"I'm sorry to have to entertain you in a shabby place like this, Gen-chan. Jun'ichi has visited you so often and had such wonderful treats at your house.... He never holds back, I'm afraid, when it comes to treats. No manners at all!... Do be sure and tell your parents how much we appreciate their kindness to Jun'ichi, won't you? I really ought to go myself to thank them, I know, but..."

Mother brought out some cakes from Mihashido or somewhere, which happened fortunately to be on hand, poured tea, and chatted about this and that with Gen-chan for quite some time. During all this I was surprised to see that Gen-chan spoke to my mother just like one adult to another. If anyone had been listening with his eyes closed, he would never have imagined that it was a conversation between a primary-school pupil and a married lady entering her middle years! Anyone would have assumed that these were two mature people exchanging pleasantries about the weather and things in general.

Gen-chan completely ignored me, as if it were quite beneath him to talk with a mere child, and concentrated entirely on Mother, answering her questions effortlessly, informing her about the Kairakuen's management policies, its methods of laying in stock, and so on. His fluency and skill in responding were nothing short of stunning. It was the first time I had seen this precocious side of him, and it was like encountering an entirely new Gen-chan.

"What an impressive boy he is," said Mother later, unable to conceal her admiration.

In general the children of restaurateurs are precocious and worldly-wise beyond their years since they learn a great deal from the cooks and waitresses who surround them from an early age. And Gen-chan was, as we have seen, a very adult child. He was a source of information on almost everything, including matters that the average primary-school pupil could not conceive of. Thus it was Gen-chan who revealed to me when we were in the second grade the secret of where babies come from. The information he provided on that topic was so startling that at first hardly any of us believed him. Our skepticism is not to be wondered at, though, since it was a time when there was no general sex education and even girls of marriageable age were often ignorant of the basic facts of life. I remember how Mother used to laugh as she told the story of a certain friend of hers who, when her first child was born, was surprised that it "came out from such a strange place!"

Then there is another story, concerning Sasanuma's wife, Kiyoko (or O-kiyo, as we called her). When they married in November 1909, Gen-chan was twenty-three and O-kiyo was an innocent girl of seventeen. Some two years later, their first child, a daughter, was born; but O-kiyo believed up to the week before the birth that babies were delivered by means of a supernatural incision in the mother's belly. During delivery, the "cutting god" and the "sewing-up god" would appear: the former would cut the belly open and take the child out, and the latter would then sew the incision up.

"Why, of course, Mr. Tanizaki. . . . I'm amazed you don't know about that!" she said with a straight face, leaving me wondering if someone had been filling her with misinformation before the marriage.

"What nonsense! Are you serious, O-kiyo?"

"It's *not* nonsense. That's the way it happens: there's a god for cutting and another for sewing up."

"Stop this silliness, O-kiyo," scolded Sasanuma from the sidelines, laughing.

But there was something in her manner that suggested she might not be making a joke, that she really might believe what she was saying.

"Listen, Gen-chan, I think she really doesn't know," I said later in a quiet voice.

"Oh, come now. . . ."

"I tell you, she doesn't know! Why don't you at least try to find out for sure?"

That night Sasanuma talked to the head waitress about "the cutting god" and "the sewing-up god" and asked her to find out discreetly whether his bride actually believed the story. The results were as I had expected. So, had things been left to stand as they were, O-kiyo too would have had quite a surprise with regard to the "strange place" from which babies emerge. I was really very pleased to have been able to return tit for tat to Sasanuma Gen-chan, who had provided me with my earliest sex education.

Gen-chan's curriculum in that area was ever developing, and the next stage was something we called "the Emergency Basket game." There was a rather large room that had once been the sole Chinese-style dining room at the Kairakuen, but was now used for storage. Later on it was refurbished as a Japanese dining room; but at the period I am describing it was a large, empty space filled with the odors of dried sharks' fins, bêche-de-mer, and other items used in Chinese cooking. The floor was of wood, not tatami, and here and there were stacks of the rectangular tables used for banquets as well as large round ones left over from the room's "Chinese period." A group of us, urged on by Gen-chan, started to make use of this space for a variety of games and pastimes. We would line up a number of the tables to make a stage and then perform a play on it. Or we would have pitched battles and hurl fire crackers at one another. Then one day someone had a fresh idea: we would "play brothel"!

Most houses in those days were equipped with one or two emergency baskets, oblong containers made of roughly woven bamboo strips, and about the size of a large chest. They were kept in case of sudden fire, when anything and everything close at hand would be pitched into them and then carried to safety. They were usually placed in a conspicuous spot so as to be ready for use in any emergency: at the Kairakuen, two were set on top of one of the round Chinese tables in the storeroom. We children, however, immediately found another use for the baskets: we converted them into "courtesans' bedchambers" for our brothel game. Three or four of us would take turns, one playing the client, another the courtesan. Gen-chan and I each played both parts several times. We would lie facing each other in the narrow basket for a while—that was all; then another couple would take our place. Those who were not having their turn in the basket watched, snickering, from below.

I suppose the idea for this came from the stories the cooks told Gen-chan about their adventures in the Suzaki red-light district. We all loved the game, which we dubbed "the Emergency Basket," and so passed many carefree days playing at prostitutes. "Let's do the Emergency Basket again today," was our constant cry.

The following story may serve to illustrate how relaxed and innocent the atmosphere at primary schools was in our time, compared with today. One day Gen-chan and I were talking quietly in a corner of the classroom about the Emergency Basket, courtesans, etc. Soon all the pupils sitting around us were looking in our direction, whispering and laughing among themselves.

"What is this? What are you all chattering about?" demanded Mr. Nogawa, turning away from the blackboard to gaze down on the class from his high perch. Immediately one of the class wags volunteered, "It's

Sasanuma and Tanizaki, sir. They're lechers!" and the whole room roared with laughter.

"They are, are they?" said Mr. Nogawa, laughing too.

"That's right, sir. That's all they talk about every day."

"Is that so? All right, let's put that on the blackboard."

He turned to the board again and in thick white letters chalked in the words "Sasanuma, Tanizaki, Lechers," provoking another storm of laughter.

I still remember to this day the rather peculiar characters Mr. Nogawa chose to use; but the point is that any schoolteacher who dared write a word like that on the blackboard today would be in deeper trouble than the worst of his students.

From that day on Gen-chan and I were treated as confirmed lechers. Once when Mr. Kuroda was giving us a history lesson, he held up a portrait of the fourteenth-century shogun Ashikaga Yoshimitsu and remarked, "See how his eyes turn down at the corners? It makes him look lecherous, doesn't it?" The whole class turned to look at us two and burst into laughter. Then some tattletale informed the teacher, "Those two over there are lechers too!"

Even though Mr. Nogawa did not particularly scold us over the lecher business, he did lay down the law on another matter.

He was living at the time near the end of a small cul-de-sac behind the Army General Staff Headquarters in Hayabusa-cho, Koji-machi; and Gen-chan and I, along with Wakita, the son of the former constable from the official residences area, went to visit him at his home two or three times, always on a Sunday. Naturally in those days we walked all the way from Nihombashi to Hayabusa-cho, and by the time we had left Mr. Nogawa's and were on our way back, we felt very much like stopping somewhere to have a bite. Without Gen-chan, we would not have had the courage to part the curtains and enter an eatery, children that we were; but with him in the lead, Wakita and I managed somewhat fearfully to follow along. The first few times, we went into a noodle shop that stood on the corner of Hayabusa-cho and Koji-machi Street; then, gaining more confidence, we chose a tempura restaurant (also on Koji-machi Street, as I recall) and boldly had a meal on the second floor. Everything went well; but Wakita, like a true constable's son, told all when he reached home and was roundly scolded by his mother. Then a few days later all three of us were summoned before Mr. Nogawa:

"You're still just in primary school. You have no business going into noodle shops and tempura restaurants all by yourselves.... If your parents take you, of course, that's another matter. But there must be no more of this going off by yourselves, just the three of you, from now on!"

Those were his words; but I no longer remember, if I ever knew, precisely how he came to know of our experiments in dining out. The restaurants in question were close to his house, so perhaps someone saw us and informed him; or perhaps we were naïve enough to have written about it ourselves in our class compositions.

Another incident from the same period: I have already described how sellers of various sweets and pastries had their stalls in the precincts of the Yakushi Temple in Minami Kayaba-cho. One day Gen-chan announced that one of the vendors had shown him something interesting: "Come on, Jun-chan—I'll show you something worth seeing!"

Leading me to a candy vendor's stand and lowering his voice so the other children standing about wouldn't hear, he asked the man to "show it to us." The candy seller said nothing, but gave Gen-chan a hard, steady look. He assumed an air of indifference but was clearly concerned about being observed by the crowd. When the other children had drifted off, he saw his chance and, reaching under the counter of his stall, drew out a large clam shell.

"OK, kid, take a quick look while there's no one around. But this is the last time!" He whipped open the top shell for an instant and then immediately shut it. I caught the merest glimpse of what was inside: candy figurines, of great delicacy and precision, showing a man and woman making love.

It will no doubt seem to the reader from all this that Gen-chan and I were regular delinquents, but I must insist it was not so. When we played the Emergency Basket game, it was purely out of childish curiosity: we had no real notion of what it was the Kairakuen cooks went off to Suzaki to do. In general I think one may say that city children tend to accumulate superficial knowledge about all kinds of things and are thus able to assume a knowing air about sexual matters too; but when it comes to actual practice, I am sure that children raised in the country are far more precocious. In the case of Gen-chan and myself, it was not until our early twenties that we had our first experiences with a woman.

Gen-chan had a reputation for being self-assured, forward, and knowing beyond his years, but even he once made a major, and exceedingly childish, blunder. There was a teacher called Mr. Ikeda who was notoriously strict. The incident happened one day while he was temporarily taking charge of Mr. Nogawa's class. Because it was Mr. Ikeda, the entire class was keeping perfect silence; not a whisper or a cough was heard. In the midst of this stillness, a great wail suddenly came from Gen-chan and tears began to pour down his face.

"What is it, Sasanuma?" demanded Mr. Ikeda.

Gen-chan kept on crying and bawling out something unintelligible as he rose from his seat holding his satchel, from which drops of liquid were falling, spattering the floor.

"What's wrong, Sasanuma?"

"I . . . I . . . I . . . peed!"

Gen-chan had been so afraid of the terrible Mr. Ikeda that he had tried to hold back his urgent need to urinate; at last, unable to stand it any longer, he had used his satchel as a chamberpot.

"You little idiot! Go home and change your clothes and then get right back here!"

And so, crying all the harder, Gen-chan made his way out of the classroom, one hand raising the skirt of his kimono, and the other carefully balancing the satchel so that its contents would not spill out onto the floor. The contrast between our usual clever, well-mannered Gen-chan and his present state was so ludicrous that the whole class roared with laughter.

*K*agura dances and *chaban* farces

There must be very few Shinto shrines left in Tokyo that still have stages for the performance of *kagura* sacred dances, and even fewer places where the *kagura* are actually performed at the shrine festival and on fair days. Besides, even if they were put on, children today would probably think them boring. Yet I find myself longing to experience once more the atmosphere of those performances on a long, slow spring day somewhere in Ningyo-cho or Kayaba-cho, with dancers in fools' masks moving to the simple, vigorous rhythms of the flutes and drums.

This was the only form of entertainment for children in the days before there were cinemas or even street storytellers with their illustrated tales. Of course one could not see the dances every day: one had to wait for a fair or festival at some shrine to come around. But near my house were the Meitoku Inari Shrine in the same block, the Junko Inari in Kamejima-cho, the Icho Hachiman in Kakigara-cho, and the Suitengu in Ningyo-cho, each of which held performances once a month.

As I recall, the pieces most frequently performed at all the shrines included ones in which the dancer, wearing a woman's mask and clothing from the classical age, shook a set of small bells which jangled as he moved about the stage; fools' dances, in which masks and movements alike were crude and comic; ones in which the dancer wore a costume of glittering gold brocade with an extraordinarily wide *hakama* divided skirt and a fox mask under a wig of fluffy white hair like that worn by the lion-dancer in the No drama *Shakkyo*; ones in which a fool gets mixed up with a fox and is in the end bewitched by it and made to do all sorts of ridiculous things; and dances where, instead of a fox, two devils, red and blue, appear and frighten a fool out of what few wits he has. There may have been other pieces, of course, but most were of this order. Usually there was no dialogue; just dance and gesture in time to the shrilling of flutes, the clang and clatter of gongs, and the rhythmical beat of the drum. But to please the children, dialogue was sometimes added. Thus the red and blue devils were usually provided with lines to say when they were threatening the fool; and their speech sounded uncanny and devilish indeed, muffled and distorted as it was by the heavy wooden masks they wore.

For me there was something very precious about even these simple, old-fashioned *kagura* of the ordinary kind; but especially deserving of note here, I think, are the dances from the "seventy-five-piece *kagura* repertoire" performed at the Suitengu Shrine on May 5 each year. The usual sort of *kagura* is popularly known as the "twenty-five pieces"; as far as I know, the dances taken from the special "seventy-five-piece repertoire" were put on only once a year, on the Suitengu stage. This was an entirely different type of *kagura*, and had the character of an archaic drama of great refinement and rich content. It could perhaps be compared with the masked dance-dramas performed annually at the Mibu Temple in Kyoto; yet the differences were too great to make this a very helpful comparison, each form being true to its own essential character. The Mibu Kyogen, as they are called, are based on popular materials from the Edo period, while the seventy-five *kagura* were mostly historical pieces based on authentic sources from the age of the *Kojiki* and *Nihon shoki* chronicles of the eighth century. Among the *kagura* that I saw performed, the one set in the most distant past was the story of Hosusori-no-mikoto and his younger brother Hikohohodemi-no-mikoto from the "Journey to the Sea Palace" toward the end of volume two of "The Age of the Gods" section in the *Nihon shoki* (the two are identified in the *Kojiki* as Hoderi-no-mikoto and Hoori-no-mikoto). This legend, often titled "The Fish-Scale Palace in the Sea," has been depicted in modern times by the painter Aoki Shigeru.

According to the legend, the elder brother Hosusori-no-mikoto has a special power called the Luck of the Sea and comes to be known as Luck-of-the-Sea Male, while his brother Hikohohodemi-no-mikoto has the Luck of the Mountains and is known by that name. Whenever a storm comes with strong winds and rains, the elder brother loses his luck and can obtain nothing from the sea, whereas the younger one's luck is unaffected. This being so, the elder brother suggests that they try exchanging their territories for a time. The other agrees, and the elder takes the younger's bow and arrows and goes to the mountains to hunt, while the latter takes his brother's fishhook and goes to the sea. Neither of them, however, is successful: both come back empty-handed. The elder brother returns the bow and arrows and asks for his fishhook; but the younger explains that he has unfortunately lost the hook at the bottom of the sea and asks pardon. When his brother nonetheless demands its return, he takes his sword, ten hand-breadths in length, and breaks it into pieces, making several thousand new fishhooks. But his brother angrily refuses them, still demanding the return of the original fishhook. The younger brother goes to the seashore and wanders there disconsolate, not knowing what to do, when he comes upon a river bird caught in a trap and releases the creature out of tenderness of heart. Shortly afterward the Old Man of the Saltlands appears, builds a small, well-caulked boat, invites Hikohohodemi to board, and pushes it out to sea. The boat travels to the bottom of the ocean, passing along "the Pleasant Road," and arrives at the palace of the god of the sea. The god himself comes to greet Hikohohodemi, welcomes him to the palace, spreads eight sealskin mats one on top of the other for him to sit upon, and sets before him many tables loaded with every sort of delicacy.

Hikohohodemi gives the god of the sea a detailed account of his problems with his brother. The god invites him to stay as his guest in the palace and gives him his daughter Toyotama-hime in marriage. The young couple live happily and lovingly together for three years, when it is time at last for Hikohohodemi to return to the world above the sea. Thereupon the god of the sea summons all the fishes large and small within his domain and discovers the lost fishhook, caught in the throat of a sea bream. The god returns it to Hikohohodemi with the following instructions: "When you get back to your native place and meet your brother, toss him this hook, facing away from him the while, and repeating these words: 'Ohochi, susunomichi, mijiji, urukechi.' " Then the god gives him two precious objects, the Tide-raising Gem and the Tide-lowering Gem, directing him to "make your rice fields in low places if your brother makes his in high ones, and make yours in high places if he makes his in low ones." The sea god calls together all the sharks in his domain and addresses them, saying: "The grandchild of the Heavenly Deity is about to return to his home and one among you must bear him safely there. How many days will it take you to reach the Land Above the Sea?" Whereupon one of the sharks comes forward and says, "I can take the divine grandchild there within a day." And so Hikohohodemi returns to his homeland mounted on the shark's back and restores the lost fishhook to his elder brother. Nevertheless, the latter is if anything more ill-disposed toward Hikohohodemi, treating him with great harshness. When he begins to use violence against him, the younger brother, remembering the sea god's instructions, at last takes out the Tide-raising Gem. At once the tide rises to engulf his brother who, on the point of drowning, cries out: "Help, help! I was wrong— forgive me!" The other, hearing these words, takes out the Tide-lowering Gem, and immediately the waves roll back and the sea is calm again. After a succession of such experiences, the elder brother begins to grow pale and thin, loses all strength, and in the end acknowledges Hikohohodemi's supremacy and becomes his servant.

Meanwhile, in the sea god's palace, Toyotama-hime finds herself with child and sends a message to her husband: "Since the child to be born is a descendant of the Heavenly Line, I must not give birth to it in the sea. When the time comes, I shall go to the Land Above the Sea. Please build a lying-in hut by the shore and wait for me there." Then, mounting a great sea turtle, and accompanied by her younger sister Tamayori-hime, she rises to the surface, shining radiantly. Hikohohodemi has begun to build a hut by the shore, thatching it with cormorant feathers, but the babe is born so quickly that the roof has not been finished. For this reason he is named Ugaya-fuki-aezu-no-mikoto, the deity Cormorant-Feather-Thatching-Not-Yet-Done.

The *kagura* from the seventy-five-piece repertoire at the Suitengu Shrine were all more or less based on this sort of material. The stage was wider and larger than usual, with, I believe, a kind of connecting bridge attached. The musical instruments were much the same as those for other *kagura*, that is to say, rather simple and limited in range. By contrast, the masks and costumes were quite splendid, and a variety of props were used. Thus, when Hikohohodemi-no-mikoto, the deity with the Luck of the Mountains, appeared on stage he bore a bow and quiver of arrows. There was absolutely no dialogue, the actors expressing themselves entirely through gesture and dance. Since there was no explanation provided of the title or contents, most of the audience would not have known just what incident from what period was being shown; we simply watched the actors and listened to the musicians without understanding much of the meaning. Later, when I began to read books of history and folklore, I would often come across something that made me realize for the first time just what it was I had been watching. Yet even as a small child I was able to grasp something of what was going on: I sensed that these were tales of the gods of ancient Japan and of their descendants, and I was somehow deeply impressed by what I saw.

In my retelling of the story of the two brothers Luck-of-the-Mountains and Luck-of-the-Sea, I relied on the accounts given in the *Kojiki* and *Nihon shoki*; but I do not mean to suggest that the entire story was presented in the seventy-five *kagura* performances. Some parts I clearly remember: the younger brother coming on stage with his bow and arrows; the elder brother abusing him; the younger one repeatedly taking out first the Tide-raising Gem and then the Tide-lowering Gem; the elder brother struggling not to drown in the sea at high tide; the elder prostrate on the ground before the younger, admitting defeat. I am not sure, however, whether such incidents as the appearances of the small, well-caulked boat, or the shark, or the great sea turtle; the figures of the god of the sea, Toyotama-hime, and Tamayori-hime; and the birth of little Cormorant-Feather-Thatching-Not-Yet-Done, were ever shown on stage.

The assassination of an Emperor has never been presented on the No, Kyogen, or Kabuki stages; yet such a scene did in fact appear in the

Suitengu *kagura*: when Prince Mayuwa creeps up to where the Emperor Anko is sleeping and slits his throat with a long sword. I saw this played at the Suitengu with my own eyes.

The historical accounts say that the Emperor Anko killed Prince Ohokusaka and took his consort, Princess Nakashi, for himself, finally making her his Empress. Now Princess Nakashi had had a child by Prince Ohokusaka, a boy named Mayuwa. This boy's father had been executed for conspiring against the throne; but because his mother enjoyed the Emperor's favor, the lad was considered free of any guilt and was raised at court. In the eighth month of the third year of his reign, Emperor Anko repaired to his summer palace in the mountains, where he held a banquet in one of the high pavilions. Having drunk heavily, he turned to the Empress and said: "I truly love you, but I am worried about Prince Mayuwa. Soon he will grow up and, when he learns that it was I who killed his father, he will surely try to avenge his death. This is a source of constant worry to me"; then, laying his head upon the Empress's lap, he fell asleep. Now Prince Mayuwa, who was seven years old at the time, happened to be sitting beneath the pavilion, where he overheard all that had been said. Taking advantage of the Emperor's nap, he "took up the sword that was lying at his side and slashed the Emperor's throat. He then fled away to the house of Tsubura Ohomi" (from the *Kojiki*).

I have very clear memories of the *kagura* based on this story: Princess Nakashi looking pleadingly at the Emperor; the Emperor lying asleep with his head pillowed on her lap; the seven-year-old prince approaching the Emperor, the sword grasped in his trembling hands—I remember it all being just as the historical records describe it.

I also saw an enactment of Prince Naka-no-oe (later to become the Emperor Tenji) killing the powerful courtier Soga no Iruka in the Grand Throne Room of the Imperial Palace. Of all the dances from the seventy-five *kagura* I remember this as being by far the most ambitious.

According to the account of the Empress Kogyoku's reign given in volume twenty-four of the *Nihon shoki*, in the sixth month of the fourth year of that reign, ambassadors arrived from the three Korean states; and Prince Naka-no-oe decided to take advantage of this opportunity to carry out his long-cherished plans. So in private he told Yamada-no-maro, "On the day when the Korean embassy's gifts are to be presented, I will have you appointed as the one to read the formal greeting before the Empress. As soon as you have finished, we will all rise together and attack Iruka."

When the day came, the Empress was ushered into the throne room, with Prince Naka-no-oe at her side. The prince's trusted follower Nakatomi no Kamatari knew that Iruka was a man cautious and suspicious by nature, who never went without his sword, so he had told the entertainers at the reception precisely what ruse to employ in order to disarm him. Iruka was taken in by the trick and, laughing good-humoredly, removed his sword before sitting down. Then Yamada-no-maro came forward and began reverently to read the memorial from the Korean ambassadors. Prince Naka-no-oe had previously warned the imperial guard to close all twelve gates of the palace at once so as to allow no one to leave or enter; he then took a pike and hid in the shadows. Kamatari and his followers were armed with bows and arrows, ready to protect and aid the prince; and two swords had been given to Saeki no Muraji Komaro and Katsuragi no Wakainukai no Muraji Amita, with instructions to be ready to strike at Iruka without hesitation once the signal was given. Komaro, who had been eating some rice gruel when this message was delivered, was so shocked and terrified that he vomited, bringing up everything he had eaten. Kamatari observed this, and said a few words of reproach and encouragement to put some spirit into them.

At the reception Yamada-no-maro, aware that Komaro and the others were making no move to attack Iruka even though he was reaching the end of the memorial, began to break out in a cold sweat; his voice trembled and his hands shook. Iruka became suspicious and demanded to know why Yamada-no-maro was in such a state. The latter replied that, being so near the august person of the Empress, he was overcome with awe, and could not keep from sweating and trembling. Prince Naka-no-oe, realizing that Komaro was too afraid of Iruka to strike on his own, suddenly gave a loud cry and leaped forward, wounding Iruka about the head and shoulders just as Komaro and his group also made their move. As Iruka struggled to his feet in terror, Komaro slashed at his legs. Stumbling, Iruka made his way toward the Empress and fell prostrate, his head to the floor: "Truly it is you alone, O Child of Heaven, who can occupy the Throne of the Sun-descended Line! Deign to see that I have committed no offense against Your Majesty!"

The Empress was greatly shocked and turning to Prince Naka-no-oe demanded, "What is the meaning of all this?" The prince prostrated himself and said: "Iruka is seeking to destroy the imperial clan and topple the Sun Throne itself! How can we allow the Sacred Throne to pass into the hands of such a man as he?" The Empress stood up and withdrew to the inner apartments; and Komaro and Amita both slashed the fallen Iruka several times with their swords. By now it was raining, and there were great puddles of water in the palace gardens. They took Iruka's corpse and placed it there, covering it with straw mats and screens.

In the *kagura* version of the scene just described, there would have appeared on stage the Empress, the prince, Iruka, Kamatari and the other conspirators (eight persons in all), together with the entertainers. And it seems to me there were others as well: courtiers in attendance on the Empress, the members of the Korean embassy, and so on. The scene was highly dramatic in content, and rich in movement and gesture; the audience must have found it as interesting as any stage play. At the point where Iruka was attacked, the Korean envoys were shown as petrified with fear, and they made their exit crawling on their knees. (Or perhaps it was not the Koreans but the entertainers—I am not quite sure.)

I have heard that since 1955 the Suitengu Shrine has revived the seventy-five *kagura*, which had been discontinued for so long, building a new stage and giving performances annually on May 5. Last year, alas, I was in Kyoto in May and so missed the chance to see it; but if some day I do manage to see the "Death of Iruka," for example, I am sure those phantoms of sixty years past will come before me in an instant.

Another traditional genre that impressed me as much as *kagura*—indeed, I think, rather more—was *chaban*. More properly called *chaban kyogen*, it is described by Shimmura Izuru in his well-known dictionary as "a comic farce employing jokes and puns accompanied by gestures and other movements of the body, and utilizing as material for humor whatever happens to be at hand," a definition that seems to me both simpler and more to the point than the one given in the *Daigenkai* dictionary. The Tokyo *chaban kyogen* was much like the Osaka *niwaka*, a genre that is now almost extinct. One difference, however, lay in the fact that the *niwaka* was performed by specialists like Tsuruya Danjuro, who were organized into professional troupes, some of which made their appearance in Tokyo as well from the latter part of the nineteenth century on. The people who did *chaban* were mostly just amateurs who were fond of the theater; it was not so much an art form as a simple pleasure or pastime. Sometimes they performed at private parties or gatherings, but it was on the *kagura* stage of the Meitoku Inari Shrine, on the evening of the eighth of each month, that I most frequently had the chance to see them. For the custom at the Meitoku Inari was to present *kagura* in association with the monthly fairs only occasionally; more typically their place was taken by *chaban*.

The performers were amateurs, with their own trades or callings; still, there was one man, using the stage name Suzume, who functioned as head of the troupe and whose authority was respected by all the members. I have forgotten what Suzume's real name or regular job was; but one of his students ran a shop where flowered hairpins and other ornaments were sold: he was called, appropriately enough, Hana-kin ("Flower Gold"). Hana-kin in turn had a student named Ko-hana ("Little Flower"). Then there was Cho-cho ("Butterfly") and Kaji-kin ("Blacksmith Gold"), the brother of a roofer who often came to work at the Kairakuen (judging from his stage name, I suspect he himself worked as a blacksmith). Hana-kin was quite popular, but he could not compare with Kaji-kin, whose stern, manly beauty and exceptional skill in movement and delivery made him the idol of the women and children who mostly comprised the audiences. Later, it seems, he became a professional actor of sorts, taking minor roles under the stage name Baishi.

There must have been other *chaban* troupes in Tokyo besides the Suzume group, but it was the only one operating in our neighborhood. The group very occasionally performed at the Junko Inari Shrine in Kamejima-cho as well; but apart from that, they could be seen solely at the Meitoku Inari. The other Inari and Hachiman shrines in the area presented only rather monotonous *kagura* dances. Thus, after we moved to the side alley near the Meitoku Inari, I gradually lost interest in the usual *kagura* (the elaborate seventy-five *kagura* at the Suitengu were another matter), and concentrated instead on the monthly *chaban* performances at our local shrine: I could hardly wait for the eighth day of the month to come so that I could go off to see Kaji-kin, Hana-kin, and the others.

The *kagura* pieces were presented in the afternoon, always ending by nightfall. The *chaban*, on the other hand, began at dusk and continued until nine or ten, or sometimes even till close to eleven o'clock. Again, in contrast to *kagura*, the *chaban* had considerable appeal for adults, about as much as the *manzai* vaudeville dialogues have for people today. So the performances were always quite crowded—though "crowded" here means not more than a hundred people at best, since the audience was limited to the women, children, young girls, and miscellaneous idlers with time on their hands from the Kayaba-cho, Kamejima-cho, and Reiganjima area. It had to be fairly dark before anything could begin, so the drum announcing the performance and inviting the audience to attend did not start to sound until around six. Then a ladder would be placed at the back of the *kagura* hall and the actors would climb up onto the stage.

"There goes Suzume!"

"Look, it's Cho-cho!"

"That one there's Ko-hana."

The girls, baby-sitters and shop assistants, would cluster around the foot of the ladder, chattering away. Some would even climb the ladder themselves and peek through the curtain that divided the "dressing room" from the stage area proper.

The first few pieces, performed while there was still some light in the sky and the audience was small, tended not to be very interesting—just short sketches, comic dialogues, and the like. As the evening went on, longer, more elaborate numbers were introduced. As in the Osaka *niwaka*, the troupe would begin a well-known Kabuki drama, playing it straight at first and then suddenly introducing comic and burlesque elements halfway through. It was, in fact, through the *chaban* that I became acquainted with many plays in the Kabuki repertoire that I had not yet seen at a regular theater: for example, the scene at the moat where Marubashi Chuya appears in the *Keian Taiheiki*; the outcastes' hut scene from *Tengajaya*; the murder of Bun'ya in *Utsunoya toge* (The Utsunoya Pass); O-han and Choemon's lovers' journey to the Katsura River in *Katsuragawa*; the slaughters that result when Fukuoka Mitsugi and Sano Jirozaemon are rejected by their lovers; the murder of Giheiji by Danshichi Kurobei; the third, fifth, sixth, and seventh acts from *Chushingura* (The Treasury of Loyal Retainers); the O-yumi scene from *Dondoro Daishi*; ghost tales like the story of the murdered wife Kasane and the famous *Yotsuya kaidan*; and Yajirobei and Kitahachi's adventures at Shioikawa and Akasaka Namiki.

In the course of the five or six years that we lived in the alley near the Meitoku Inari, I saw all of these, and more. On *chaban* evenings,

I would finish my supper in a leisurely way and then set off for the shrine when I thought that things would be reaching an interesting point.

Very few props were used, and there was no scenery or backdrop except for a persimmon-colored curtain with "The Suzume Troupe" or something of the sort inscribed on it. The wigs were for the most part made of cotton or papier-mâché, though in time more money came to be spent on such things and regular theatrical wigs and splendid costumes were acquired. Originally, in keeping with the character of *chaban*, most of the things they did were comic; but afterward that changed, and they began to perform more serious pieces like "The Earth Spider." Still, they continued to do burlesque versions of scenes like O-han and Choemon's journey: the audience would roar with laughter at the sight of an oversized man playing dainty O-han, dressed in a long-sleeved Yuzen muslin kimono, and borne on the back of a panting smaller actor in the role of Choemon. Struck by O-han's heaviness and thinking her pregnant, Choemon says, "Have you conceived?" She answers, "Conceived of what?"; to which he replies, "Conceived of such a mess as we're in now!" When Choemon recites the poem "Sharing a pillow for one night at the inn at Ishibe . . . and you with an unborn babe of seven months besides," O-han says in reply "But babes, like bibs, are easily misplaced. . . ." And so on. In the end Choemon tires of it all and flings O-han off his back onto the ground.

Of course those two Edo comic figures Yajirobei and Kitahachi were perfect material for this kind of farce, and all kinds of ludicrous action was devised to "keep the audience rolling in the aisles." In the scene at Shioikawa, Yajirobei and Kitahachi play a trick on the two blind masseurs Inuichi and Saruichi, substituting themselves in succession for Inuichi and having Saruichi carry them across the river on his back. In the next scene, at the teahouse on the far bank of the river, the *chaban* version differed a little from the original *Hizakurige* (Shanks' Mare) text. There the two rascals enter the teahouse where Inuichi and Saruichi are drinking together and, seating themselves next to the two blind men, proceed to steal their saké. In the *chaban* it is not saké but a dish of greens in sesame-seed dressing. I remember feeling a bit hungry myself as I watched Yajirobei and Kitahachi snatch away the rice bowls from which the masseurs had started to eat, and proceed to stuff the just-cooked, steaming-hot rice into their mouths; or lift the dripping green strands onto their waiting tongues.

I am not really sure who played what role in this piece, but I think Hana-kin was Kitahachi in the Shioikawa scene. Kaji-kin's most memorable role was Danshichi Kurobei: his wig and costume were just like those used on the regular stage; and when Danshichi Kurobei is wounded between the eyes by Giheiji, puts his hand to the spot and, seeing the blood, becomes enraged and cries out "You'd cut a man's face?" Kaji-kin was in his element. I must have seen him in this role any number of times: when he came to the part where he kills Giheiji, he played it straight, like a Kabuki actor, and did the killing with a display of savage cruelty.

Speaking of cruelty, in the old days scenes like the murder of Yoichibei in *Chushingura* were not played on the Kabuki stage in the simpler, more restrained way they are today. There would be a long dialogue beginning with the line often used in *Otsu-e* illustrations of the episode, "Hey, old man!" and continuing with other well-known lines: "No, no, it's not the money . . ."; and "Here are the rice balls, sir, all ready for you . . ."; and "There is a ringing in my ears . . . a mist before my eyes." Only after this long, wordy exchange would the climactic action come: Yoichibei thrown onto his back; Sadakuro mounted on his chest like a horseman; the knife slowly, carefully carving away at Yoichibei's entrails; his last, agonized breath.

That is just the way the scene was played in the *chaban* performances too. The audience was more interested in watching some good swordplay or a grisly murder scene or two than in the ordinary comic pieces: they considered themselves lucky to be able to see real plays, however vulgarly staged, for free. And the actors enjoyed it more too, and put more of themselves into it. Thus gradually the Suzume troupe moved away from the original spirit of *chaban* and more often than not performed bloody dramas of mayhem and murder, rendering them still more grotesque in the process. They even went farther afield than the Kabuki stage in their search for the thrilling: imitations of plays about nationalistic bully-boy heroes, dramatizations of newspaper accounts of violent hoodlums and murderous females—they all provided opportunities for the favored scenes of binding people hand and foot, throttling them, and disposing of their corpses in traveling cases; of pistols being fired until the air was heavy with gunsmoke, of bodies sticky and running with blood. Every month the audience could look forward to at least one or two scenes like this.

I daresay most people of my generation will remember the notorious "O-kono murder case" at Ochanomizu in the spring of 1897. On April 26, the night of the Bishamon fair, Matsudaira Noriyoshi, aged forty-one, killed his common-law wife, Gozeume Kono, a former bar girl who had managed to save up a small sum of money. He then carved several long cuts on her face so she would not be easily recognizable, stripped her naked, bound the corpse with ropes, wrapped it in straw matting, and tried to toss it into the Kanda River at Ochanomizu. But the bundle rolled to a point about five feet short of the river, and stopped. It was almost immediately discovered, a hue and cry was raised, and Noriyoshi was soon under arrest.

Needless to say, the newspapers splashed the story all over their front pages. In addition, three-by-four-inch photographs of O-kono's knife-slashed face were on sale everywhere, ranged alongside those of popular actors and geisha. I saw them myself many times, at the stalls set up for the monthly Suitengu fair.

O-kono had been forty, only a year younger than Noriyoshi; but reportedly "her charms lingered still, like a cherry tree that has lost its blossoms but not its leaves. Though her eyebrows had been shaved away, their outline remained, blue against her pale white skin." Hers was a story that the popular theater could hardly leave untouched; and as early as June of that same year it was turned into a play with the title *Fame* and presented, along with *A Comic Tour of Hell*, at the Ichimura Theater by the combined troupes of Ii Yoho and Yamaguchi Sadao. I did not see the production then, but I heard about it, probably from my uncle at the print shop who was so fond of the theater: Yamaguchi Sadao played Noriyoshi and Kawai Takeo O-kono, and the latter's portrayal of O-kono quarreling with her husband, showing her true colors as a woman of questionable character and reviling him with the utmost bitterness, was highly praised. At any rate, within a month, Suzume's troupe was ready with its own version, based on the earlier one, for presentation on the Meitoku Inari stage.

I cannot recall the actor who played Noriyoshi, or indeed the name of the one who took the part of O-kono; but he was the troupe's leading player of female parts, and his face is still clear in my memory. He was not exceptionally good-looking, having a large-jawed, squarish face, but he was fair-complexioned and had an attractively full figure, and there was a certain voluptuous femininity in the way he stood and moved. The

authors of the play showed greater sympathy for Noriyoshi, representing O-kono as an extremely spiteful, hysterical woman, and suggesting
that he could hardly be blamed for feeling murderous toward her. The
actor's portrayal of O-kono screaming abuse at Noriyoshi in a shrill voice,
spitting out insult upon insult, was clearly a close imitation of Kawai's
version, and was really quite well done. At last, unable to bear her abuse
any longer, Noriyoshi strangles her, then takes a knife and carves cut
after cut into the corpse's face. (This part was played with great skill.)
Finally he grasps the head by its hair and lifts it up for the audience to see.

Looking back, it is amazing that such a play could be shown to the
public on an open-air stage facing a major thoroughfare. But if we consider the standards of the period, when actual photographs of O-kono's
mutilated face might be sold in every wayside shop, perhaps it is not
so surprising after all. The stage looked out onto the main road going
through "Back" Kayaba-cho, a major artery that crossed the Kamejima
River and went on toward Eitaibashi. Thus, in the daytime there was
a good deal of traffic and many pedestrians about. But by the time the
eerie murder dramas were shown, it was quite late, and passersby were
few.

The whole area, in fact, was enveloped in thick darkness, the only light
coming from the single dim bulb of the lamppost at the entrance to the
Tokyo Electric power station. In its faint glow, great puffs of steam could
be seen rising whitely from the wide ditch outside the station. But in
the surrounding darkness the small, square stage alone was brightly lit;
and from it the woman's blood-covered and ravaged face floated up, glaring into the void. A momentary cry of terror went up from among the
people watching below. Yet no one left: everyone held their breath, and
looked. (The space that separated the audience from the stage was narrower here than at the Ichimura Theater. Everything was done literally
before one's eyes, and so the effect may have been more grotesque even
than in Yamaguchi and Kawai's production.) At last Noriyoshi lowered
the body to the stage and began to tie the legs with a hempen rope; the
act was over.

I want to stress that this kind of *chaban* performed at the Meitoku
Inari was peculiar to the Suzume troupe; the regular *chaban kyogen* were
more humorous, lighthearted affairs. At first the Suzume troupe had
also aimed at more conventional productions, but gradually they began
to move in stranger directions and became something altogether dif-

ferent. Nonetheless, for better or worse, between the ages of about ten and fifteen or sixteen, on the eighth of every month, in the darkness of night in "Back" Kayaba-cho, I was shown these weird and ghastly dreams. I do not regret it for a moment.

I spoke earlier of the Osaka *niwaka* troupe headed by Tsuruya Danjuro, and how they came to perform in Tokyo: although I have forgotten the precise year, I suspect I may have seen them perform even earlier than I did the Suzume troupe at the Meitoku Inari. In those days there was a first-class theater called the Yurakukan, similar to the Kinkikan in Kanda; it was located in Kakigara-cho 3-chome, on a corner near the riverbank. I was taken there by my mother and uncle to see Danjuro play the role of Tombei in *Shinrei Yaguchi no watashi*. The key scenes were done seriously, but here and there Danjuro inserted amusing business for comic relief. He was very skillful, so much so that I remember mistakenly thinking that he must be a talented Kabuki actor.

There were only a few good places like the Yurakukan, falling somewhere between a legitimate theater and a vaudeville hall. The result was that a variety of interesting and unusual entertainments were presented: it was there that I saw my first motion picture and my first Western-style marionette show. According to *One Hundred Stories of the World of Meiji* by the late Yamamoto Shogetsu, the first presentation of a motion picture in Tokyo was around February 1897 at the Kabukiza; and the Yurakukan must have begun showing them soon after. They were either simple records of actual events taken on the spot or trick shots, and the ends of the reel would be joined together so that the same film could be projected over and over. I can still remember a scene, endlessly repeated, of high waves rolling in on a shore somewhere, breaking, and then receding, and of a lone dog playing there, now pursuing, now being pursued by the retreating and advancing waters. There was also a scene of a long line of horses in the distance at the edge of a broad plain, looking as small as grains of millet. They came rushing straight toward the camera, growing bigger moment by moment until finally they were upon us. Suddenly they veered away into the distance, to be succeeded by another thin line on the horizon.

Then there were scenes reminiscent of the upheavals that attended the French Revolution or the persecution of the Protestants after the Reformation: aristocratic-looking women are being dragged to the place of execution, placed on a great pile of bundled faggots, and burned to

97

death; the smoke billows forth and the women are enveloped in flames; at last the fire and smoke die down to reveal only ashes—not even the outlines of the bodies remain.

There was yet another scene in which two beautiful, almost naked women stand, one on either side of a devil dressed like Mephistopheles. He summons one of them and orders her to lie on a table shaped like a chopping block. He then wraps her body in a huge sheet of glistening black material like carbon paper. A sign is given, and the body of the woman in its black wrappings rises into the air. Then from the area of her feet flames appear and begin to lick at her body, moving upward and finally consuming her, paper wrappings and all.

These were only a few of the motion pictures I saw at the Yurakukan.

Incidentally, I remember Mother telling me how one evening on his way back from a performance by the celebrated monologist Encho, Grandfather Kyuemon encountered a mugger behind the Suitengu Shrine and came home pale and shaking. Now, Encho often performed at the Yurakukan, so I daresay it was on the way home from that theater that Grandfather had this frightening experience. At any rate, the reader can imagine from this how lonely and desolate the streets behind the Suitengu could be.

Memories of great Kabuki actors

My earliest memory of the Kabuki is of the play *Nachi no taki chikai no Mongaku* (Mongaku's Vow at the Nachi Falls) with Ichikawa Danjuro in the lead, presented at the Nakamura Theater in Torikoe, Asakusa, from June 23 through July of 1889, when I was four years old. I have a very faint recollection of a huge waterfall virtually covering the stage and for years have wondered just when and where and in which production it occurred. Then just the other day I mentioned the matter to a well-known Kabuki critic and was told that it was probably a production in Torikoe. I then checked in the third volume of Tamura Nariyoshi's *Kabuki Yearbook* and was indeed able to find it. *Mongaku* was apparently the first of three items on the program, yet I retain nothing of it, apart from the instant when the curtain fell on that scene of an immense waterfall flowing over the stage; I have no idea how Danjuro looked or sounded. The Nakamura Theater was a historic one, having been known also as the Saruwaka or Torikoe Theater at various times; but in January 1893 it burned down, and then Nakamura Kanzaburo XIII died, and somehow it was never rebuilt. Thus, I think this was my only visit to that celebrated theater.

The next Kabuki play I saw was *Kanjincho* (The Subscription List) at the Shintomi Theater, starring Danjuro, Kikugoro, and Sadanji, and beginning on May 22, 1890. I have fairly clear memories of being taken into this building, with its outer walls of black tiles separated by thick, protruberant lines of white plaster; it remained standing until the Great Kanto Earthquake of 1923. The first play on the program was *Satsukibare Ueno no asakaze*, based on the "Ueno War" of 1868, and the concluding one was *Omi Genji senjin yakata*; yet here again all I can recall is the middle piece, *Kanjincho*. As for the actors, I remember Danjuro's portrayal of Benkei and Sadanji's of Togashi, but only by reference to the *Yearbook* did I learn that Kikugoro V played the part of Yoshitsune.

It was around this time too that Nakamura Ganjiro came to Tokyo for the first time to perform at the Kabukiza and the Shintomi Theater.

The Shintomi Theater.

There was considerable discussion as to what role would be best for his debut on the Tokyo stage, and the final choice made was that of Moritsuna in *Omi Genji*; the *Yearbook* informs us, "It was proposed that, as a special treat for the audience, Danjuro and Kikugoro would appear in the production in the minor roles of army scouts, and the cast list was accordingly made up. Ganjiro was extraordinarily pleased at this news and lost no time in proudly reporting to his patrons in Osaka that those two great stars of the Kabuki world were going to help him shine in his first performance in the capital, and that this would be the greatest honor that could ever be done him. At the last minute, however, both Danjuro and Kikugoro began to raise objections and ultimately said that they did not wish to appear in a joint performance. Even the redoubtable Kan'ya was at a loss as to what to do; but, by arguing that it was now too late publicly to cancel their appearances, he finally persuaded them at least to let their names appear on the cast list."

Kanjincho is the only Kabuki play I remember seeing when I was five; but in the following year, 1891, I saw performances at the Kabukiza in March, June, and November, and at the Kotobuki Theater in June, as I was able to ascertain with the help of the *Yearbook*. The program for March at the Kabukiza consisted of *Buyu no homare shusse Kagekiyo* (The Glory of Martial Valor, Kagekiyo Victorious) as the opening play and *Ashiya Doman Ouchi kagami* to follow. This was just ten months after the performance of *Kanjincho* at the Shintomi Theater, yet when I consider the fact that I can still remember certain points about both the principal pieces performed at the Kabukiza, it is obvious how greatly my powers of observation and memory had improved between the ages of five and six. Thus even before learning about the history of the struggle between the Genji and Heike clans from Owada Tateki's *Tales from Japanese History*, I knew from the Kabuki play that there was a Heike warrior known as Akushichibyoe Kagekiyo. The one I saw was based on Chikamatsu Monzaemon's *Shusse Kagekiyo* (Kagekiyo Victorious), with the plot slightly amended by Fukuchi Ochi, and the whole turned into a five act drama for the Meiji Kabuki stage by Kawatake Mokuami. I still vaguely remember the part where Danjuro as Kagekiyo, hoping to attack Yoritomo, enters the Todai-ji temple disguised as a carpenter during the reconstruction of the Great Buddha, but is discovered and taken prisoner—all this against a backdrop of petals from the huge lotus throne on which the Great Buddha sits; also the part where Kagekiyo, having escaped from his cell, attacks and kills Juzo, the elder brother of his mistress Akoya. I have forgotten the famous scene in which Akoya brings Kagekiyo's son to visit him in prison; but at the point where Kagekiyo tramples on the prostrate Juzo and cries out "Wait for me, villain, in the courts of Hell!" Danjuro's tremendous dramatic skill made a deep impression even on a mere child like me. For a long time thereafter, whenever occasion arose, I would imitate Danjuro's voice and manner and announce "Kagekiyo escapes from prison!" or command "Wait for me, villain, in the courts of Hell!"

In Chikamatsu's original text, the bodhisattva Kannon from the Kiyomizu Temple in Kyoto takes the place of Kagekiyo in distress: "Mysterious and wondrous to relate—where Kagekiyo's head had been, there now appeared the sacred head of the Thousand-armed Kannon, emitting rays of supernal light!" This scene was included in the new production, but with certain changes: I remember how a beam of electric light was made to shine forth from the shadows of the bodhisattva's shrine. But in my eyes the most impressive scene of all was in the last act when Kagekiyo, acknowledging his great debt of gratitude to Yoritomo, says "Henceforth, I cannot take up arms against you, my lord. If, when I see your visage, thoughts of revenge continue to assail me, is it not the fault of these two eyes?" Then, raising his dagger, he pierces each eye. At this point in the action, Danjuro, seated on the steps, would lean back with his face to the sky and perform the act of self-mutilation. Kagekiyo, now blinded, with blood streaming from both eyes, stumbles first in one direction and then the other, and at last passes tottering before Yoritomo, and makes his exit.

But with whom did I see this drama? With my mother, certainly; but was my father along too, or my uncle from the printer's? I cannot be sure. No doubt it was only with the help of Mother's explanations that I was able to understand the reasons for Kagekiyo's act. But why is it that I can now dredge up from somewhere in the depths of my memory the details of this particular performance? One reason must have been the abnormal nature of this act by a hero of olden times. Another was the fact that one scene was set in the Hall of the Great Buddha at Todai-ji, of which I had earlier been told. And a third reason must have been the consummate skill of Danjuro himself, an art great enough to have left a deep impression even on the mind of a child.

As for the second major piece, *Ashiya Doman Ouchi kagami*, Mother had previously told me the story of Kuzunoha the fox; but she had said that when the time came to write the poem "If you miss me, come and see me . . ." on the sliding screen, Danjuro's Kuzunoha would be holding her child in her arms and using a brush held between her teeth. I was greatly looking forward to seeing that and was as a result a bit disappointed when Danjuro did the inscription in ordinary fashion, by hand.

Years later, in my forties, I happened one day to see the puppet master

Bungoro present Kuzunoha at the Bunrakuza in Osaka; and it brought back distant echoes of Danjuro's performance. At the same time, I seemed to see the figure of my mother leaning close and whispering in my ear the meaning of what was happening on stage; and I felt a helpless yearning for those days so long and so irretrievably gone. In 1931 I wrote a work called *Yoshino kuzu* (Arrowroot), and the links between that work and Danjuro's portrayal of Kuzunoha which we saw so many years before are impossible to deny.

In June of 1891 the offering at the Kabukiza was, first, *Kasuga-no-tsubone* (Lady Kasuga) and, second, *Banzui Chobei*, with Danjuro playing Lady Kasuga, the shogun Ieyasu, and Chobei. I have some recollection of these plays: of Lady Kasuga dressed for a journey, resting at the foot of a pine tree in the scene at Otakano in Sumpu; and of the scene entitled "The Retired Shogun's Last Instructions" where Ieyasu draws a sharp distinction between the statuses of Hidetada's two children Takechiyo and Kunichiyo, ordering the latter to move to a lower seat and coldly tossing down a sweet with the words "Do you wish to be allowed to eat with your brother?" Kunichiyo, accepting the rebuke, moves to a lower place where, prostrating himself, he meekly answers "Yes, my lord," and picks up the sweet. This episode remains with me still because of its poignancy; but who, I wonder, was the child actor, a boy of about my own age, who played Kunichiyo? He performed under the juvenile name Ginnosuke, but to whom among the later adult actors this corresponds I do not know.

Of the drama *Banzui Chobei* I remember only the bathroom scene: I can still almost hear the sound of Gonjuro's voice in the role of Mizuno Jurozaemon, to say nothing of the great Danjuro. In later years, Kichiemon acted the part of Chobei in the bathroom any number of times, but it seems to me that the scene ended differently in the two versions. Danjuro's version had Chobei lying face up on the floor and impassively receiving the thrust of Jurozaemon's spear, with the curtain closing on Jurozaemon standing astride him, twisting the head of the spear deep into his chest.

In the same month of June, I also went to the Kotobuki Theater to see the "Tokaiya" section from *Yoshitsune sembonzakura* (Yoshitsune and the Thousand Cherry Trees) with Danzo VII, then still performing under the name of Kyuzo. This time too I must have been taken by my mother. Little of the program now remains vivid, only Kyuzo playing

Gimpei the boatman (actually the Heike warrior Taira no Tomomori in disguise) in the "Tokaiya" scene, and Kigan (perhaps the father of the present Taganojo) as Sagami Goro. I may not have fully appreciated Kyuzo's artistry, but I was thrilled by his portrayal of Tomomori dressed as a ghost, wearing white-laced armor with arrows embedded in it; and by the part where Tomomori winds an anchor rope around his body and throws himself backward from a rock into the sea. I was so impressed by it that later I often played at "Tomomori with the anchor," wearing an improvised suit of cardboard armor in the Kairakuen storeroom or in the parlor at Yukiuchi the wigmaker's house.

"Tomomori with the anchor" in *Yoshitsune sembonzakura.*

The young Kyuzo already had the hoarse voice that was to become his trademark after he assumed the name Danzo; and there was a rumor that it was the result of his having been fed quicksilver by someone. At any rate, when, after a lapse of twenty years, I happened to see him perform on the stage again, what pleased and moved me most was that voice of his, still unchanged after so many years.

In November the Kabukiza presented *Taiko gunki Chosen no maki* (The Military Chronicle of Lord Hideyoshi—the Korean Campaign), with Danjuro playing Hideyoshi, Kiyomasa, and the boatman Yojihei, who is, in reality, the Korean Kim Myong-sok. From this piece I can remember a sudden upheaval occurring in the boat; a great many people being cut down by Yojihei's sword and falling into the water; Hideyoshi fleeing from the boat to a rock in the sea; and Yojihei pursuing him, only to be cut down by his adversary's long sword. (Yet surely my memory must be playing tricks on me here, since it has Danjuro playing both Hideyoshi, the attacked, and Yojihei, the attacker, simultaneously!)

Thus, in 1891 I had been taken to see the Kabuki as often as four times; but in the following year I saw only *Sakai no taiko* (Sakai's Drum) which opened at the Kabukiza on May 28. Here again, nothing much impressed itself on me apart from Danjuro's portrayal of Sakai Tadatsugu, and Torii Mototada as played by Chusha when he was still known as Yaozo. I also recall an actor portraying a shaven-pated tea master who, stunned at how numerous the attacking force appeared to be, rushed stumbling down from a turret, half-paralyzed with fright—it was very amusingly done.

In March of 1893 I had the chance to see Danjuro and Kikugoro acting together on the same stage for the first time in a long while. The program consisted of *Azuma kagami haiga no maki*, followed by Danjuro's *Kagamijishi* lion dance, and Kikugoro's *Kurotegumi no Sukeroku*. Of this last play I have no memory whatsoever. However, since I was already eight years old and had developed some interest in history and geography, I must have watched with special interest scenes like the one in *Azuma kagami* in which Sanetomo (played by Fukusuke) is killed by Kugyo (Kikugoro) in front of the Tsurugaoka Hachiman Shrine in Kamakura. I had heard a great deal from my mother about Fukusuke's beauty and elegance, and to see the graceful figure of Sanetomo, Minister of the Right, beheaded at the hands of Kugyo was somehow unutterably sad and painful, even if it *was* only a play. According to the *History of Meiji Drama* by Ihara Seiseien, Danjuro, in acting the part of Hojo Yoshitoki in this drama, portrayed him as a great villain by "showing him secretly inciting Kugyo to his murderous act against Sanetomo"; and this especially in the scene where "as a member of Sanetomo's retinue during the visit to the Hachiman Shrine, he feigns illness and begins to move away along the elevated ramp that runs from the stage to the rear of the theater, clutching at his stomach; then, pausing and looking back toward the stage as if lost in thought, he relaxes his hands for a time; finally, as if changing his mind, he again presses them violently against his belly and disappears beneath the curtain." But, according to Seiseien's history, "this was an extremely subtle, intuitive sort of art, which most of the audience could not grasp." And, alas, I myself remember nothing of Danjuro's performance on that occasion; all I can recall is Kikugoro as Kugyo emerging from beneath a curtain, Fukusuke as Sanetomo lying dead on the stage, and Kugyo approaching him to sever his head.

Kagamijishi (The Mirror Lion), the lion dance that was later to be revived by Kikugoro VI and achieve instant popularity, was written around this time by Fukuchi Ochi on the basis of the *nagauta* piece *Makurajishi* (The Pillow Lion). Thus the mantle of Danjuro who, according to Seiseien, "was applauded for the skill with which he imitated the manner and movements of a young girl," was passed on in time to Kikugoro VI. It was in this production that Danjuro made use of his two daughters in the roles of attendant butterflies; of this, Seiseien remarks that "by using his eldest daughter Jitsuko and second daughter Fukiko in these parts, Danjuro provided a precedent for the admission of women to the Kabuki stage." The *Yearbook* likewise states that "this was the first instance of a joint male-female performance on the stage of a major Kabuki theater in Japan." I do clearly remember watching the two girls, later known under the names Suisen and Kyokubai, dancing with their father; and, if my memory does not fail me, at certain points in the dance Danjuro as the spirit of the lion would turn to the girls and utter a little cry—"Oh!" or "Ah!"—to help them with their timing.

For the next year, 1894, even a perusal of the helpful *Yearbook* brings back no memories of plays attended. A play about the Sino-Japanese War entitled *Kairiku rensho nisshoki* (The Rising Sun Flag, Victorious on Land and Sea) began at the Kabukiza on November 1, with Danjuro as Minister Omori (for the historical Otori); Kikugoro as Sawada Jushichi (for Harada Jukichi); the previous Ennosuke, later known as Danshiro II, as the Chinese general Hsu Ting-juan; and Matsunosuke IV as the Taewon'gun, the father of the Korean king Kojong. I remember seeing a large, three-sheet color print of Danjuro and Kikugoro in costume for sale in front of the Shimizuya bookshop; but I never saw the play itself.

My guess is that, since our family finances had worsened greatly over the previous two years, going frequently to the Kabuki was a luxury we could no longer afford. According to the *Yearbook* the admission fees at the Kabukiza in those days were four yen fifty sen for a first-class box, three yen fifty for a good raised box in the orchestra, two yen fifty for an ordinary box in the orchestra, thirty-five sen per person for seats in a second-class box, and twenty sen per person for seats in the boxes on the third tier. And though Mother still seemed to go from time to time at my uncle's invitation, I was now included in these parties less and less often; presumably, as I got older and bigger, it became a nuisance to try to find space for me in one of the good raised boxes that we always rented.

I can still remember how it felt to go with Mother by rickshaw from Minami Kayaba-cho toward Tsukiji, where the Kabukiza was, my heart beating fast with excitement as we raced along. Mother still referred to Shintomi-cho, which in the 1870s had housed a licensed quarter called the "New Shimabara," by that name; and so, crossing Sakurabashi bridge, we passed through "Shimabara," where the Shintomi Theater now stood, turned south along the bank of the river just in front of Tsukiji Bridge, and, approaching Kameibashi bridge, caught our first glimpse of the large, cylindrical section crowning the roof of the Kabukiza. The theater had been built in 1889, so it was only four or five years old at the time. Nearby were some eleven teahouses affiliated with the theater, and these displayed bright flowered hangings on their second floors whenever the Kabukiza was open. We always left our rickshaw at an establishment called Kikuoka and then, with hardly a moment to rest in the guest room, we were bustled off by the maids. Slipping into the "lucky" rush sandals supplied by the teahouse, we crossed a wooden-floored corridor and entered the theater. I remember how, after we had slipped off our sandals and stepped up into the theater corridor, the smoothly polished wooden floors felt strangely cool even through the thick soles of my *tabi* socks. Generally one felt a kind of chill in the air as one came in, with a breath of wind as cool as mint entering from the sleeves and from below one's holiday kimono and prickling the underarms and nape of the neck. The slight sensation of chilliness was like the fresh, bright days of plum-blossom viewing in very early spring, making one shiver pleasantly.

"The curtain's going up!" Mother would call, and I would hurry so as not to be late, running down the cool corridors.

I remember that often as we returned from the play it was raining. Perhaps this made our visit to the theater all the more memorable for me. The rickshaw in which we rode was fitted out with an oilcloth awning—the same material as those table covers used in Chinese restaurants. The odors of the oilcloth and the oil in my mother's hair blended with the sweet fragrance of her kimono, filling the darkened cab. As I took in these smells and listened to the sound of the rain beating upon the awning, the images of the various actors we had seen on stage that day, the sounds of their voices, and the stage music came alive again for me there in that dark, enclosed world. On nights when I had watched scenes of a woman about the same age as my mother having to part with a beloved child, or stabbed by a furious husband, or driven to kill herself for the sake of fidelity or chastity, I asked myself what Mother would do if she found herself in such straits. . . . Would she too abandon me or let me be killed for some principle? Thinking such thoughts, I passed along the streets that led toward home, swaying with the motion of the rickshaw.

In 1895, quite unusually, I was taken to a play at the Engiza theater in Akasaka. A new program began on June 8 and included *Kaidan jissetsu sara yashiki* and *Kochiyama*. The cast was made up of second-ranking actors: Shinzo, Enzo, Somegoro, Metora, and the like. My uncle from the print shop was a fan of Shinzo's, and we doubtless went to see him in particular. He was universally touted as the only candidate fit to succeed to Danjuro IX's name, and so I must have felt some curiosity about him as we set out that day. But, to tell the truth, I was too young to appreciate his particular kind of skill. *Sara yashiki* as a whole has faded from memory; but I do recall how, when Shinzo as Kochiyama strode onto the side ramp at the close of the entrance-hall scene in the second play and delivered the famous line "You fool!" my mother and uncle and all the people in the nearby seats exclaimed in wonder at how exactly like his teacher Danjuro he was.

Beginning on January 6, 1896, at the Meiji Theater, Kikugoro V's troupe performed a complete version of *Yoshitsune sembonzakura*, including *Michiyuki hatsune no tabi*. Toward the end of the same month the Kabukiza presented *Jishin Kato* and *Dojo-ji* starring Danjuro. Why then, I wonder, did my print-shop uncle choose the Meiji Theater that month, despite his passionate devotion to Danjuro (or "Narita-ya," as he was also called by his fans) and consequent disdain for Kikugoro? Was it that, out of kindness and goodwill toward Mother and me, he wanted to take us to a play sometime within the auspicious first twenty days of the New Year? Anyway, since Danjuro did not appear in this production, the artistry of Kikugoro made an especially strong impression on me, then a boy of eleven. The drama critic Sugi Gan'ami, writing in the *Mainichi News*, stated: "In the first Kabuki production of the New Year at the Meiji Theater, the famous Onoe Kikugoro performed three separate roles—Tadanobu the fox, Gonta, and Kakuhan. He met with raves throughout Tokyo, and as a result of his popularity the other theaters, both great and small, were devastated at the box office."

As I read Gan'ami's quite detailed review, I recall various points in the play, so I shall go on to quote him in part. First, with regard to "quarrelsome Gonta":

> This is a superb interpretation of the role, quite without peer in contemporary theater. . . . It has been a very long time since I have seen such a splendid Gonta. . . . Kikugoro's Gonta bares one shoulder and moves to the edge of the set, where he begins hurling stones at a pasania tree and using his sedge hat to gather the nuts that fall to the ground. His movements and timing in this scene are even more masterful than in previous years; it is hard to believe it is a performance rather than reality. . . . The beauty of form shown when Gonta swiftly presses his left foot against Kokingo's arm as the latter tries to draw his sword is indescribable.
>
> Gonta listens to his wife's reproaches, and then things become still more interesting. He shows his little son Zenta how to gamble. (In the Association's performance last year, there were doubts as to the propriety of exhibiting a gambling scene in the presence of members of the imperial family, and this piece of action was cut. This year, however, it was duly performed, to my great gratification.) Then, when Gonta withdraws, he carries his son on his back; but, wanting to keep his hands free, he has the boy take hold of his shoulders. Thus, he is able to make his exit with his arms folded nonchalantly across his chest. I do not know whose idea this was, but it is very effective.

Of the scene in the sushi shop, he writes: "Kikugoro's fans were concerned that the scene in which he appears on a midwinter's day with one shoulder bared and covered with stage-blood, delivering lines of great length, might tell on the constitution of one no longer young."

With regard to the portrayal of Tadanobu, Gan'ami praises the part where the fox-skin drum is handed to him in front of a shrine gate as being particularly unusual in conception:

> On his head he wears a hero's wig that might have come straight from a classic Kabuki wood-block print; his face is painted white with red flame-like accents; he wears a red kimono decorated with Genji

carriage wheels and held back by exaggeratedly large braided cords; and he appears on stage barefooted. . . . As he stands protecting Lady Shizuka and directs his scornful laughter at the blustering Tota, he seems splendidly larger than life. In the fight scene, his execution of the set gestures and postures was almost faultless. . . . As for the episode in which Tadanobu the fox, carrying on his back the suit of armor with scarlet braiding that Yoshitsune has given him, makes his exit, the actor skillfully imitating the movements of a fox, one can only say that it is the high point of this marvelous production. Even the journey through Yoshino and the palace scene do not compare with this exit. I have seen many famous actors' versions of this fox imitation, but Kikugoro truly gives the impression of being a phantom fox, without a trace of the human about him.

He says of the palace scene:

As the audience, hearing a jangling sound along with that of the drum, turns back to look toward the ramp's exit curtain, Kikugoro, who has swiftly changed into a lilac-colored kimono embellished with scattered chrysanthemums, suddenly appears on the black wooden steps in the center of the stage; the sight of him sitting pensively there is unforgettable. As he sits listening, lost in the sound of the drum made from the mother fox's skin, Lady Shizuka suddenly cries "You are not Tadanobu!" and slashes at him with a sword. His gesture of surprise at this attack is not overdone, and his rapid, staccato delivery of the last part of the line "I have done nothing to make you attack me!" is wonderfully fox-like rather than human. Then, after being interrogated by Lady Shizuka, he listlessly descends the black steps and, to the sound of drums, disappears. Almost immediately, the figure of a fox dashes out from behind a revolving partition on the right of the stage. Before the play opened there were rumors that Kikugoro had spent a great deal of money on a special costume, and it proved to be true: even from a distance the effect of his fox costume was stunning. . . . Kikugoro played with brilliance the scene where Tadanobu painfully parts with the drum made from his mother's skin; there was not a person in the audience who was not moved to tears. When he appears as the fox for the second time, it is on the left side of the stage, where he leaps over a passageway and hedge and vanishes. The third time, the fox, drawn by the sound of the drum, appears unexpectedly near the very front of the auditorium and, receiving the precious drum from the hands of Yoshitsune, goes almost mad with joy. Then, as always, he runs along the palace balustrade to the tumultuous applause of the audience.... Carrying the drum, he stops for a moment at the edge of the set and executes a fixed pose before disappearing. Truly, Kikugoro's is a divine art; and I doubt there will be anyone in the future who can match him.

Thus Gan'ami employs the highest terms of praise for all aspects of Kikugoro's performance, and concludes by remarking, "The *Waseda Literature* editors refer to us as 'people who blindly delight in the old-fashioned Kabuki'; but I must insist that it is not without reason that we praise such productions as this. If we praise something, we are accused of 'blindly delighting in it,' and if we criticize, we are accused of 'reviling.' It is indeed a hard thing to be a critic nowadays."

I have quoted Sugi Gan'ami's critical comments at such length not merely out of nostalgia for the past, but to make a point: the importance of coming in contact with really first-class works of art in one's childhood, whether they are dramas, paintings, or music. Parents should not allow themselves to think that "the child won't understand," or "a masterpiece like that will be wasted on him"; if one is going to expose a child to art, let it be of the first order. If an adult understands a particular work of art, it is likely that a child will as well. The notion that children cannot appreciate such things is a fundamental mistake. And even if something is beyond a child's present powers of apprehension, if the work is truly first-rate it will leave its traces in the child's mind, to revive one day when the time is ripe. The passages from Gan'ami quoted above all describe scenes that I myself remember from my childhood play-going: Gonta hurling stones at a pasania tree in order to knock down some nuts; or the gesture with which, still reclining, he raises one foot and presses it against Kokingo's elbow as he is about to draw his sword; or Gonta going through the motions of gambling in front of his little son. How often, in later years, those scenes came to mind! Certainly even as a child I sensed the beauty of form and dramatic power of Gonta's gesture in restraining Kokingo with his foot. In the part where Gonta teaches his son how to gamble, I did not understand exactly what was going on, but from the reactions of the other people in the audience, their amused smiles, I could get a general idea. And how could I ever forget the scene at the sushi shop, where Gonta is slashed by his father and drenched in his own blood?

Gan'ami speaks of Kikugoro "on a midwinter's day with one shoulder bared and covered with stage-blood"; and indeed I now recall what a cold January day it was when my uncle took us to the theater. "His fans were concerned that it might tell on the constitution of one no longer young," Gan'ami goes on; but, though Kikugoro would have been fifty-three at the time, he did not look his age. Stripped almost to the waist, half his upper body bare except for a length of bleached cotton wrapped around his stomach, he still looked youthful and strong.

The scene in the palace is rich in fairy-tale elements that would delight the heart of any child—the point where Tadanobu suddenly changes into a fox, the unexpected appearances and disappearances of the fox from unlikely places on stage, and his traversal of the balustrade, for example. Naturally, I watched them all with the greatest excitement.

Arrowroot, my novel of many years ago, depended not only on my memories of Danjuro's portrayal of the fox Kuzunoha in *Ashiya Doman Ouchi kagami*, which I saw with my mother when I was six, but also, even more significantly, on Kikugoro's Tadanobu the fox in *Yoshitsune sembonzakura* seen some five years later. Had I not seen the latter performance, I doubt that the fantasy of *Arrowroot* would ever have come to be. In the novel, I speak through the mouth of Tsumura, a youth born in Osaka:

> How I envied the Abe child in the play *Ashiya Doman Ouchi kagami*, wishing that my mother too might have been a fox in disguise. For if she were a mere human, then there was no hope of ever meeting her again in this world; but if she were a fox in human form, then there was a chance that she might appear again in the guise of my mother. Any motherless child who saw that play would feel the same way, I am sure. But in the *michiyuki* journey scene in *Yoshitsune sembonzakura*, the figures of mother, fox, beautiful woman, and lover are even more closely interwoven than in *Ouchi kagami*. In *Sembonzakura* both mother and child are in fact foxes, and even though the relation between Lady Shizuka and Tadanobu is that of mistress and retainer, the scene is designed to have the appearance of a traditional lovers' journey. Perhaps that was why I loved this dance-drama

more than all the others. I used to put myself in Tadanobu's place and imagine how it must have felt to follow Lady Shizuka through the clouds of cherry blossoms at Yoshino, drawn on by the sound of the drum made from the mother fox's skin. I even thought of studying traditional dance and performing as Tadanobu in some amateur recital.

The late Baiko when he was still known as Eizaburo once acted the part of Lady Shizuka opposite his father as Tadanobu, and the latter was so displeased with the way Eizaburo played the drum in the palace scene that he shouted from beneath the stage, "You'll never get the fox out with drumming like that!" Eizaburo says that in fact his father took a good long time to appear, and he was terribly embarrassed. But Gan'ami states that "Eizaburo's Lady Shizuka was played with a fine sense of rhythm, and even now I can see in my mind's eye his skillful, well-paced turns upon the stage."

Of the scene at the mansion of Kawazura Hogen, Gan'ami writes: "In front of the temporary curtain, a great crowd of warrior monks was shown, bewitched by the fox; meanwhile, behind the curtain, Kikugoro was changing into Kakuhan's costume. When he had finished his preparations, the curtain was dropped to reveal Kakuhan rising into view from below the stage by means of a trapdoor mechanism; he was restraining the fox with his halberd, to the accompaniment of samisen music. The entire audience broke into loud applause." I remember thinking that of all the actor's appearances that day, this, with Kikugoro sitting with his halberd held aslant, was the most impressive. And many little rag-doll foxes were featured in the same scene, delighting the audience with their prettiness. Shortly before World War II, I had a chance to see this scene again for the first time in many years, with the late Tomoemon as Kakuhan; but his stage manner was so different from the refreshing style of Kikugoro that I was quite disillusioned. As for the charming little foxes, there was of course no question of their being allowed to appear on the more intellectualized contemporary Kabuki stage. For the same reason, Gonta in the sushi shop scene as played by Tachibana-ya or Kikugoro VI was no longer daubed with stage-blood as in the past. All of this is a reflection of modern trends in Kabuki and there is no use complaining, but one cannot help regretting the gradual loss of the real flavor of traditional Kabuki with each passing year.

Eizaburo's Lady Shizuka was certainly pretty, but, for true refinement and beauty, there was no one to match Fukusuke IV's Yoshitsune. One prominent critic called him "a perfect Yoshitsune"; and indeed, watching him, it seemed as if the Yoshitsune we had imagined as boys, the one from the *ukiyo-e* prints, had come alive before our eyes. But all this has reference only to the period when he acted under the name Fukusuke. When, after taking the name Utaemon V, he played Yoshitsune to the late Koshiro or Ennosuke's Benkei in *Kanjincho*, he was already well past his prime. But seeing him in the New Year's performance at the Meiji Theater in 1896, I was able to understand for the first time just why Mother and my Manazurukan aunt, as well as O-kiku and my other cousins, had been so excited about the twenty-six-year-old actor while he was staying at the inn at Oiso some years before.

Fukusuke also played the part of O-sato in the sushi shop scene in *Sembonzakura*, but he was not nearly so impressive in this role. It is true that O-sato's face was beautiful, but for some reason Fukusuke had not applied any white stage makeup to his feet, which were bare. It was January, after all, and O-sato's feet were red from the cold. Child though I was, the disharmony bothered me a lot. "Since her face is painted so white, she should have put some on her feet too!" I remember thinking in dissatisfaction.

Utaemon V (the former Fukusuke).

Danjuro IX as Benkei in *Kanjincho*.

Kikugoro V.

From April 30, 1896, the Kabukiza presented *Fukigusa Heike mo-nogatari* with Danjuro, Kikugoro, Shikan IV (Fukusuke's adoptive father), and Fukusuke; the second major play was *Totoya no chawan*, and as a middle piece *Sukeroku* was performed, with Danjuro as Sukeroku, Fukusuke as Agemaki, and Shikan as Ikyu. I was dying to see this last piece, but it proved impossible so I spent my days loitering in front of the Shimizuya bookshop and gazing at the large three-leaf prints of Sukeroku displayed there. In the illustrated booklets that circulated at the time, the ruddy, bearded face of Ikyu as played by Shikan made the strongest impression on me, more so even than Danjuro's Sukeroku or Fukusuke's Agemaki.

In fact, though, I was still more eager to see the *Heike monogatari* play than *Sukeroku* itself. I had developed an intense interest in tales of the twelfth-century wars between the Genji and the Heike through reading Owada Tateki's works, so I was convinced that plays featuring such characters as the lay priest Jokai, the monk Saiko, Lord Keeper of the Privy Seal Shigemori, and New Grand Councillor Narichika could not fail to be fascinating. Then by chance it happened that the chrysanthemum-doll exhibition at Dangozaka for that year was based on the current *Heike monogatari* play, with figures representing Danjuro as Saiko, Gonjuro as Narichika, and the late Chusha in his Yaozo days as Kiyomori. Seeing the displays, I regretted all the more that I had been forced to miss the play itself.

Then in April the next year I saw a complete performance of *Otokodate harusame-gasa* at the Kabukiza. Ihara Seiseien wrote that "Danjuro's attempt to look much younger than his age in playing the townsman Gyou does not suit him. After all, even a great actor cannot contend with the passage of the years . . . ," and my own memories confirm Seiseien's judgment. On the other hand, in the scene where Gyou delivers the line "It stinks, it does!" in an indirect insult intended for Tsurigane Shobei, Danjuro's voice was so splendidly sonorous that for some time afterward I went about saying "It stinks, it does!" on every possible occasion in as close an approximation of Danjuro's voice as I could manage. This famous line came to be omitted when Ebizo and Kichiemon played Gyou but was reinserted by the late Kan'ya when he performed at the Teikoku Theater, as I recall. But his voice could not begin to compare with the bold, free sound of Danjuro's, a voice that still resounds somewhere within me. Kikugoro VI played Shobei opposite Kan'ya's Gyou, and the present Sadanji the same role opposite Ebizo's, and obviously both of them were quite good. Still, it seems to me that Yaozo playing Shobei opposite Danjuro's Gyou was by far the best. There was something very real about the figure of Shobei, bested in a fight and crestfallen, following Gyou down the side ramp barefoot and with the skirts of his kimono tucked up behind; or the melancholy expression on his face when he sits opposite Gyou in a second-floor room, in the hara-kiri scene; or his look of disgust when, reaching for the tobacco pouch that normally hangs at his waist, he finds he has lost it. It is said that when Kikugoro VI played the part at the Teikoku Theater he was subjected to threatening letters and hostile visitors: it must have been a difficult role for Kikugoro or Sadanji to play, since the plot was out of keeping with the temper of the times. At any rate, Yaozo's performance of the role in that first production seemed the most effective, perhaps because playing opposite Danjuro released his energies to a special degree. Seiseien remarks that "Yaozo's Shobei had real presence and pluck, but after his suicide the play was quite disappointing." Yet to this young spectator there was nothing disappointing about the performance—it seemed splendid, both before and after the hara-kiri scene.

When Shobei kills himself, Gyou exclaims "What a man we've lost today!" As performed, it was very moving. Okamoto Kido in his *Lamplight Talks on the Meiji Drama* reports that "Danjuro's Gyou and Yaozo's Shobei were very well received by the audiences, which were much larger than they have been in recent years. . . . Because Gyou appeared on stage carrying a tannin-dyed umbrella, that type of umbrella became all the rage for some time afterward."

I also have various recollections of the interval piece performed along with *Harusame-gasa, Wada kassen onna maizuru*. It was the first time I became aware of Ushinosuke, for example, later to assume the name Kikugoro VI. He had appeared as Gonta's son in the production of *Yoshitsune sembonzakura* that I had seen the previous year, but I only realized the fact many years later, looking at the *Kabuki Yearbook*. The first time I learned that Kikugoro V had a son one year older than myself, an appealing lad with the juvenile stage name Ushinosuke, was when I saw him in the part of Ichiwaka, the son of Hangaku the woman warrior, who was played by Danjuro. Ichiwaka was shown encased in a suit of armor, about to leave for the army encampment, despite his age; then other child-warriors appeared on stage and engaged in a spirited exchange with him. I was consumed with envy to see these boys of about my own age being allowed to wear helmets and armor and all the other trappings of martial valor.

With regard to Danjuro's portrayal of Hangaku, Kido writes:

> The traditional script of *Wada kassen onna maizuru* was used unchanged; but the audience was amazed when the "breaking down the gate" scene came and Danjuro as Hangaku appeared dressed in realistic historical drama style, with a headband bound behind over long, flowing hair, warrior's formal garb, gauntlets and shin guards, and furred boots. There were some who criticized this style on the grounds that "one can't even tell whether the character is supposed to be male or female!" ... Part of the original charm of this play was the sight of a beautiful woman in an elegant overrobe pushing against the gate with a wad of thin paper in her hands.... This point was quite disregarded in the new production, and it was because of such willful misjudgments on the part of Danjuro that his realistic interpretations of historical plays often met with fierce criticism from a section of the audience. Thus, Danjuro's Hangaku was as unpopular as his Gyou was popular.

Now I did not understand anything about the details of realistic historical drama; but I did notice that Danjuro, who was not particularly good-looking to begin with, actually seemed rather ugly when costumed and made up for this part. In addition, he looked very small on the stage that day, though usually his artistic technique succeeded in making him appear taller and larger than he really was. (Or was it perhaps that he intentionally made himself look smaller to stress the fact that the character was indeed a woman, despite her male dress?) Kikugoro VI's comment about the Dojo-ji maiden as danced by Danjuro applies also to his Hangaku: "When he first appeared on stage, you were struck by how unattractive he was; but when he once began to dance, you no longer noticed such things: he turned into a stunning woman." In the scene where little Ichiwaka commits suicide, Hangaku appears in a woman's graceful over-robe, and the beauty of her movements made one forget entirely Danjuro's great bulging eyes and thick lips. One felt as one watched the part where Ichiwaka begins to chant his last prayers from the other side of a partition and his mother, hearing his voice, cries out and collapses in tears, that only Danjuro could do justice to it. Many years later I had an opportunity to see Baigyoku play Hangaku in *Onna maizuru* (I had not seen it in the intervening years, except on the puppet stage). Watching him, I couldn't help recalling Danjuro's performance of the same part. Baigyoku too was a fine actor, but, in comparison with Danjuro's art, his that day seemed dry and charmless.

Having seen the future Kikugoro VI as Ichiwaka at the Kabukiza in April, I was able quite by chance to see him from close by in street dress, some two months later in Kakigara-cho. His foster brother had died on June 28, and on the thirtieth the funeral procession left the family house in Shintomi-cho, crossed Sakurabashi and Yoroibashi bridges, and passed through Ningyo-cho on its way to the Daiun-ji temple. The route was known in advance, so the streets were crowded with young girls eager to catch a glimpse of the famous actors who would be part of the cortege. I too took my stand near the Miharado cake shop on Yoroibashi Street, waiting for the procession to pass. (I can hardly believe that I would have dared to skip school in order to do this, so either it must have been a Sunday or the funeral was at a late hour, after we had been let out of school.) I was certain that Ushinosuke would be taking part in the procession, and indeed he was, riding in a rickshaw and wearing a formal crested kimono with *hakama* divided skirt, topped by a small derby hat. I was already twelve at the time, so I no longer wore black silk crested kimonos and *haori* coats, or stiff Hakata sashes, or fine Sendaihira divided skirts (the expensive clothes that I had worn when I was younger had by now been passed down to my little brother Seiji).

"When our family was rich, I used to have clothes like that too," I thought as I watched Ushinosuke ride by; and I was overwhelmed with longing for those easy, innocent days of early childhood.

On July 7, little more than a week later, Ichikawa Shinzo, known as one of the "four great disciples" of Ichikawa Danjuro, also died. Again I watched the funeral procession pass down Ningyo-cho Avenue. According to Seiseien's history, Shinzo was the son of a man who had served the noble Tayasu family as a steward; like his fellow student Yaozo, he was good not only at martial arts and realistic portrayals of steady, loyal types but also at love scenes and female roles. The two young actors were natural rivals, but Shinzo enjoyed an advantage in that he was also an excellent dancer, while Yaozo was not. He possessed a certain rich, full quality of gesture and voice; and the latter, closely modeled on his teacher Danjuro's, was clear and sonorous. He was eloquent in speech and a gifted writer, publishing a novel entitled *The Cold Winds of Winter* and contributing articles to the magazine *The Friend of Learning*. He studied traditional Kyogen farces of the Sagi School under Yata Keisai, calligraphy under Ichikawa Man'an, and painting under Nakano Kimei, from whom he received the sobriquet Setsudo. With this background, he had an impressive knowledge of dramatic scripts old and new and was in fact assured of a brilliant future as the next Danjuro. What a loss it was, then, when he died before reaching the age of forty. His teacher Danjuro, in a published conversation with the playwright Fukuchi Ochi, said of him, "I have no hopes any longer that my ideas for reform of the Kabuki will be put into practice. When I'm on stage, the other actors defer to my wishes, but, left to themselves, they do as they like. Shinzo could put up with that, and carry on. He was a fine actor—that's why he was able to do what he did.... If he had lived, perhaps my reforms could have been carried out, even after I'm gone...."

Shinzo himself seemed to have cherished the same ambition, declaring "I will be the next Danjuro"; and he soon acquired the nickname "the Tenth" (i.e., Danjuro X). I saw him two or three times at the Engiza theater around 1895 when he was engaged in a heated contest for popularity with Yaozo. I know that he sometimes appeared on stage with a patch over one eye when it was hurting; but the only memory I retain of his performances is of Kochiyama, which I mentioned earlier. The *Yearbook* describes his funeral, stating that "since he had been an officially recognized religious teacher before his death, he was buried according to Shinto rites at the Yanaka Public Cemetery; the body was placed in a coffin, dressed in white Shinto robes, with a traditional court cap placed on the head." The funeral was extremely simple and sparsely attended despite his fame as an actor. A lot of people resented him and were jealous of his rapid rise in the theater; and he seems to have taken a rather too obvious pride in his own skill. Probably this accounts for the poor show of mourners at the funeral. The tragic eye ailment that killed this giant of the theater (as important in that sphere as that other victim of blindness, Hishida Shunso, was in the world of Meiji painting) first appeared around 1893. It grew worse, leading to frequent stays in a number of Red Cross and university-related hospitals. Shinzo was treated by the celebrated Dr. Scriba and seemed for a time to get better. But from 1896, when he played Munemori in *Shigemori kangen* (Shigemori's Remonstrance) starring Danjuro, the problem recurred, leading to Shinzo's complete collapse. On the day of the funeral I heard several people who stood waiting for the cortege to pass say that "Shinzo's illness was no ordinary eye disease: it was a result of syphilis." The rumor may have been true, since he had enjoyed the favors and patronage of an older woman called Okamoto Mitsu, the mistress of a steamship agent in Yokohama, and eventually became her adopted son.

On July 11 Mokuami's play *Kozaru Shichinosuke* opened at the Kabukiza with Kikugoro in the main role. I did not see it, but I remember hearing my mother and uncle talking about it in the back parlor at the print shop. It seems that the newspapers, with *Current Events* in the lead, loosed an attack on the production as cruel, indecent, and immoral, with the result that within a week of opening it was ordered closed by the police.

In November the Kabukiza presented *Chinsetsu yumiharizuki* and *Shihei-ko nanawarai*. Since his favorite actor, Danjuro, was playing in them, Uncle Kyuemon went to see both and brought back a program for us, but Mother and I were not invited to accompany him. It must have been around 1897 that I overheard him complaining about the rise in prices at the Kabukiza: the good boxes in the orchestra which had cost three yen fifty in 1893 now cost twenty yen, if you included all the miscellaneous expenses. "I can't afford to just go to the theater when I feel like it any more!" my uncle exclaimed.

Perhaps it was for financial reasons, then, that he took us to the cheaper Masago Theater in Nakasu for the New Year's performance in 1898. The program consisted of, first, *Shiranui monogatari*, then *Keisei Tadanori* as the first interval piece and *Yamatobashi* as the second, and finally *O-shizu Reiza* as the concluding play. Sazanami Tayu (in fact, Tadanori, the governor of Satsuma) and Reiza were played by Uzaemon XV under his previous stage name Kakitsu; Sanshichi Nobutaka and O-shizu by the late Sojuro under the name Tossho. No doubt both of these young actors were still technically immature, yet they were at the peak of youthful freshness, and I was fascinated by the sensuous beauty they embodied. The *Yearbook* says that when Kakitsu performed at the Masago Theater the previous year, "he was an immediate success: his portrayals of O-han and Chokichi in 'The Obi Shop' interval piece were well received, and in the second play on the program he looked exactly like his uncle Kikugoro." From this it is apparent that he was already beginning to win acclaim, but I daresay it was initially his physical charms that assured him success. It must have been around this time, or a bit later, that I emerged from the Kairakuen restaurant one day to see Kakitsu getting into a rickshaw parked at the gate. I stood and gazed at him, awestruck that anyone could be so beautiful. Then, as he stepped up into the carriage, the bottom of his kimono opened slightly to reveal a glimpse of almost translucently fair skin. Again, I was amazed that any man could have such beautiful legs.

Kakitsu was sharp and lively, so the gallant roles of Tadanori and Reiza suited him better than that of Sazanami Tayu, the courtesan. Tossho, on the other hand, was somehow soft and ample in appearance and could play the female role of O-shizu more naturally than the male Nobutaka. It seems that, generation after generation, the actors who bear the name Tossho have had a particular erotic quality of their own. Thus the present Sojuro when he was acting under the name Ensho had a voluptuous charm that no woman could ever match; and the present Tossho VI too carries on the style of his father and grandfather. But Tossho IV conveyed a certain eerie fascination when he played a scene like the outcastes' hut in *O-shizu Reiza*. Reiza is depicted as a strikingly handsome man, a modern Narihira, while O-shizu is known by the nickname Komachi, after the great beauty of long ago; so the two parts were perfect for Kakitsu and Tossho respectively. The strange, disquieting beauty of O-shizu as she collapses weeping after her lover Reiza is forced by his sense of honor to part from her left an indelible impression on my young mind. And Mother also watched this scene, sniffling and on the point of tears. When for some reason we had to leave before the last scene, she seemed relieved, and said "I'm glad we're going—I've cried enough for today."

In any case, I must say that of all the actors of female parts I have seen on stage over the years, from childhood to old age, none has ever come up to Tossho IV as he was then, in point of sheer sensuous beauty.

I have other memories, of course—of Danjuro as Tonbei or Kikugoro V as Mitsuhide; but I no longer remember when or where I saw them and, besides, I have run on too long about my beloved Kabuki. So I shall bring this section to a close here—an appropriate enough point, I think, since very soon after the time I have been describing, my uncle's print shop went bankrupt and there were no more invitations to the theater. At best, Mother and Father would take me to hear a comic monologue at a vaudeville house. Then in 1902 at the age of seventeen, with my father facing absolute ruin in his business ventures, I went to work as a live-in tutor at the house of the family that ran the Seiyoken restaurant in Tsukiji. For the next few years I passed the familiar front entrance of the Kabukiza almost daily, yet I never had so much as a glimpse of the inside; thus I missed seeing Danjuro and Kikugoro perform during the last four or five years of their careers.

In February of 1903, Kikugoro V passed away, followed by Danjuro IX in September; and the Kabuki theater entered a period of stagnation. Of all the kindnesses my uncle showed me during my childhood, the greatest, it seems to me, was to teach me from such an early age to appreciate the excellence of these two truly great actors. What an immeasurable gift it was to an impressionable young boy like me! And it was not that he acted simply out of a sense of duty toward my mother— no, I am convinced that he knew I could appreciate the delights of the theater, and wished to give me that pleasure and joy.

Growing up

While Father was still running the Marukyu business in Komeya-cho, a third male child was born and, as explained earlier, sent off to be raised in rural Chiba. Then, in 1896, a year or two after we had moved to our second house in Minami Kayaba-cho, Sono was born. Since she was the first daughter in the family, it was decided not to send her away, but to raise her at home. (Later two more girls came, and finally Shuhei, the youngest child; but the two girls were given to other families.) The year of Sono's birth was Mother's thirty-third, an inauspicious one for women. This time she had no milk to give the baby, so I was often sent out to buy condensed milk for her. In those days there was only one variety available as a substitute for mother's milk: Eagle Brand, which is still being sold. Usually it was referred to as "condense milk," but the last word was often mispronounced as "melk," and if you just asked for "melk" you were sure to be given Eagle Brand. I always went to a liquor store called Okura's on the west side of Nihombashi Avenue to buy it. When it was time to feed the baby, a teaspoonful of this thick, rich liquid would be mixed with a little warm water. Often, when Mother wasn't looking, I would take a spoonful of the unwatered milk right from the can and swallow it down. Even now I find it pleasant-tasting, and when I was a boy it seemed the most delicious thing imaginable. I knew that if I took it too often Mother would find out, so I limited my thefts to two or three per can and relished the sweet taste of each precious spoonful all the more.

Apart from the condensed milk, I was also sent to buy "simple syrup" and Bordeaux wine at Okura's. This "simple syrup" appears to have been used chiefly to mix with medicines; and as for the Bordeaux, Father liked to drink it occasionally in place of saké. Having once run a liquor store which stocked some very fashionable goods—wines, brandies, liqueurs, vermouth, sherry, and the like—he knew a good deal about Western wines and spirits and would sometimes get the urge to have something familiar from the old days. Then too there was the health factor: it was generally believed that Western wines were purer and healthier than saké.

I went to the Nihombashi area frequently on other errands as well. The Haibara stationery shop was then located on Kaiunbashi Avenue, and whenever some special occasion came up I was sent out to buy the kind of stiff paper and colored paper cords used when presenting formal gifts. (This special paper was actually thin, soft Sugiwara paper that had

The Haibara stationery shop.

been stiffened with a kind of paste. In the Kyoto-Osaka area, they use the ordinary, untreated Sugiwara paper alone, while in Tokyo the stiffened type is common.) I was often dispatched to the Yamamoto shop for dried laver, to Nimben for dried bonito, and to the Yamamotoyama for tea. For *mochigashi* sweets of rice dough and bean jam, Mother always insisted on the Mihashido shop in Koami-cho. (Nowadays in Tokyo the term *mochigashi* has been replaced by *namagashi*, or perishable sweets, but they were always called *mochigashi* in the old days.) I remember how, when you entered, a man wearing an apron and with his sleeves tied up would come out and pack the cakes you had chosen; I don't know if he was the owner or simply a clerk, but he was around thirty years old, with a rather long, pale face. There was also the Saruya shop in Yoshi-cho, where I usually went for old-fashioned toothpicks and toothbrushes. Traditional toothbrushes with tufts of shaved wood or bamboo instead of bristles continued to be used in the teahouses and brothels of the Yoshiwara up to my university days, and the same was true of ordinary Shitamachi households in general until the early 1900s. Every morning after you cleaned your teeth, you found your mouth full of little bits and pieces of the brush.

The Nihombashi area had numerous bookstores—Suharaya, Okura Shoten, Aoki Suzando, Maruzen, and Hakubunkan, among others; and from about the age of thirteen or fourteen I made it a practice to save up any spending money I received from Father or Mother or my Yamaju uncle to buy books, often difficult ones which in fact I could barely read at the time. My first trip to Hakubunkan was in search of a special supplement of the *Boys' World* magazine. I was so eager to get my hands on it that I couldn't wait for it to appear in the ordinary retail stores but went straight to the publisher's outlet. From then on I often did this, going directly to buy the Teikoku Bunko edition of Bakin's epic adventure tale the *Hakkenden* and the *Taiheiki* (Chronicle of the Great Peace).

I purchased the *Taiheiki* first and well remember beginning to read it on the way home from the bookshop, filled with excitement and pleasure, and feeling somehow a very grown-up and consequential person as I held in my hands the thick, thousand-page volume with its sober cloth cover and leather spine. Since all the students of that day were united in their devotion to the Emperor and Fatherland, I was taken aback when I read in volume one the sections "On Yorikazu's Transfer of Loyalty" and "On Suketomo and Toshimoto's Descent to the Kanto," containing such passages as "If the *Emperor's conspiracy* does not succeed...," or "When the *Emperor's conspiracy* gradually came to light...." It seemed very strange to me to see Emperor Go-Daigo's plans to subdue the Hojo clan termed a "conspiracy."

Again, consider the last line of the last section of volume forty, "Hosokawa, Captain of the Right Horse, Comes to the Capital from the Westlands," with which the entire *Taiheiki* concludes: "The age was one of peace and good governance, and all was well." I thought it a very odd statement, given the fact that the Southern Court had been defeated and power had fallen again into the hands of the warrior caste, and that the Ashikaga shoguns' rule was wracked by continual strife and disorder.

When I learned that Ueda Akinari's eerie collection *Ugetsu monogatari* (Tales of Rain and Moonlight) had appeared in the Teikoku Bunko *Anthology of Rare Works*, I went to buy it; then later, hearing that there was a single volume wood-block edition as well, I searched that out at Suzando, which also provided me with an edition of Oshio Chusai's *Senshindo sakki*. It was due to the influence of Mr. Inaba, when he took over as my teacher, that I tried to read such difficult works while I was still in primary school; but more of that later, in its proper place.

A Teikoku Bunko double edition of the classic Chinese romance, the *Saiyuki* (The Journey to the West), together with Bakin's *Yumiharizuki*, published in April 1898, was priced at fifty sen, judging from a copy that is at hand; and the *Taiheiki* published in January 1899 was sixty sen. If I was able to spend such sums on books from time to time, it must have been largely due to the generosity of my uncles. I had no idea then of my father's real financial situation—how he supported us, or how much of a monthly income he had. All I knew for certain was that Father was by now no longer going to his old haunts in Kakigara-cho but to Kabuto-cho instead. I had no clue as to where he went in Kabuto-cho, whether he had a fixed salary, whether he was running his own dealership or not, whether he was dealing in rice or in stocks. But it was all too clear that things were not going well for him. As the last day of the month approached and it was time to pay the bills, Father would look depressed and anxious. He was becoming increasingly peevish and given to constant complaining. On the other hand, he almost never absented himself from the family evening meal, or came home late, drunk as a lord, as so many of the Kabuto-cho dealers did. He was always home in time for supper; sitting across the long brazier from Mother, he enjoyed his evening cup of saké and talked with her about a wide range of topics, from what was happening in the world at large to the day's trivial events. But whenever his expectations of something were not fulfilled and things did not go as he wished, he would begin to grumble about "those Kabuto-cho people," or indeed people in general. He would complain at great length, making an appeal for Mother's sympathy. According to him, most men were liars and cheats, with whom nothing could be done; he alone was a model of rectitude. As I sat listening quietly beside them, everything he said seemed true: if we were poor, it was not because of any lack of ability on Father's part, but because society would not make use of someone as honest and virtuous as he was. I sincerely believed this and sometimes felt such indignation at the wicked world that I would express it in a composition and show it to Mr. Inaba.

Like me, Mother always tried to see things Father's way, to believe that everything was society's fault, not his. Yet there was another side of her which seemed never to forget that it was Father's incapacity for business that had caused us to lose everything, including the inheritance Grandfather Kyuemon had been at such pains to leave her. Sometimes she would remember the old days and seem vexed beyond endurance at the painful contrast of her present state. She often described how it had been: how in the 1870s, before the railroad had gone that far, she and her father or sister would take rickshaws to Hakone, or Enoshima near Kamakura, or Ikaho and enjoy an excursion in the country; how you could hire as many rickshaws as needed in Tokyo and travel about with them, spending the night here and there. Then there were the Kabuki plays: it seemed she never missed a month's performance. She had a little box in which she kept photographs of old actors like Nakamura Sojuro, Bando Kakitsu, Hanshiro VIII, Tanosuke III, Shucho II, Kosuke IV, and Metora II, about whom I knew little more than their names. After her death, I preserved that box with its photo collection until the Great Kanto Earthquake of 1923, when it was destroyed in a fire.

Occasionally my parents exchanged very bitter words as they sat opposite one another across the brazier, most likely because Father's calculations had gone awry that month and there was no money to tide them over. Mother would usually begin to sniffle and demand to know just whose folly had brought them to such a miserable pass, or ask what he planned to do, with things going from bad to worse with every passing year. In the face of these complaints, Father sat wordlessly staring at the floor. There was a look of remorse on his face and, though he said nothing, it was evident that inwardly he was begging Mother's forgiveness. But even he was not always reduced to helpless silence, and once or twice a major quarrel suddenly flared up. Of course there was never a knock-down drag-out fight; but once, when Mother threw a ball of tissue she had been wiping her tears with into Father's lap, he did start to do something. Granny Miyo, who was still in good health then, dashed from the kitchen and tried to calm them both down, but things had gone too far for either of them to be able easily to back down. Crying, Mother opened the clothes chests and started packing, refusing to listen to Granny's attempts to mollify her. When she was done, she set off for the main house at Kakigara-cho. After she had gone, Father sat leaning against the brazier, looking very unsettled as he waited for a message from Grandmother or Uncle Kyuemon. And, sure enough, in about an hour one of the young men from the printer's appeared at the door. Father then went with him to Kakigara-cho and late that night succeeded in bringing Mother back home. Even so, it was a good two or three days before they would speak to each other.

"Jun-chan, aren't your Mama and Papa speaking yet?" Granny asked anxiously from time to time.

In those days there was a fish shop called Uobun in the old official residences area, and the wife of the owner would come every morning to take our order. Everyone in the neighborhood acknowledged that Uobun's fish was excellent, freshly caught in the waters just off Tokyo; and the shop took pride in its reputation. However, the prices matched the quality: they were much higher than those of the ordinary pedlars who came by offering their wares. As Father's finances worsened, he would warn Mother, "We're going to have to economize from now on. Quit buying such expensive fish! We don't need bonito sashimi—mackerel and sardines will do fine." But we had been dealing with Uobun even when we were at No. 45, and the owner's wife came to take our order personally, so it was not so easy for Mother suddenly to stop buying good fish. Around ten each morning, after Father had left for Kabuto-cho, the woman would appear at the back door, sliding open the oilpaper *shoji* and calling out, "Good morning. Is there anything I can do for you today?" She then took out a small piece of wood on which were written in simple characters the sorts of fish available that day, and read off the list. But she was in no hurry to make a sale: after reading the list she would spend perhaps twenty or thirty minutes chatting about this and that, leaning against the wall in the entranceway, while Mother remained on the raised wooden floor of the kitchen. (Truly, it was a leisurely age!) Yet as they stood there indulging in this extended twaddle, I am sure Mother was secretly wondering if there were not some way to get rid of the woman without ordering anything; or, if she had to buy something, at least to hold it down to a single half-dried bonito. The woman from Uobun, on the other hand, seemed to be on to Mother's weak point—her desire to keep up appearances at all costs—and no doubt was telling herself that after such a long, friendly conversation Mother could hardly fail to order *something*. In the end it was always the fishwife who won: she never left without an order of some kind in her pocket.

Actually, Mother felt strongly that she should provide at least a single portion of sashimi for Father, to go with his evening cup of saké; she and the children could do without, but Father should have that much. And no matter what he might say about economizing, when the sashimi was laid before him he never showed any displeasure. "They've got good fish, Uobun does . . . ," or "Mm, this is delicious!" he would say, smacking his lips.

But for the family as a whole the main daily fare, apart from rice, was vegetables, perhaps because they were considerably cheaper than fish, beef, chicken, or other meats, or perhaps simply because Mother was fond of them. Mostly it was lotus roots, taro, sweet potatoes, arrowhead bulbs, burdock roots, carrots, broad beans, green soybeans, kidney beans, bamboo shoots, radishes, and the like, flavored with soy sauce, sugar, and dried bonito flakes—hardly the kind of food to appeal to a child! These roots and vegetables were a little better when they were cooked in oil, so we preferred fried burdock root and eggplant, chopped devil's-tongue in a sesame and bean-paste dressing, or a kind of vegetable stew done with oil. But we could not have them as often as we would have liked, probably because they were more trouble to prepare than the plainer foods. Fish cakes from the Kammo shop too were more appealing to us than vegetables. There was just one vegetable dish I did like: the thick gruel made from grated yams called *tororo*. Even after being warned "If you eat too much of it, you'll get a stomachache," I always asked for seconds. Fish was usually served boiled rather than grilled: typically, flatfish, sole, rock trout, mackerel, codfish, herring, shark, and half-dried bonito would be boiled, while pre-steamed sole, gurnard, sardines, and flying fish might be grilled. I *hated* boiled fish.

On Sundays and other special occasions, we sometimes had fish and vegetable tempura; not very often, though, for it required the combined efforts of the whole family, with even Father being called into the kitchen to help out.

In the summertime cooked rice would occasionally go bad. If, for example, we had cooked too much the previous day and Father's sense of economy required that we finish the leftovers, it could be really ghastly. When the smell of the old rice was too strong, it would be made into rice balls and grilled with soy sauce. No matter what we did with it, it smelled awful.

By contrast, I always looked forward to the tenth of every month, the anniversary of Grandfather Kyuemon's death. The actual anniversary was the tenth of June, but it was our custom on that day each month to set up a lacquered papier-mâché table in the storeroom parlor with a large photograph of Grandfather enshrined there and some "Occidental cuisine" set before the photograph as an offering. This was chosen because Grandfather, with his fashionable tastes, had enjoyed eating it in his last years, and also probably out of kindness to me and Seiji, who were the ones designated to devour the offering eventually. At first there were sometimes several different plates of food, but in time these were reduced to one. It was always the same dish—a ham omelet with a sprig of parsley, delivered from either the Yayoiken or the Homero restaurant. The grown-ups had decided on an omelet because it was easy to divide equally between the two of us, in a fair and friendly manner. After coming home from school on the big day, I would frequently go before the altar to pay my respects to Grandfather, and also to fix the ham omelet with a steady, though sidelong, gaze. I waited impatiently for supper-time to come, and when at last I was seated at the table I made a careful comparison of the portions, and then proceeded to eat the little mound of egg before me very slowly, relishing each bite.

I have used the term "Occidental cuisine" because that is what we called it then—never simply "Western food," as nowadays. At any rate, apart from Grandfather's monthly anniversary, we hardly ever ordered food in from a Western-style restaurant. But my uncle at the print shop had come to share Grandfather's tastes, so when we were invited there for supper we sometimes dined off things brought in from the Azumatei restaurant on Yoroibashi Street in Koami-cho.

"What was that Occidental dish we had the other day? . . . I'd like to have that again, but I can't recall the name. . . ." Then, after a moment's thought, "Ah, yes, I have it!" and, taking a sheet of paper from the drawer of his inkstone box, my uncle would write "Minced Extract" or whatever and hand it to the maid.

The Occidental cuisine of the Meiji period was a faithful copy of European cooking and not at all Japanized; it was therefore more authentic and elegant than today's "Western food." Take the matter of "Worcestershire sauce," for example—there was only one kind then, real Worcestershire sauce, made in England. As for breads, rolls and croissants had not yet been introduced; there was English-style bread (we called it "square bread") and "twist bread," seldom seen nowadays, with the two ends twisted together.

Apart from foreign dishes, the food we ate most often at the print shop was chicken from the Tamahide restaurant nearby. (We called it *kashiwa*, which in my dictionary is written with characters meaning "yellow chicken" and is said to refer either to a chicken with yellowish-brown feathers or to chicken meat of high quality. Even today chicken meat is called *kashiwa* in the Kyoto-Osaka area, as it was also in Tokyo when I was a child. Now, though, the term is no longer used in the capital.) One reason my uncle ordered from Tamahide was that it was very close, just one or two doors down from us. But another was that the meat was so tender and delicious, with a light, non-greasy flavor typical of Tokyo tastes in food and quite different from its Kyoto counterpart.

Another favorite treat was eel from the Kiyokawa restaurant in Koami-cho, which I believe is still in operation.

Father's stomach ailment had given him no trouble for a long time after he went to the Shima hot springs for the cure; but a few years after we moved to No. 56, he had a sudden attack of ulcers in the middle of the night and collapsed in the hallway on his way to the toilet. "Jun-chan, there's something wrong with your father!" I was awakened by Granny's voice, and found her and Mother carrying him back to the bedroom in the storehouse. Then Granny rushed off to get the doctor while I ran, panting, as fast as I could to Kakigara-cho, having been told to "tell the people at the print shop right away." For once, I felt no fear as I raced through the night streets.

Father began to recover from this acute attack after about a month's rest, but he continued to have constant problems with his stomach. "The food doesn't taste good to me today," he would say; or "I think I'd better give up saké for a while"; or "Actually, though, I feel more like eating after a drink." Often he would massage his stomach in a worried way, or emit a sudden, loud belch.

Mother, on the other hand, had never known real illness. She was graceful and slender-looking, but in kimono she looked thinner than she was: in fact she had a rather ample figure. On a very hot day she would often roll her kimono sleeves up, exposing most of the arm, and cool herself with a fan. I suspect too that she enjoyed displaying the exceptional fairness of her skin like this. She had been raised in luxury and had never been toughened by hardship, yet she was quite strong—she seemed to have been born with a healthy constitution. When she contracted the erysipelas that led to her death at a little over fifty, it was

Tanizaki's mother, at about the age of fifty.

the first time I had ever seen her take to her bed with an illness. Even in the midst of that fatal sickness (which nowadays could probably be easily cured), her doctor remarked on how exceptionally strong her heart was. And in fact neither Mother nor I thought she was in any real danger. I suppose it is because I have inherited her good constitution that I escaped serious illness until I was sixty-six or -seven. Apart from measles, which I contracted along with my brother Seiji when I was about ten, and two or three bouts of flu, I have hardly ever been unwell enough to be confined to bed; and unlike my father's, my stomach has continued strong and healthy up to this very day.

Sad things, happy things

Of all the children in our family, the one who gave my parents the most trouble was surely myself, "the first born and least clever." Nonetheless, I was not scolded very often by either of them. My earliest memory of being punished was once in our first house in Minami Kayaba-cho when I was six or seven. Mother, angry over something I had done, said "All right, if you're going to be like that, today we'll really do it!" and had Granny help her apply a cone of moxa to my little toe. From then on, whenever I was being difficult Mother would say "It's moxa for you, young man!" and take out the dreaded cone and incense stick. But then Granny would intervene and smooth things over by having me kneel on the tatami to make a formal bow and apologize: "I'm sorry. I'll never do it again." I soon took the whole process for granted, until one day, when I must have been especially naughty, Granny actually changed sides and joined forces with my mother.

"I'm sorry. I'll never do it again," I cried frantically as loudly as I could. In the end, though, they succeeded in pinning me down and applying the moxa, lit from a burning incense stick. "It's hot, it's hot!" I yelled over and over at the top of my lungs, beating my feet against the tatami. But Granny just tightened her hold on my legs so I could not move.

"There now, it's all over. . . . Yes, it's all over now," said Granny, as Mother placed two burning cones on each of my little toes. To tell the truth, it was not so much the heat of the cones that I feared as the sensation of being forcibly held down by two adults to be punished. Moreover, the moxa did not hurt very much at the time, but it left marks that remained for two or three days and continued to sting in a very unpleasant way. Whenever I felt that penetrating pain, I remembered the day I was punished, and felt miserable.

This sort of thing happened perhaps two or three times in all. I recall that once, just when the moxa was being applied, Father came home and immediately picked me up and began to comfort me with such unaccustomed gentleness that I found it odd:

"What happened to you? Don't cry. . . . Poor little fella. . . . Did Mama give you the moxa? Did she? Well, never mind. She won't do it any more. It's OK. . . ."

This is not to say, however, that Father never scolded or punished me himself. He had his own methods. Once when we were invited by the Yamaju family to go by boat to the Battery in Tokyo Bay to dig for shellfish, I jumped into the ocean as soon as we neared the shore. It was deeper than I had expected and my feet could not touch bottom so I immediately clambered back on board. In front of all the relatives, Father said very roughly:

"You idiot, always making a mess of everything! You don't even know how to swim, so why the hell do you have to jump in in front of everybody else? . . . Just to show off!"

It is probably true that he was surprised to see me leap into the water like that; but more than that, he was vexed at being embarrassed by his son's stupidity in the presence of my uncle and his family. I in turn was full of resentment toward him: "It was just a little mistake. . . . Why does he have to make such a big thing out of it and humiliate me like that? What a father!" I thought disgustedly. And since Mother, who disliked boats, had stayed home that day, he rehearsed the whole incident again after we got home, for her benefit. Then I was subjected to further scoldings, from both of them.

I remember another, slightly earlier incident: it was a Sunday, and I was trying to carve myself a wooden sword. I have always been clumsy with my hands, and I was having a hard time—the sword just would not come out as I wanted. Father, who couldn't bear to watch me struggling on my own, good-naturedly called me over:

"OK, bring it over here. What d'you want done with it?" At first he willingly did whatever I asked, without seeming in the least put out by my various requirements: "So you want me to make it like this, eh?" As I watched my longed-for sword taking shape, I was delighted, looking forward to covering it with tinfoil as the final step. But I became a bit too demanding, asking him to "take a little more off there" or informing him that "it isn't right yet." At last Father flew into a rage, and shouting "What the hell do you want? Aaah, do it yourself!" he smashed the sword into smithereens. I couldn't understand why he did that, after all the trouble we had gone to. My sword lay in broken pieces, and my tears of frustration and disappointment would not stop.

Granny Miyo died when I was twelve or thirteen, fourteen at most—I have no precise memory of the date. Since there was no longer any need for a nurse, she had taken up the duties of a maid, working mostly in the kitchen. One evening when she was bent over the sink washing the dishes after supper, she suddenly slumped over to the left and blood began to pour from her nostrils—a huge quantity, enough to fill a kitchen bucket and more. The doctor came at once and diagnosed a cerebral hemorrhage. We put Granny to bed in the maid's room, and in a few days her married daughter, who lived in Azabu Juban, came to get her. Soon afterward, we received word that she had died. She had been with us since my birth, and our relationship was much closer than the usual master–servant one. But her death came at a difficult time for us, and I am afraid we were not able to show the consideration to her surviving relatives that was their due. One of her granddaughters came to work for us for a time, but she soon left; and we had to hire maids through an agency. Actually, we could not afford to keep a maid; and the girls would come and go, often leaving us with no one to do the kitchen work, which Father, Mother, and I would then have to divide among ourselves. It was not unknown for a newly hired maid to take off without a word to us and flee back to the agency. We might send her on an errand and, seeing that she had not come back after several hours, look in her room only to find it empty, all her things gone.

"Another one's gone off and left us!" my parents would say, exchanging shocked glances. And the following days or even weeks until the next girl came would be terrible ones for me.

Even though he could not provide Mother with the luxurious style of life she had enjoyed earlier, my father was determined at least not to have her do such everyday chores as washing and scrubbing and cooking the day's rice. Mother was entirely unused to such hard work, having about her something of the young lady of good family who does not even know how rice is cooked. Thus, no matter how straitened our family circumstances became, there was a real need for at least one maid. When none was available, Father would get up first and light the fire in the stove; or sometimes I would be told to do this and other tasks in his place. Early on a winter morning I would get up by myself and begin to perform the kitchen tasks while my parents were still in bed in the storehouse parlor, where the night lantern glowed softly in the darkness. More than the nightly cleaning of the oil lamps, more than the frequent errands I was sent on, I disliked this early dawn duty. I often recalled the stories I had heard about the hard childhood of Ninomiya Kinjiro, that late-Edo model of filial piety; but instead of being inspired by them, I only felt all the more keenly how very disagreeable a thing it was to be poor.

Only once did Mother punish me severely. I have forgotten the cause, but it must have been something very upsetting for her to have become so angry. Anyway, it obviously involved a person other than myself, someone whom a confession on my part would have implicated. I am certain it had nothing to do with money, but I cannot remember who the other person might have been. I had resolved from the beginning that no matter what happened I would not reveal his identity. When Mother summoned me, I sat stiffly in the formal posture in front of her and repeated

"I don't know" to every question. Angered at my stubbornness, Mother too refused to give in and, taking a thin metal rod from the kettle stand on the long brazier, she struck me on the thigh with it. It was about five or six inches long, and polished on one side to a silvery sheen. I was probably twelve or thirteen at the time, since I remember Granny trying to intervene on my behalf. This time, though, Mother would not listen to her: she continued to hit me, though the blows were not very hard, and my kimono gave me some protection.

"Why can't you tell me? What do you mean, 'don't know'? Come on, out with it! I won't stand for this!"

Every time I repeated the words "I don't know," Mother struck me again. No matter how restrained they may have been, the repeated blows falling on the same spot on my thigh began to sting painfully. I could have offered some resistance if I had wanted to, or tried to get away; but I only cried noisily and kept saying, over and over, "I'm sorry—forgive me," without ever revealing the reason for my denials.

I have forgotten how this punishment was brought to an end, but I certainly did not give in and reveal what Mother wanted to know. I trembled at the thought of the additional punishment that awaited me when Father came home and was informed of what had happened, but to my great surprise Mother said nothing about the matter in his presence. I had no reason to think that she was, in her heart of hearts, sorry for having chastised me so severely, and I was thus completely at a loss to understand why she kept the whole affair secret.

But enough of these painful incidents; it is time to move on to happier ones, though it is perhaps a bit difficult to say into which category the next one falls.

Occasionally one of Father's schemes turned out well and he would return home with a fair amount of money in his wallet. At once there would be noticeable changes in our daily menu, such that even we children could guess that business was going better than usual.

"Today you can have whatever you want! How about beef hot-pot? Or Occidental cuisine?" At times like these, he would order great quantities of anything we asked for so we could eat our fill. Mother looked very happy, watching her brood stuffing themselves greedily until their bellies could hold no more. But my own feelings were quite mixed. Loving food as I did, I was delighted to be able to eat my favorite dishes to my heart's content. On the other hand, I could not help feeling sad when I thought how miserable my father's life was, and how the little money he had managed to bring in would be wiped out by a few of these feasts. Yet, sad as I was, I ate until it seemed my stomach would burst—and then felt sadder still.

Though he himself was one of them, Father was forever deploring the meanness and petty-mindedness of the Kakigara-cho and Kabuto-cho people, whose moods rose and fell according to the state of their wallets. And in truth, though it may seem that I am playing favorites with my relatives, I do believe that Father and my Yamaju uncle were several cuts above the usual class of dealers in the area. Almost all of our relatives on the Tanizaki side were engaged in stock or rice dealing in Kakigara-cho, Kabuto-cho, or Suginomori, so I inevitably came into close contact with the people of that world and got to know their character. A man might be leading the life of a millionaire in a splendid mansion one day and then find himself ruined and living in a narrow room in some squalid slum the next. Then the rumor mills would start to operate: "So-and-so's dead broke"; and suddenly everyone's attitude toward the unfortunate man would change. His friends of yesterday hardly took notice of him now. But even the victim himself did not complain of this treatment: it was the way things were in this world. And if, on the other hand, some poor bedraggled specimen managed to "score" one day and make a comeback, from that instant anyone and everyone would flock to do his bidding. I saw several instances of this even at the Yamaju shop. A nod of the head or the words used in greeting someone could indicate with awful clarity just who had power and who did not. At the end of this process of violent ups and downs, there were a few who, having had the good fortune to land on their feet, were able to spend their last days comfortably; but the great majority—eight or nine out of ten—would find themselves having to eke out their days wretchedly and in poverty. As I have mentioned before, my father knew nothing but failure; but even my Yamaju uncle, who was the most honest and hard-working of any of the dealers in Komeya-cho, and who had amassed a considerable amount of money, in his last years (just about the time I was making my debut in the literary world, around 1912 or 1913) ran into some unexpected difficulties and died a broken man. His last words to his children before he died were "No matter what, don't keep on in this business. Find a better, steadier line of work." Unfortunately, there was no way for my Yamaju cousins to switch to a new business at that point, so they were forced to ignore their father's final advice and continued dealing in rice and cotton thread. In the end, all of their enterprises went bankrupt. That, of course, was much later; but even from childhood I found it impossible to respect the people involved in the dealers' world, including my own relatives. In my heart, I was determined not to walk the same path as the other Tanizakis; I had no wish to become "one of them."

Since those distant days when they went several times to stay at the Shorinkan in Oiso, my parents had never been able to afford a train trip together. Only once, while we were living in the second house in Minami Kayaba-cho, did they manage to go sight-seeing, to Nikko, taking us children along. It must have been while Granny was still with us, and our party would have included Father, Mother, myself, and Seiji, who was not yet quite ten. In fact this was the only trip that we four ever took as a family. It was at a very hot time of the year, toward the end of the midsummer vacation; and I remember being unable to sleep the previous night out of sheer happiness. But here again there was a tinge of sadness mixed with my happy anticipation. The reason was that I had naturally assumed we would stay the night in Nikko, since Father had been doing exceptionally well lately and our financial situation seemed quite good. But he had said, "We won't be able to stop overnight.... We'll make it a day trip." When I realized that the much-anticipated Nikko tour would be over in a day, my pleasure in it was cut in half:

"But we won't have time to see anything except the Higurashi Gate and the carving of the sleeping cat at the Toshogu Shrine; there'll be no way to see the Kegon Falls or Lake Chuzenji or anything!"

In addition, I had been pointedly told by both my parents that I was not to say a word to anyone about the trip: "Don't talk about it when you go to the printer's or the rice shop, all right?"

We left early on a bright Sunday morning. Our Yamaju uncle often dropped by on Sundays, and Father was concerned that he might show up that day too, so he left instructions with Granny: "The master of the rice shop may come by today, and if he does, be sure to tell him that the whole family went to Ueno Park for the day." If my father felt it necessary to hide, not only from the main house but even from our Yamaju uncle, his beloved brother Jittsan, the fact that he had recently made a little money, it could only have been because he had run up debts with almost all our relatives. And an overnight stay on this, our first family excursion in years, would have made them more likely to become suspicious and find out the truth about it. When I understood what lengths Father had gone to in planning this treat for Mother, Seiji, and me, I felt both very grateful and very sad for him.

We boarded a second-class car in a train bound for Nikko from Ueno Station, my second such experience. The first time was when I was taken by the head clerk of the print shop to stay for a few days with Uncle Kyuemon and his wife at the Gunkakuro in Oiso, and then traveled back with them to Tokyo. For Mother too it must have been eight or nine years since she had been able to sit in a comfortable seat on a train like this, carefully dressed like any prosperous middle-class matron, and gaze at the scenery flowing by beyond the window. It was also the first time any of us had ever set foot in Nikko. I remember a good many details about that journey: how the seats on the train to Nikko were arranged so that the passengers on both sides faced each other across a long aisle, with the windows at their backs; while on the way back we all sat facing forward, with the windows beside us, as in the contemporary "Romance Car" trains to popular sight-seeing spots. On the ride up, we had seats on the left-hand side of the car, with the Ueno hills behind us. But why should I remember such an insignificant detail from so many years ago? It is because sitting diagonally across the aisle from me was a most elegant-looking, remarkably fair-skinned young lady obviously from the Yamanote uplands of Tokyo, accompanied by her parents; even now I have not forgotten her. It is hard for a boy to make accurate judgments about the age of a woman older than himself, so I cannot say with certainty how old she was; but not, I think, more than eighteen or nineteen. In the then popular *Boys' World* magazine, I had often seen illustrations showing beautiful, well-bred women, but now I realized for the first time that such persons actually existed, outside the world of fantasy. I was clearly aware of a physical awakening within me, yet I continued to stare at that lovely face, turning my gaze toward her again and again, with a boy's boldness. And not only her face: I looked at her hair, her neckline, her teeth, her fingers, her *tabi*-clad feet, feature by feature—carefully, repeatedly, tenaciously, tirelessly. . . . She had a rather long, oval face of the sort that was regarded as ideal in those days, with a high nose and bright, clear eyes. Sensing that the attention of everyone in the car was beginning to focus on her, she seemed embarrassed and sat with her head bent slightly forward, which made her look all the more gentle and refined; the air of distinction about her seemed to suffuse the carriage. Not only her face, but each single finger showed white and elegant. In the midsummer heat, everyone else was flushed and sweating, but as I gazed at those white, white fingers, I felt the sweat all over my body vanish, leaving me refreshed.

"So this is what a real Yamanote lady is like," I thought, sinking into a kind of rapture. Then, to my surprise, she looked toward me and give me a pleasant smile (perhaps she didn't know where else to look, in that car full of attentive observers). Startled, I smiled faintly in return. And that moment of surprise and joy, that shudder of emotion, may have been my first experience of love.

Her smile soon faded, and she turned to look in another direction; but, of all her features, the beautiful whiteness and evenness of her teeth at the moment she smiled stayed with me the longest.

"Can't hold a candle to her, can she?" said Father, leaning over to whisper in Mother's ear. "They're from different worlds. That one doesn't even come near her. . . ." Father jutted his jaw toward the people sitting across the aisle, and Mother gave a silent nod. I could tell from snatches of their conversation that they were talking about the young lady, and I was pleased that they seemed to share my high opinion of her. But I wondered who it was that was being compared unfavorably with her; just where this person from a "different world" might be. When I looked in the direction indicated by the slight movement of my father's chin, I noticed a woman sitting on the same side of the car as the young lady, but a bit further up. She seemed to be in her late twenties or early thir-ties, and had a slightly dark complexion. She might well have been a former geisha, and a man who could have been her husband or patron sat alongside her. She resembled Uncle Kyuemon's mistress, O-sumi, in the darkness of her skin but was not even as attractive as she. Why would Father try to compare someone like that with the pure and spotless figure sitting opposite us, even while admitting they were "from different worlds"? How strangely adults acted sometimes. . . . It was sacrilegious! Almost unable to contain my indignation, I inwardly bowed before Her shrine and prayed: "Dear Lady, my father is saying ridiculous things, but please forgive him. I would never, never think of you that way."

Nothing in particular happened at Nikko. I remember only a few things: our resting at an inn called the Konishi, which Father somehow knew about; my feeling that a long-cherished desire had been at least partially fulfilled when for the first time I saw the Otani River and the Gammagafuchi river valley; how I was determined to see more than just the Toshogu Shrine and immediate surroundings, and pleaded to be allowed to go at least to Urami Falls, the closest of the outlying sights; how Father had said, "Well then, go on by yourself. You'll probably be able to make the return train if you hurry, and, if not, you can stay the night at the Konishi inn," and then handed me some money "just in case"; how I went off by rickshaw as the sun sank low over the mountain road until the rickshaw man dropped me somewhere, telling me to "walk the rest of the way, since it's just a bit further up the mountain. I'll wait for you here." I started to climb on my own but soon began to feel rather lonely, and eventually gave up and went back without seeing the waterfall. In fact, I was just barely able to avoid being marooned by myself in Nikko for the night.

In the end, the thing that made me happiest on that day trip was the sight of the beautiful young lady sitting opposite us on the train for those few hours between Ueno Station and Nikko itself.

The print-shop uncle and rice-shop relatives

For about ten years after our own family moved to the shabby obscurity of Minami Kayaba-cho's back streets, the printer's in Kakigara-cho carried on, the clack and clatter of its machinery evidence of continuing life. But as Uncle Kyuemon became more and more addicted to the pleasures of the geisha house, he spent less time and energy on the print shop; gradually business began to fall off, as people lost confidence in the Tanizaki enterprise. After his wife O-kiku returned to her parents' house, his mistress O-sumi was ensconced in the back parlor of the main house; but this arrangement lasted only a very short while. Soon she was back in the Yanagibashi geisha district, engaged in her old profession. Even so, her connection with my uncle was not severed: they continued to meet from time to time somewhere near the Daichi embankment. Uncle Kyuemon was by this time selling off most of his property and possessions in order to pay his debts, and also imposing heavily on our Yamaju uncle's good nature. But even though he no longer had the money for his accustomed pleasures, he did not break off his relationship with O-sumi.

Uncle Kyuemon got along well with my mother, who was his immediate elder sister; and when he had time on his hands, he would often appear in the afternoon, when Father was at work, and involve her in long conversations. One day when I came home from school, I found him waiting at home:

"Jun'ichi, I'd like you to go on a little errand for me."

When I agreed, he sat down and wrote a letter then and there; and, taking from his sash a tobacco pouch of dyed and embossed leather, he said, "Here you are, then. Take this to the Katsumi purse shop. You don't have to say anything, just show it to them with the letter attached."

Katsumi was a pouch and purse seller located on the corner of "Back" Kayaba-cho, diagonally across from our first house at No. 45. Uncle Kyuemon always bought his tobacco pouches, pipes, expensive gold and silver accessories, and netsuke at this shop; and when I showed the head clerk the pouch he took it in a friendly way and, saying "Just a moment, please," went to the back of the shop. He seemed to be discussing the matter with one or two assistants in a kind of code language and doing calculations on an abacus, so that I could not see clearly what was going on. But before long he returned with a little bag of coins, which I was told to take home with me. The bag must have contained about as much as my uncle had been hoping for, since he gave me a quite unexpected tip, with the words "This is for your trouble."

Since he had no one else to tell about his amorous adventures, he sometimes cornered Mother and recounted in great detail, and often in a highly amusing manner, his intimate relationship with O-sumi. Of course he said nothing about it in front of us children, but at supper Mother would repeat the stories for Father's benefit, and I was able to take in every detail as I sat beside them with a blank, uncomprehending look on my face.

"What a fellow! Do you know, he told me all about O-sumi today."

"A lot of nonsense probably," commented Father, yet he continued to listen without any show of anger.

It was obvious that Uncle Kyuemon was in love with O-sumi, but I don't know how much she loved him. However, judging from my own memories and also from surviving photographs of him at the age of twenty-three, he was quite a handsome man in his youth: had he been a woman, he would probably have been as attractive as my mother was; so perhaps O-sumi did return his feelings. At any rate, somehow or other my uncle managed to persuade Mother to let him use our house for rendezvous with O-sumi. These took place in the afternoon, around two or three o'clock, when Father was at work; and he was not to be told. Sometimes my uncle would arrive early and sit waiting uneasily for O-sumi to appear; at other times she would come first, proffering a little gift in a rather embarrassed way and then making small talk with Mother until my uncle came. When they had both arrived, she conducted them to the parlor in the storehouse, while we children stayed hushed within the six-mat parlor or went outside to play, responding to a silent look from Mother. I did not feel any particular guilt about cooperating with her in keeping all this a secret from Father. Mother sympathized with her younger brother's love affair, and there was nothing sordid or underhand about her desire to help him with this daring plan. Besides, I enjoyed the atmosphere of gallantry it entailed, which reminded me of the Kabuki. And when I considered how this uncle who had been so kind to me from my earliest childhood had now drastically come down in the world, I too wanted to comfort him in some way. So I could only approve of O-sumi's generosity in coming all the way to our shabby back lane in order to meet him.

Meanwhile, things were going extremely well for our other uncle at the Yamaju shop; and as we could depend less and less on the main house, we found ourselves relying still more on him. Uncle Kyubei, though he was disgusted with "Sho-chan's" irregularities, must have felt sympathy for "Wasuke," my father, who was incompetent and therefore poor, but honest and principled. He often came over on Sundays, and he and Father would take Seiji and me to the kind of place children enjoy; and on the way back he always treated us to supper somewhere. We would first go to Etchujima or Tsukudajima to hunt for locusts and then go on perhaps to the Kawai restaurant in Minami Temma-cho or the Imayo in Moto-Osaka-cho for beef hot-pot (as we called sukiyaki in those days—it was only afterward that the latter word became current in Tokyo). When we went bathing on the Omori beach, Uncle "Sho-chan" from the printer's also came along. Uncle Kyubei could not swim so he stayed in the shallows and paddled about with Seiji and me; but Father and Uncle "Sho-chan" swam very well. Once, Uncle S. offered to teach me how to swim and began sporting about in the ocean, providing me with more seawater to drink than I had bargained for.

By then our Yamaju uncle would have been perhaps the vice-chairman of the Chamber of Commerce, and yet he was still willing to give this much time and energy to his nephews. He did so partly, I am sure, out of love for us; but even more so out of pity for his unfortunate younger brother, I suspect. As he became increasingly successful, the social and economic gap between the two of them grew. Didn't he secretly want sometimes to do as he had done in the old days when as children they worked together at the Tamagawaya, and put his arm around him? I think it must have been so, and find it all the more impossible to forget this uncle's gentleness and kindness.

Nor am I likely to forget his wife, O-hana, my mother's elder sister and sister-in-law to my father in a double sense, and thus my aunt on both sides. O-hana had been born in 1858, as the eldest of Grandfather Kyuemon's three daughters, and was some six years older than my mother, who was the youngest. I am not sure what year it was that she married Ezawa Jitsunosuke, who was one year older and who, having been adopted into the Tanizaki family, took the name Tanizaki Kyubei and started a new branch family. If my own parents were married around 1883–84, then I would guess that O-hana and Jitsunosuke wed around 1877 or so. She gave birth to three boys and two girls in all; but in 1891, when she was thirty-three and her youngest girl, Ryu, was born, she became ill. From that autumn until her death in 1901 at the age of forty-four, she was bedridden and unable to walk.

I can recall seeing her in good health only once or twice. This was when we were still living in our first house in Minami Kayaba-cho: I remember one day when she came to visit and chatted with Mother in the first-floor parlor, which faced the street behind a latticework grille. Yet even then she was not entirely well, since I remember hearing her complain about her legs. Her problems began in the autumn of 1891 when she slipped and fell while out shopping. She felt a pain in her right hip joint, which she had treated with massage therapy for about a week. Since there was no improvement and she found the pain hard to bear, she entered the Kashimura Hospital; but still the cause of her pain could not be determined. Then she was examined by a university doctor and underwent electric therapy at the Red Cross Hospital, all without results. Finally, she consulted the well-known Dr. Sato Sankichi who said that it was impossible to make a diagnosis without exploratory surgery. Entering the No. 2 Hospital at Izumibashi in Kanda, she underwent a major operation that lasted over two hours and involved removing some two inches of rotten bone from her hip joint. The diagnosis was arthritis, and if proper treatment had been begun before the illness invaded the bone, all might have been well. Given the state of medical knowledge at the time, however, the cause could be discovered only through surgery, and by then it was too late for a cure.

Earlier I wrote that Aunt O-hana looked very different from my mother, and that there was something a little severe and forbidding about her face. She seems to have had something of this temperament from the beginning; but I also think that the experience of spending ten years as an invalid and having to bear those pains and constraints must have strengthened a natural tendency to harshness in her and in the end made her a hysterical and selfish woman. She was, after all, the eldest daughter and an heir, even if only head of a branch family; and as the printing business at the main house began to fail, the Yamaju shop managed by her husband gradually overtook it in prosperity and power within the extended family. As a result Aunt O-hana became supremely self-confident and aggressive, ordering about everyone in the family from Uncle Kyubei on down. Since she had been in a position always to have her own way, it must have been all the more vexing to be subject to such a disabling illness.

She entered the No. 2 Hospital twice. The first time was from December 1892 to March of the next year, and during the first month of that period Uncle Kyubei was not allowed to leave her bedside, even to attend to business at the shop. Of course she had a private nurse and a maid; but, in addition, from morning till early evening each day she was constantly attended by our aunt from the Manazurukan inn, my mother, or her own eldest daughter, O-kiku, in turn. Since she disliked the hospital food, whoever was on duty was obliged to make and bring something Aunt O-hana would enjoy. In the evening, when the women had to return to their families, the head of one of the print shop's subsidiaries would come to sit with her from around seven till twelve. After the first month, Uncle Kyubei was finally allowed to go and live at home; but as soon as his business at the exchange ended around 3:00 P.M., he would rush to the hospital and stay with her, without even eating supper, until the following morning.

Even after her release from the hospital, her right hip joint never recovered its free movement; so she would lie in bed with her leg stretched straight out, or sit up in a chair in the same position, or move about the house, carried on someone's back. I remember her sitting on the only chair in a small parlor with a long brazier, in the rear of the rice shop, her bad leg stretched out before her, chatting with the family members and other relations who sat grouped at her feet. I often went to pay my respects, kneeling before her and making a low bow; but Aunt O-hana never responded even with a smile: she glared down at me with a peevish expression on her face, as if the strain of enduring the physical pain were too much for her. Frightened, I fixed my eyes on the floor.

From what I could see, the only thing wrong with her was her bad leg; that, and her sallow complexion and scrawny, nervous-looking frame. Dr. Sato came to examine her about once a month, but ordinarily she depended on the ministrations of two local doctors who took turns looking after her. According to her daughter O-kiku, whom we all called O-kii-chan, Aunt O-hana insisted on variety in her daily menu, since she had little else to distract her from the tedium of her existence. So food was brought in for her from various restaurants at both lunch and supper; nonetheless, she hardly touched most of the dishes—nothing was really to her taste. As a result, most of the food found its way into the mouths of O-kii-chan and the other children. In the morning, the kitchen entrance was busy with the comings and goings of delivery boys from local restaurants specializing in sushi, grilled eel, noodles, and more formal Japanese cuisine, who came to pick up the empty plates, bowls, and layered boxes.

The illness persisted, and Aunt O-hana's demands continued to cause everyone in the family a great deal of trouble, so they tried to encourage her to go to the Shonan coast in Kanagawa "for a little rest." However, she did not care to be away from home, and on those rare occasions when they did manage to persuade her to go to Hiratsuka or Oiso, near Tokyo, she would return almost immediately. Then everyone would join forces to beg and plead with her to go back "for just a little longer." Once, declaring that she would not go anywhere too distant, she agreed to stay for a month or so at the Shibahamakan inn in Shibaura. When she got there, though, she discovered that there were too many unmarried couples staying for a single night and, insisting that the hotel "didn't know how to look after proper guests," she sped home within four or five days.

My mother once said of Aunt O-hana's behavior during this period, "Even Her Majesty the Empress doesn't wield the power she does!" In fact everyone in the family complained of her in private, giving her nicknames like "Lady Kiyomori" and "Mother Superior General." We all greatly respected Uncle Kyubei as the man who had made the Yamaju shop a first-class establishment in the world of Komeya-cho, but Mother and the others sometimes commented, "He doesn't dare stand up to her at all." And once when Aunt O-hana showed her contempt for Uncle Kyuemon from the printer's, really humiliating him, he came to our house and tearfully expressed his bitterness toward her in front of my mother: "Who does she think she is? Trying to make a *fool* of me like that!"

I often wonder who was the happier: my aunt, who was always in comfortable circumstances that provided her with everything she wanted, but who died worn out by years of illness; or my mother, who was poor but lived in peace and safety, enjoying the love of an admittedly ineffectual husband until her death. Grandmother Tanizaki, who outlived O-hana by some ten years, often told O-kii-chan, "Your mother was so lucky. Her husband was such a fine, capable man. It's true she died young, but she led the life of a princess. Not everyone gets to live like that." One can certainly look at it that way, but it is not, I think, necessarily true.

Mr. Inaba Seikichi

Mr. Inaba was my home-room teacher when I entered the first grade of the Sakamoto Primary School at the beginning of the second term, in September 1892. But in April 1893, after giving me failing marks for that first year, he was put in charge of another level, and I received instruction from Mr. Nogawa for the next four years until I finished the lower course there. However, when I started my first year of the upper level of the school in April 1897, Mr. Inaba, as if it were fated, once again became my teacher and remained so for the next four years.

Mr. Nogawa, for his part, was put in charge of one of the girls' classes in the upper level. One day as we were being led from the classroom into the hall by Mr. Inaba at the end of our lesson, we saw Mr. Nogawa walking down the corridor on the other side of the playing field, at the head of a file of girl students. "Hey.... Hey!..." we shouted, wide-eyed, waving our hands and making an uproar to attract his attention. But Mr. Nogawa just looked embarrassed and, smiling but saying nothing, passed down the corridor.

A primary-school group. From left to right: Nomura, Wakita, Mr. Inaba, Tanizaki, Mr. Kuroda, Okada, Kimura, and Sasanuma.

Mr. Inaba was no longer the inexperienced teacher fresh from normal school who had failed me four years before, but he was still young and energetic, full of enthusiasm and with many dreams he hoped to fulfill. In a few years he was to marry his wife Chiyoko, who has survived him and is still in good health; when I had him as teacher for the second time, though, he was single. After his marriage he moved to Toyooka-cho in Mita; until that time he lived in a house located on the west side of the broad avenue that runs through Tamachi, from the Ginza to Shinagawa. Every morning, he walked to school—a distance of over two and half miles. There was already a horse-drawn trolley running from Shimbashi, and soon afterward a line was established for the area between Shibaguchi and Shinagawa as well; but Mr. Inaba continued to walk. I often encountered him by the front gate as he came across the bridge at his usual slow, steady pace, a dignified figure with a rather strained look on his face. He wore Japanese clothing more often than Western, and usually had a favorite book stuck into the folds of his kimono, one corner peeping out as he entered the classroom. The range of his reading was very broad, from the works of ancient Chinese sages and Buddhist (particularly Zen) philosophical texts, to Japanese poetry and romances from the ninth century on. He brought slim Japanese-style volumes that slipped easily inside his kimono, or occasionally just ten or twenty sheets of rice paper on which he had carefully copied in brush and ink passages from the ancients that he particularly admired.

Mr. Inaba's ideas were those of the Wang Yang-ming School of neo-Confucianism, and of Zen, with an admixture of Platonic and Schopenhauerian idealism—in contemporary terms, a position perhaps rather close to that of Dr. D. T. Suzuki. Of course Mr. Inaba lacked the broad knowledge and profound scholarship of Dr. Suzuki, but nevertheless he was notably studious in comparison with most teachers coming from normal schools, and was also possessed of a firm, unswerving faith. I remember how he would sometimes bring to school a volume from the ten-volume *Collected Works of Wang Yang-ming*: it was a straight, unpunctuated Chinese text solidly printed in No. 6 movable type, and was for sale at the Aoki Suzando bookshop. Mr. Inaba wrote two poems by Wang Yang-ming on the blackboard and explained their meaning:

> Neither troubles nor ease remain long within the heart,
> They are like clouds that float across the limitless sky.
> The night is quiet, and the sea stretches for thirty thousand
>   leagues,
> The moon is bright and, plying my staff, I walk on as Heaven's
>   winds direct.

and

> To destroy the robbers in the mountains is easy.
> To destroy the robbers in one's heart, that is difficult.

From what I observed, Mr. Inaba's knowledge of classical Chinese was considerably greater than that of the average primary-school teacher of those days—and standards then were of course higher than they are today in the same subject. He was apparently not very good at English, the normal vehicle for the acquisition of knowledge of Western culture at the time; but there were doubtless partial translations of, and introductions to, Plato and Schopenhauer available in Japanese, and he must have come to know those philosophers through such secondary or tertiary sources.

What he most frequently talked of, though, and with most fervor, were Buddhist works and ideas. From very early on, I remember seeing him walking about with Japanese Buddhist classics like the *Indications to the Three Teachings* by Kobo Daishi and the *Eye-Treasury of the Right Law* by Dogen Zenji. (Though at that time, at any rate, he read the title of Hakuin's work *Orategama* in the highly idiosyncratic way *Enratempu*.) He sometimes lectured to us on such relatively easy Edo-period works of moral philosophy as Shibata Kyuo's *Talks on the Way*, but he was even more enthusiastic when discussing the ideas of Suzuki Shosan. All of this, let it be remembered, was directed at pupils in the first through fourth grades of the upper level of primary school—for the most part, boys like myself between the ages of twelve and sixteen!

With a teacher like Mr. Inaba, the pedagogical method used in the classroom was by no means standardized or formalistic. He believed in free, living education and refused to be bound by textbooks, taking advantage of whatever opportunities presented themselves from day to day; and this was true not only in the hours of moral-ethical instruction, but also during reading and history lessons as well. As a result, he would occasionally go off on a tangent totally unrelated to the textbook or curriculum. One winter day, for example, as the lesson was about to begin, the weather suddenly turned much colder and large flakes of snow began swiftly to fall. Mr. Inaba immediately stood up and, taking a piece of chalk, wrote on the blackboard the well-known Japanese poem:

> Snow and sleet and hail are separate
> Yet, melting,
> All become water
> Flowing in the valley stream.

Then he wrote Fujiwara Teika's famous poem,

> Stopping my horse,
> No place to shake the burden from my sleeves—
> A snowy dusk in Sano.

As this last example shows, Mr. Inaba did not introduce us to exclusively didactic or moralistic poetry and prose literature; he also taught us other works by Teika:

> A spring night's floating bridge of dreams,
> Breaking—
> Parted by the peaks,

Clouds trail across the dawn sky.

and

> Through the frost-filled sky
> A wild goose flies homeward.
> On its weary wings
> The gentle spring rain falls.

Mr. Inaba also loved the priest-poet Saigyo and was very fond of his *Mountain Collection*. At various times he put on the board such poems as:

> Blown by the wind
> The smoke from Fuji disappears,
> Who knows where?
> So too my thoughts.

and

> Show it to one who has a heart—
> At Naniwa in Tsu,
> This springtime view.

and

> Even one without a heart
> Can feel the sorrow—
> A snipe rising from the marsh
> In the autumn dusk.

During a history lesson, he told us the story of Sugawara no Michizane and quoted his best-known poems:

> When the east wind blows,
> Send forth your fragrance—
> O flower of the plum,
> Though your master be absent,
> Do not forget the spring!

and

> If I, adrift,
> Like seaweed strands
> Should float away,

Become a weir
And hold me.

He then said he would introduce us to an even better, more profound
poem by Michizane, and wrote:

Parting at the mountains,
The clouds fly off.
Yet when I see them once again return,
So does my hope.

After teaching us the lines,

"There is tomorrow,"
My heart, as vain as cherry blossoms, says ...

Mr. Inaba went on, "One of the ancient sages of China wrote this for
his disciples:

Youth easily turns to age, but learning is not easily attained.
Do not neglect a single moment, then.
One has not awakened from a dream of spring grasses by the pond
And already the paulownia leaves before the steps are heeding the
    voice of autumn."

Then he told us about its author, Chu Hsi, and even added an explanation of the White Deer Grotto, the poets' retreat in T'ang China.

On another occasion, he showed us a Japanese translation of Thomas
Carlyle's poem *Today*, included in the book *Best-loved Poems* by the Christian thinker Uchimura Kanzo:

So here hath been dawning
Another blue Day:
Think wilt thou let it
Slip useless away.

Out of Eternity
This new Day is born;
Into Eternity,
At night, will return.

Behold it aforetime
No eye ever did:

So soon it forever
From all eyes is hid.

Here hath been dawning
Another blue Day:
Think wilt thou let it
Slip useless away.

When Mr. Inaba wrote these examples of Japanese, Chinese, and Western poetry on the blackboard, he always read them in a strong, clear voice, with a characteristic intonation and rhythm; he would repeat each one several times, as if unable to leave off reciting something he loved so well.

On Sundays he would often invite some of his students to go on excursions to the Hakkeien garden in Omori, the Fudo Temple in Meguro, or the Myoho-ji temple in Horinouchi; we also went to view the plum blossoms at Kamata, the peonies at Yotsume, the irises at Horikiri, and the autumn leaves at Takinokawa. On the way to and from these spots, he never tired of reciting some favorite poem or song and telling us how it came to be written. One day we were joined by pupils from a lower class; and as Mr. Inaba and the other teacher walked along together, he began to chant with great feeling the poem that begins "Gone to ruin, the capital at Shiga where the little ripples play. . . ." The other teacher soon joined in, and later remarked, "I'm afraid children can't really appreciate songs like this . . . ," with which opinion Mr. Inaba concurred. The two of them then went on chanting "Gone to ruin . . ." a few more times, energetically.

Nowadays Ueda Akinari's *Tales of Rain and Moonlight* is known not only throughout Japan but even in Europe and America, thanks largely to the film version starring Kyo Machiko. But when I was in primary school, people had just begun to get excited about the works of Saikaku and Chikamatsu; hardly anyone outside academia knew anything about Akinari. The *Tales of Rain and Moonlight* first appeared in a movable-type edition, I think, when it was included in the second volume of the *Anthology of Rare Works* published in the Teikoku Bunko series. Even before then, though, I had read the story *Shiramine* in Mr. Inaba's hand-written copy of the work. He often made brush and ink copies of old literary texts, folding sheets of modern "improved" paper in half and then binding them together with string. In the case of *Shiramine*, he divided the work into several sections and provided each with a commentary and critique for his students' benefit. Thus, he made a break after the opening section, which reads:

> Going through the barrier at the Osaka mountain pass, Saigyo found it hard to put the crimson leaves of autumn behind him; he passed through Narumigata, where plovers leave their tracks upon the beach; to Fuji, where smoke wreathes the high peak; and then to Ukishimagahara, Kiyomigaseki, and the bays of Oiso and Koiso.... All were hard to leave, so beautiful were they. But, wishing to see some Westland places famed in song, in the autumn of the third year of Nin'an he passed through Naniwa where the rushes grow thick, on to Suma and Akashi, whose sea winds he endured, and then still further to the woods at Miosaka in Sanuki, where for a time he planted his staff.

Mr. Inaba commented on this passage, saying things like: "The above lines give an account of Saigyo's wanderings through the various provinces. Note carefully the beauty of style and charm of natural description in such phrases as 'Narumigata, where plovers leave their tracks upon the beach,' and 'Fuji, where smoke wreathes the high peak.'" Thanks to Mr. Inaba, I read *Shiramine* over and over until I could recite this opening section by heart. Then I learned that Koda Rohan's *A Tale of Two Days* and chapter twenty-five in the last part of Takizawa Bakin's *Yumiharizuki* (The Crescent Moon), "Hachiro, Intent on Dying, Visits the Sacred Mound," were both based on the *Tales of Rain and Moonlight*; and I began to read the works of these two great authors, comparing them with Akinari.

Since the Sakamoto Primary School had no indoor sports facilities at that time, gymnastics was canceled whenever it rained, and in its place the teacher in charge of each class would assemble his pupils in the classroom and tell them stories. It was, I think, Mr. Nogawa who read us pieces from the series called *Children's Literature* published by Hakubunkan: *Koganemaru* by Iwaya Sazanami, *Treasure Mountain* by Kawakami Bizan, *The Sage of Omi* by Murai Gensai, *Major General Shintaro* by Takahashi Taika, and the like. He also told us tales from Chinese history, like the story of the meeting at Hung-men from the martial tales of Han and Ch'u, or the account of how Hsiang-yu, surrounded on four sides by enemy troops singing the songs of his own native land of Ch'u, bids farewell to his beloved wife Yu-mei-jen at Kai-hsia.

Of them all, I was most impressed by the account of Nakae Toju, "the Sage of Omi," when he was still a child with the name Totaro. I wanted to know more about him than was said in class, so I went and bought Murai's book and perused it on my own. (I no longer have it, and wish I could find another copy somewhere to help bring back the past.)

The story went something like this: Totaro is sent to his uncle in Ozu in the province of Iyo at a very young age in order to be trained for a life of scholarship. In his hometown of Ogawamura in the land of Omi, his mother lives alone, waiting for him to return some day. She has told him that he must give himself entirely to his studies and not come home until he has completed his training and become a gentleman-scholar. One day Totaro happens to see a letter sent by his mother to his uncle, in which she mentions that, unused to the heavy work she must now do by herself, her hands and feet have become chapped and blistered: "My skin has cracked and the flesh become raw; on snowy mornings and frosty nights I feel the pain especially." Overcome with feelings of love, gratitude, and sympathy for her, little Totaro, now eleven or twelve years old, visits Nakada Chokansai, who is a fugitive from the "secret Christian affair" and now lives at Niiya about five leagues from Ozu, and obtains an excellent remedy from him. Then, saying nothing to his uncle, and in defiance of his mother's instructions, he sets out alone on the road home. He goes from Matsuyama to Imabari and then by boat to Hyogo. As he hurries along the mountain roads on his way to Ogawamura, he encounters a snowstorm and is almost frozen to death. But at last, early one morning, he reaches his village and stands before the gate of his longed-for home. The door is still shut, but he hears from behind the house the creaking sound of a bucket being drawn from the well. Wondering who could be doing this arduous work, he goes around to the back and there he finds his own dear mother.

"Let me do it, Mother," he cries, catching hold of her arm.

"Is your uncle with you?" she asks sternly. Totaro looks down, abashed, and notices his mother's feet, the skin cracked and bloody.

"Oh, your feet are so chapped," he cries and, kneeling, begins to apply the ointment he received from Chokansai, as he tells her the story of his long, lonely journey home. His mother, struggling to control her emotions at such an open display of filial love, says finally "But this isn't what you promised—you must go back at once to your uncle's. . . . Thank you for this medicine."

Thus Totaro has to leave home again and make his way back to Shikoku, using the money his mother insisted on giving him, which he accepted with gratitude, reverently raising it to his forehead. "The mother gazes after him, the son turns back to look; wind and snow fill the sky, the way seems endless."

This, at least, is the gist of the story; the original was written in a warm, sentimental style which any child would find moving, and I remember reading it many times with tears in my eyes.

But it was not only Mr. Nogawa who exercised a literary and moral influence. Mr. Inaba, for example, told us about *Keikoku bidan* (Edifying Tales of Statesmanship), the story of Epaminondas, Pelopidas, and the other Theban heroes.

The first half of this historical novel by Yano Ryukei appeared in March 1883, and the last in February of the next year. Until Mr. Inaba discussed it in class, however, I was unaware even of its existence. He did not tell us the title at first, but simply promised "a good story today," and began to recount the events in the first section of volume one, "How a wise king and wise noblemen performed the great work of saving the people; and how a group of boys were moved by their deeds." (This must have been in the spring of 1897, shortly after Mr. Inaba took charge of our class.)

Opening the first volume, we find it begins as follows:

The setting sun inclined toward the western peaks, and the day's lesson ended. After the crowd of boys had left, there remained seven or eight who ranged in age from fourteen to sixteen. Facing them was a gentleman of a little over sixty, with a snow-white beard and eyebrows, and the appearance and manner of a teacher. He spoke, pointing to a statue that stood in a corner of the school hall.

Mr. Inaba put the passage into easier language for us, virtually word by word. As its subtitle, "The Heroes of Thebes," indicates, the book tells the story of a group of valiant young men who rose to prominence in the ancient Greek city-state of Thebes, and of how under their leadership Thebes defeated the armies of Sparta and gained hegemony over Greece. It was the first time our eyes were opened to the ancient world of the West, the names of many of whose countries we had never heard before. It was only natural then that we listened with extraordinary interest and curiosity to everything, that each place and personal name seemed strange and wonderful.

> Now in Phocis in the northern part of Greece, there was a remote mountain called Parnassus, on whose slopes was the town of Delphi. From ancient times the people of Greece had held in profound reverence and awe a shrine located there, dedicated to the great god Apollo. Apollo was the deity of art, music, and medicine, and had the power to see all future events. Throughout the land, there were none who did not worship him.

This is a passage from the tale of the old gentleman "with a snow-white beard and eyebrows," and it was here that I first learned the word "Parnassus" and heard of "the great god Apollo." Most of the Greek names were then pronounced in an approximation of the English fashion, rather than of the original Greek, and expressed by means of Chinese characters used for their phonetic rather than semantic value. The names of the seven or eight youths "who ranged in age from fourteen to sixteen" were given in this way. The members of this youthful band, comprised of Pelopidas, Epaminondas, Mello, Theoponpus, Pherenikus, Phyllidas, Charon, Kephisodorus, and Damokleidas, all grew up to take major roles in national affairs and perform great services to their country, assuring themselves of a place in history. Among them, Pelopidas was especially notable for his ability and resourcefulness and also for his grace and dignity of manner: "It was this youth who was later to promote the fortunes of Thebes, finally raising it to the rank of head of the league of city-states." And as for Epaminondas, "he had great breadth of character, and proved to be a skillful commander. In later years, together with the others, he expanded Thebes' influence, destroyed its powerful enemy, and caused historians to number him among the noblest men of ancient Greece. Such was the wise and greatly virtuous Epaminondas."

Mr. Inaba told us how these youths heard from the white-haired old man about the wise king of Athens, Codrus, who, when the city was in danger from an attacking Spartan army, sacrificed himself and so saved his country; and of how, when Athens was suffering under the rule of an oligarchy that had no concern for the people's welfare, there arose a hero named Thrasybulus who inspired the cruelly oppressed citizens, mustered military forces, brought down the evil "gang of thirty," and once more made Athens a democracy. The effect of these patriotic tales on the young Thebans was equally inspiring, and they vowed that in future they would devote their energies to the cause of the nation and the people.

Having carried the story that far, Mr. Inaba announced "Well, that's all we have time for today; but it's just the beginning. Around 394 B.C., when these events took place, Thebes was beginning to develop into a powerful city, and Heaven sent this band of youths to make it chief among the allied states. And so they too in turn took on the great work of governing the nation and protecting the people. But let's save the rest for another day."

From then on, Mr. Inaba continued the story whenever time allowed; but since the original book was immensely long, with well over five hundred pages divided into twenty sections in the first volume and twenty-five in the second, he naturally skipped over much of it, recounting parts that seemed likely to appeal to his pupils. He ended with section seventeen of volume two, entitled "The great armies of the various states fight a major battle on the plain of Leuctra," and telling how Epaminondas as general of the allied armies and Pelopidas as second-in-command led a force of one hundred and sixty thousand men into the field on the plain of Leuctra against two hundred and fifty thousand Spartans; and how the two massed armies clashed in bloody battle from eight in the morning until noon on the twenty-first day of the third month in 371 B.C., with the final great victory going to the allied forces led by Thebes.

In 1890, six years after *Keikoku bidan* appeared, Yano published a novel called *Ukishiro monogatari*, with prefaces by various scholars and writers including Tokutomi Soho, Mori Ogai, and Nakae Chomin. Mr. Inaba, however, touched only on the first section of it in class, and then left off telling us about it. I imagine this was partly because, in contrast to *Keikoku bidan*, which was a collection of historical accounts of the ancient West cast in the form of fiction, *Ukishiro monogatari* was purely the product of the author's imagination, and was in addition left unfinished. But he must also have objected to its wildness and absurdity, and he probably felt it was wrong to instill in young children the notion that it was right and proper for Japan to invade the territory of other nations at will and help itself to their possessions.

In his own preface to this novel written some sixty-five years ago, Yano states:

> During the reign of Napoleon I, a certain Belgian painter portrayed the Emperor fallen into hell and tormented by a band of devils. The artist's outrage at the fate of his country, small in territory and population and always subject to the depredations of the French army, all his pain and sorrow at this, found expression in this painting. Now we of later generations feel pity at the sight of it. And if those who read the work that follows should be forced some day to feel similar pity for the author and his nation, would that, too, not be lamentable? Our national power continues to grow day by day, and I trust that such a sad turn of events will not come to pass in *our* case.

When I read these pages and look back on the vicissitudes of the past decades when Japan tried to realize in the lands of Asia the fantasies spelled out in *Ukishiro monogatari* and then found itself reduced once again to the status of a small, weak country, I realize that at times the ebb and flow of a nation's fortunes can be more swift and unpredictable even than the shifts in a man's life, and I am struck by the painful contrast between what is and what has been.

Graduation from primary school

I recall hearing many other stories from Mr. Inaba besides those in *Keikoku bidan* and *Ukishiro monogatari*. There was, for instance, his account of the first part of Bakin's *Yumiharizuki*, in which Tametomo engages in debate with Shinzei at the Sutokuin palace and astounds the onlookers by demonstrating his extraordinary skill with the bow. Mr. Inaba's own skill in the telling was enough to make our palms begin to sweat; but he limited himself to this first section and did not go on to other parts of Bakin's tale, as he had with *Keikoku bidan*.

For the first three years or so of primary school, Sasanuma and I alternately occupied the first place in the class, outstripping all our companions. Then, from the fourth year, two pupils appeared who suddenly overtook us both. One was a boy named Sato Kotaro, the son of a roast sweet-potato vendor who lived near Kyuanbashi; the other was Ise Yoshio, the son of a doctor in Kitajima-cho 2-chome. At Mr. Nogawa's suggestion, both of them were allowed to skip a year when they shifted from the lower to the upper level of our primary school, joining us as second-year students. Soon afterward, Sato entered the Municipal Middle School in Hibiya while Ise went to a branch of the same school in Tsukiji, where the Togeki Theater now is. In those days it was felt that primary school was quite enough for the children of Shitamachi families; and indeed there were few who even finished the upper level of primary school itself. Thus it was unprecedented for the son of a sweet-potato vendor to aspire to middle school, and Sato's parents must have strained themselves to the limit financially for the sake of their talented and promising son.

When I was bested by Sato and Ise, my parents criticized me endlessly, alternating expressions of vexation, contempt, and incitement to do better: "Aren't you ashamed of yourself? ... Can't you work a little harder?" But I never really lost confidence because of my classmates' successes. In fact, it occurred to me later that if I, like them, had been allowed to skip a grade, I wouldn't have had the chance to study under Mr. Inaba. Considered in that light, a delay of one or two academic years was nothing, and it was no doubt my good fortune to have been left behind.

When Sasanuma finished the third year of the upper level, he too entered the Tsukiji branch of the Municipal Middle School, and again I remained behind. (Under the system in force then, the lower level of primary school lasted four years, followed by another four at the upper level, leading to graduation; but a student who had completed the second year of the upper level was eligible to take the entrance examinations for middle school.) Observing Sato, Ise, and Sasanuma, I felt a tremendous desire to advance to middle school myself; but our family circumstances made things difficult, and it was by no means certain that my hopes would be fulfilled. Father's finances were as bad as ever, but Mr. Inaba was encouraging me by all means to go on, and my parents also wanted that, if it were at all possible. So it was decided that I should finish the regular primary-school course of eight years, and then we would see. The family's fortunes might improve by next year, or perhaps our Yamaju uncle would agree to help with school fees—such was my father's facile optimism. My uncle, however, had fairly conservative views on the matter of education. He saw no need for a child of our class to pursue higher studies; it would be far more sensible to send me out as an apprentice somewhere so that I could master the ways of commerce through practical experience. Those were his views, and since he had taken his own eldest son out of school at thirteen and sent him to a broker's in Osaka for training, it hardly seemed likely that he would approve of sending me, his nephew, on for more education at the cost of considerable financial strain on the whole family. Even so, I desperately wanted to get into middle school and had no desire to become an apprentice. So, revolving several uncertain possibilities in my young brain, I passed my last year of primary school in a very dark frame of mind. At the same time, I tried to gain as much as I could from Mr. Inaba's instruction, since the future was so unsure.

After Sasanuma left, another pupil emerged to compete with me for first place in the class; and indeed he took the lead and held it until we graduated, reducing me to second place. His name was Kimura Gakunosuke, and he lived in Yorozu-cho or Hiramatsu-cho near Nihombashi Avenue. I forget just when it was that he began to stand out from among his classmates, but one day Mr. Inaba wrote on the board a poem in praise of Otonomiya Shrine which ran:

> When I think of the past, how sad!
> On a summer's night the moonlight seems cold
> In the shrine at Kamakura.

He did not reveal the poet's name, but he had a broad grin on his face; and before long we learned that it was Kimura's composition. When I recited the poem for my father, he exclaimed "Really? That's damned good for a kid. First he says 'a summer's night,' and then 'the moonlight seems cold'—it's impressive! I bet *you* could never write a poem like that...."

Father had a habit of disparaging his own son more than was perhaps necessary while generously praising other people's children; but it was certainly true, as he said, that the poem was an excellent one for a boy of fourteen or fifteen. I began to have real respect for Kimura and became friends with him, occasionally going to "Gaku-chan's" house to visit. His father seemed to be not very well off, and Gaku-chan had no hopes of going on to middle school. After graduation, a friend of the family found him a job as a waiter at the Mitsui Bussan Company; but later, I understand, he was able to advance to a degree unprecedented for a primary-school graduate and attained quite a high position in the company. And though we have not met for many years, rumor has it that he is alive and well and working somewhere in Kyushu for one of the companies in the Mitsui group.

Thus, among Mr. Inaba's pupils there were two or three who did better in school than I did; but they either left his tutelage earlier than I to attend other schools, or decided to abandon their studies altogether in favor of business. And so it was I who remained longest as Mr. Inaba's favorite pupil. Later, I fortunately managed to avoid the fate of becoming an apprentice and was able to enter the First Municipal Middle School, but I continued to feel great respect for my former teacher and to visit him both at the Sakamoto school and at his home in Mita. In fact, I learned more from him than I did from my new teachers. Earlier I mentioned Oshio Chusai's work, the *Senshindo sakki*: I believe it was around this time that I first read it, at the urging of Mr. Inaba. He was himself reading the works of Wang Yang-ming, such as the *Denshuroku* (*Ch'uan-hsi lu*), and Inoue Tetsujiro's *The Philosophy of the Japanese Wang Yang-ming School*; in short, he was deeply immersed in the study of that school of neo-Confucianism. At his suggestion, I also bought from Maruzen the English original of Carlyle's *On Heroes, Hero-Worship, and the Heroic in History* and fiddled about with that, to me, incomprehensible text, having frequent reference to Japanese translations. This too must have been during my first year in middle school.

Is it only self-conceit that makes me believe that Mr. Inaba at one period had focused all his hopes on my future; that my presence in his class made everything worthwhile? Of course, he was also fond of Sasanuma and Kimura, but they were more inclined toward the sciences and did not show the same strong response to his comments on philosophy, history, and literature that I did. Was it not, therefore, only natural for Mr. Inaba to try to cast me in the same mold as himself? But, despite his literary interests, his real commitment was to the path of the ancient sages, and he seemed to want to educate me after a Confucian or Buddhist pattern. In the end, he was to be disappointed, for as I came to realize that my interest in philosophy, ethics, and religion was a temporary affectation, a mere borrowing from Mr. Inaba, and that my own province was to be that of pure literature, I found myself drifting away from him.

His educational method was close to what would now be called early, elite education, designed to produce a kind of child prodigy, and as such it may have been inappropriate to a Shitamachi primary school of that period. Probably the majority of his pupils were unable to keep up, but he was determined to benefit the few very bright students in his classes at the expense of the duller ones, if necessary. Perhaps that was why, after Mr. Kishi was replaced as head of the Sakamoto school, Mr. Inaba became an object of dislike to the new principal and was ultimately driven from the school where he had taught for so many years.

Whether because there was no appropriate position available elsewhere in Tokyo, or for some other, more personal reason, he became a teacher at an isolated country school in Asahimura, Tachibana-gun, Kanagawa Prefecture, where I sometimes visited him until my university days. I do not know how the public transportation to that area is now, but in those days one would get off the Tokyo–Yokohama line at Tsurumi, cross a line of low hills that stretched to the northwest, and then walk the equivalent of several blocks through the rice fields. It was a very out-of-the-way spot, and the small building that served as a school directly adjoined the teacher's house. Since Mr. Inaba was the sole teacher, the school must have offered only the first four years, the lower level of primary education; and while he was teaching his pupils in the afternoon, his wife would assemble the young women of the village and give them lessons in needlework. One year I went to Futagomura in Tachibana-gun to visit Onuki Shosen and then set off on foot for Asahimura. I was surprised to find that there was such undeveloped country in a prefecture bordering Tokyo: the way from one village to the other seemed immensely long, and apart from the regular undulations of the hills that covered the countryside, there was no variation in the extremely monotonous landscape.

Among the "Songs of the Eastlands" in the *Man'yoshu* is a poem:

> That lass
> Of Koba in Tachibana
> Must be longing for me now—
> How sweet!
> I think I'll go to her.

It has been suggested that "Koba" here is a place name from this area of what is now Kanagawa. Moreover one hears that there are many old tumuli and shell mounds in the region, as well as the tomb and shrine of a figure from antiquity, Ototachibana-hime. With its air of archaic simplicity, this may have been the ideal place for Mr. Inaba, one where he could lead the life of a country schoolmaster and think back with reverence to scholars like Nakae Toju, the Sage of Omi. At any rate, for a long time he lived in retirement in Asahimura; but then sometime in the 1910s he stopped teaching and, moving closer to the railway line, began to work as a watchman at a warehouse in Shibaura belonging to the Oki Electric Company. He commuted each day on the Tokyo–Yokohama line from a station in Kawasaki until one December morning in 1926 when, trying to run across the tracks, he was struck by a train and killed. He could not have been more than fifty-four or -five at his untimely death.

The Akika Academy and the Summers' school

A year or two before I was to graduate from the Sakamoto school, I entered two private part-time academies to study classical Chinese and English for a while. I did so because I feared that I might not be able to proceed to middle school and therefore wanted to acquire as much knowledge as I possibly could over and above the regular curriculum. Father took my feelings into account and made the effort to send me to these private schools despite our financial difficulties.

It seems to me that I began to attend the classical Chinese lessons first, before going to the Summers' place in the foreign quarter in Tsukiji. At any rate, in those days there were a number of Chinese schools in Shitamachi run by retired classical scholars. For example, in the Minami Kayaba-cho neighborhood, there was one operated by the well-known calligrapher Takabayashi Goho; it was on the south side of the street that ran through the old official residences district, which you reached by passing through the grounds of the Yakushi Temple in the direction of Kitajima-cho. It was rather grand in appearance and had many students.

The school I went to, however, the Akika Academy, was more like one of the little temple schools for children of the Edo period. There was a famous scholar named Nakamura Akika who was active around that time, but it had no connection with him. I no longer remember the name of the people who ran the place, but it was located around No. 41 or 42, Kamejima-cho 1-chome, on the way from my house to Wakita's—

the former constable's son. Wakita enrolled first and urged me to join him, but later I became the more enthusiastic student. There was a weather-beaten sign in front announcing the school's name; then, passing through a narrow entranceway, one entered a six-mat room where the lessons were held. I received instruction here for about thirty minutes each morning before going to the Sakamoto school. My teacher was an elderly man of about sixty with a long beard, who emerged from the inner rooms emitting from between his whiskers quiet belches redolent of the bean-paste soup he had apparently just had for breakfast. He would seat himself across from me, a traditional low desk between us. There were many of these desks piled against the walls, and the whole scene reminded me of the point in the Kabuki piece *Terakoya* (The Temple School) where Matsuo says "There is one desk too many here!"

I went to primary school wearing only a kimono, but for my Chinese lessons I donned a *hakama* divided skirt as well. Okinawan-style tatami are no longer much used anywhere, but in those days they were always to be found in the classrooms of private schools of this sort. When you knelt in formal posture with your lower legs folded under you, without a cushion, the pattern of the tatami would impress itself on the insteps of your bare feet.

Beginners were usually given easy texts in classical Chinese with a Japanese flavor, like the Edo Confucianist Rai Sanyo's *Nihon gaishi* (An Unofficial History of Japan) and *Nihon seiki* (Political Chronicles of Japan); but I had already been introduced by Mr. Inaba not only to Oshio Chusai's *Senshindo sakki* but also to works like Otsuki Bankei's *Kinko shidan* (Historical Tales, Old and New) and to collections of classical Chinese poetry by Chinese and Japanese authors, even if in an unsystematic way. Thus at the Akika Academy I was able to progress from the Confucian *Great Learning* through the *Doctrine of the Mean*, the *Analects*, and the *Mencius* and on to *Eighteen Histories Abbreviated* and *The Pattern for Prose*. Proceeding through these works meant for the most part simply reading them aloud, turning the classical Chinese into its Sino-Japanese equivalent; it did not involve explanation or discussion of the meaning of the text. Passages like the well-known one from the commentary on the *Great Learning* would be gone through in this way, with the teacher first reading the text aloud and the student then repeating it:

> If the mind is not present, then one looks but does not see; listens, but does not hear; eats, but does not know the flavor. This is what is referred to in the saying "Cultivating oneself lies in rectifying the mind. . . ."

If one managed to repeat the text aloud properly, with correct grammatical constructions and appropriate readings for the characters, no more was required, and the teacher moved on to something else.

The characters in the main text of the *Great Learning* in the woodblock edition were about the size of No. 1 type in movable print, and the instructor would move his pointer from character to character as he read. Primary-school teachers were generally equipped with rattan canes but teachers of Chinese always had text-pointers. These could be of wood, bamboo, ivory, or metal, and some were engraved with fine patterns; usually, though, they were simple bamboo sticks, very much like those used in washing and stretching cloth. It was one of these that my instructor employed, tapping each character as he read on.

The Akika Academy, where he lived with his wife and a daughter of about twenty, did not seem to be doing all that much business; even so, if one went very early in the morning, it was often his daughter who gave the lesson, and in time these "substitute lessons" became more frequent than the regular ones. The girl was not a great beauty, but her full, fair-skinned, vigorous-looking body was attractive, in the plain *meisen* silk kimono she wore. My attitude toward her was entirely that of a pupil toward his teacher, so I had no special longings in that direction. Still, sitting just across from her, with only the narrow desk separating us, I sometimes felt the fragrant warmth of her body wafting toward me. Then too, as with her father, there was often a strong scent of bean-paste soup about her early in the morning, and the odor of her breath at such times worked on my feelings in a curious way. In her nasal voice, reminiscent of the high-pitched whirr of cicadas in season, she would read from the appointed text: "It is written in the *Book of Songs*,

> How young the peach tree,
> Its leaves how full!
> When this girl marries,
> It will be well
> With the people of that house.

The benefits she brings to the people of that house will later serve the people of the whole nation."

Not satisfied simply with reading such passages aloud, I sometimes asked questions about their content, and both the teacher and his daughter were able to respond easily to the kind of problems I raised. Even at home, if I asked Mother about some difficult characters in the *Eighteen Histories Abbreviated*, she could usually give me the answer. In those days, even among townsmen, any household with a decent income would have the children (including the girls) take lessons in classical Chinese, just as children study English nowadays. My mother too must have benefited from such training when she was a girl.

For a long time I believed that the young woman at the Akika Academy was the teacher's daughter, but then one day I heard from someone that she was in fact his mistress. The source could have been Wakita, relaying the rumors in the neighborhood; or the ladies gossiping at the well on the way from my house to the Kairakuen; or, again, the hairdresser who came regularly to tend to my mother's coiffure. At any rate, it was soon the talk of the neighborhood: "They say she's the old man's mistress! Isn't that something?"

As for English, it was Mr. Inaba who first taught me the rudiments of that language. Lessons in English began from the third year of the upper level at the Sakamoto school, though whether it was a required subject or an extracurricular one I am not sure. (They also taught accounting, and I sometimes had to carry a ruler and ledger with me to and from school; but I never cared for this subject and made little effort to master it.)

I remember how, at the outset of the first English lesson, Mr. Inaba taught us the equivalent of "I have a pen": *Ai habu e pen*. We were all interested and excited, repeating the phrase over and over. This was the first time I had ever heard or spoken an English sentence. The teacher wrote it out on the board in the English alphabet and had us learn it. (We learned other words too, but I have forgotten which.) From then on for some time we concentrated on spelling (which we pronounced "speruring"): "b, a, ba; b, i, bi; b, o, bo," etc. We looked at the letters on the blackboard and repeated them after the teacher: we were practicing production of English sounds, without concern for meaning. In short, the English taught in Meiji primary schools was little more than the alphabet itself; it was of no use at all, not even permitting us to read the first book in the National Readers series.

However, the foreign quarter in Tsukiji had a private English school where only real English ladies taught, without even one Japanese instructor. This district was located in Akashi-cho, Kyobashi Ward, and had been open as a residential area only to Westerners until the treaty revision

The foreign quarter in Tsukiji.

of 1899, after which they were allowed to live wherever they liked. Even after the revision, however, the district preserved something of its former character, at least for a time: there were rows of exotic-looking Western-style houses, and the whole atmosphere was somehow un-Japanese. And it was here that the Summers, an English family, had opened a private language school. Its official name was the Obun Seiko Gakkan, the Grand Academy of European Culture: this was written in Chinese characters on the wooden signboard that hung on the painted clapboard gate. No one called it that, though; it was usually referred to simply as "Summers'."

I say "an English family," but there is no way of knowing whether they were all really English, or whether it was simply a random collection of Caucasians of various types who had drifted over from Shanghai or Hong Kong. They were a group of "lady foreigners" of charming appearance ranging in age from eighteen or nineteen to about thirty, and claimed to be sisters. There was also an old woman who was said to be their mother, but there was not a single male in evidence. The youngest, as I remember, was a girl named Alice, who said she was nineteen. Then there were the others—Lily, Agnes, Susan. All of them could understand some Japanese and write the simple *katakana* script, but Lily was unusual in that she spoke Japanese fluently, almost like a native. Finally, it must be said that, for sisters, they bore very little resemblance to one another.

There were three or four levels of classes at the Summers' school, and each level was divided into two groups, one of which met at around four in the afternoon and the other at seven in the evening. Each class lasted about an hour, and the sisters divided the teaching responsibilities among themselves. When I entered the school, Alice, the youngest, was in charge of the first-level afternoon class, which consisted of about thirty students. From the second level on, a conversation book written by the Summers was used; but, at the first level, Alice would write a piece of English dialogue in each student's notebook and then distribute a handout with the readings of the English words spelled out in *katakana* alongside— this was our text.

In addition there were private lessons for rich, upper-class students who had some proficiency in English conversation; apparently they used no textbook, but engaged in "free conversation." Seeing that even the ordinary classes cost one yen per month, the charges for the private lessons really must have been quite steep. One yen was by no means an insignificant sum for that time, but since the British standard of living was so much higher than our own, and since they were regarded as representatives of a more advanced, civilized nation come to enlighten our backward countrymen, everyone accepted such high fees as natural and inevitable.

As I mentioned before, I started attending Summers' at the urging of Wakita, who had enrolled earlier. His two elder brothers had been attending for some time; and while I was still in primary school, the second eldest went to America to study. The eldest brother also made the trip overseas to visit him. I remember how Wakita left school early and in great high spirits on the day his eldest brother returned from abroad. As a present from America, he had brought Wakita a bicycle which the boy gleefully rode around on for a long time afterward. (This must have been when I was in the second or third year of the upper level.) Anyway, through his brothers, Wakita was on friendly terms with the Summers from the very beginning. Lily, who was so good at Japanese, would engage him in conversation, laughing and exchanging compliments with him in a very relaxed way.

The first floor of the house was taken up by classrooms, while the ladies lived on the second floor. When lessons were over, the foreigners all went upstairs, and we ordinary Japanese were never permitted a glimpse of those upper precincts. Wakita claimed, though, that his brothers had sometimes been allowed to go up, and that he too had had a chance to ascend the stairs, just once. He said that the second-floor rooms were furnished with luxurious carpets and fine lace curtains, and that the arrangement of the chairs and tables and beds made one feel as if one were actually in a foreign country: it was like awakening to a strange new world. Then, lowering his voice, he told me something that he appeared to have learned from his brothers: that the foreign women were in the habit of secretly accepting upper-class Japanese gentlemen as "clients." He went on to say that some Kabuki actors, including the late Baiko, came to Summers' to buy (or was it, perhaps, in their case, to be bought?). Furthermore, the so-called private lessons were all somewhat suspect, being held on the second floor at night. As evidence that Wakita's accounts were not just fabrications, there is an article by Kawarazaki Gonjuro which appeared in the "Conversation Salon" column of the *Tokyo News* for January 27, 1954. In it the author touches on the Summers' establishment:

> There used to be a private English school called Summers' in Tsukiji, and I was sent there for lessons. Before I began going, the late Uzaemon and Baiko as well as Fukusuke (the late Utaemon) attended the same course, but their real purpose lay somewhere other than in learning English. There was a pretty young girl named Susan among the teachers, and it was for her they went.

Later, when Sasanuma also enrolled in the school to keep me company, he and I were discovered stealthily mounting the staircase for a peek at the second-floor rooms, and ignominiously chased away. Actually we did succeed in catching just a glimpse of the gorgeous, brightly colored furnishings within.

My first teacher, Alice, was in fact a rather ugly girl, but she was then in the full bloom of youth, no more than three or four years older than I. At the same age, a Japanese girl would still have been very girlish indeed and quite incapable of teaching a group of students. But in the eyes of the poor stunted Japanese of that time, she appeared a person of dignified and commanding presence, a member of the superior White race; so we were all well behaved in class, at least at first. Her features were almost the opposite of the Japanese ideal of beauty in those days —a narrow, oval or "melon-seed shaped" face; she was pug-nosed, with a large mouth and prominent, fleshy cheeks. But a closer look revealed a charming, innocent expression, hair that was thick and glossy, and a figure bursting with youthful vigor. I now had the chance steadily to inspect a Western woman for the first time in my life, and as I watched Alice in the thin, short-sleeved blouse which showed most of her arms on that hot summer's afternoon, I was lost in wonder at the extraordinary whiteness of her skin, almost doubting the evidence of my eyes.

Alice was big in stature but really still a child at heart, and she would burst out laughing at the slightest excuse. Even during class she would begin to titter at nothing at all and have to struggle hard to control herself; and the many apprentices and Ginza shop clerks in the afternoon class soon began to make fun of our young "Miss Alice," teasing her in vulgar Japanese and greatly enjoying it when they succeeded in making her blush a deep red.

I never had the courage to tease Miss Alice, but I did walk about with Sasanuma and Wakita and peer over the fences of the Western-style houses in the area. If we found any foreign children playing there, we tried to provoke them with our newly acquired English. Once, having mastered the word "pickpocket," I tried it out on a cute little boy about two or three years younger than myself, whom I discovered crouching by a flower bed in his yard: "Yuu, aaru, e, pikkupokketto!" I said. The little boy, without the least show of anger, replied clearly "I am *not* a pickpocket!" I was incredibly happy because I had been able to communicate in English, and for some time after that, I loitered in front of the same house every day; but the little boy never appeared again.

If I still remember clearly that the monthly fee for the Summers' lessons was one yen, there is a good reason. At some point both Sasanuma and Wakita quit going and I had to keep on by myself. To get to the Tsukiji foreign quarter I used to go through Kamejima-cho, past the Hatchobori triangular intersection, across Nakanohashi or Inaribashi bridge, and then on in the direction of Teppozu. But on dark winter nights on the way home, one could be sure that the young hoodlums who liked to prey on still younger boys would be lying in wait somewhere in the shadows of the foreigners' houses or the church. I was terrified of them, so I often played truant from my evening lessons, going instead to local fairs here and there or just strolling about Ningyo-cho, Nihombashi Avenue, or the Ginza, killing time. I managed to keep my parents in the dark about this, but once when I had stayed away from English class for a full month, I was hard put to know what to do with the one-yen bill my mother gave me for that month's tuition. Ten or twenty sen would have been easy to use up, but it was very difficult to spend an entire yen in installments and still keep the matter hidden from my parents. For a long time I kept the one-yen bill tucked into a school book I carried around with me. Sasanuma Gen-chan, who knew I was skipping classes, found out about the money as well: "Hey, I bet that's the Summers' money!" he declared. At any rate, I ultimately found some way of spending it all.

Despite my fears and evasions, I continued to attend the Summers' school at least sporadically until I moved from the first level taught by Alice to the next class. The school, however, was extremely casual and haphazard in its organization; instead of giving set examinations at fixed intervals, they simply admitted anyone to a higher level whenever it seemed convenient to do so. Thus I cannot be sure exactly how long I stayed there altogether. Their selling point was instruction in English by young, attractive English ladies; but the methods of instruction were almost whimsical, lacking any system. In fact the program was of little help in language learning. I remember how once in the second level, which was taught by either Lily or Agnes, we were told that the Twelve-Story Tower in Asakusa was best rendered in English as "the Eiffel Tower." I could understand the "Tower" part all right, but I could not imagine what "Eiffel" might mean. Why not simply translate the Japanese for "Twelve-Story" into its proper English equivalent? Unable to accept the translation, I opened the Summers' conversation text and saw the same thing printed there. I realize now, in retrospect, that since the Eiffel Tower was only built in 1889, and the Asakusa tower three years later, the one in Paris was not yet at all well known here, so the Summers probably just made their translation carelessly, in an off-the-cuff sort of way. Even so, their failure to provide any explanation of what in fact the Eiffel Tower was, and their use of the English rather than the French pronunciation of the word, give a fair indication of the quality of their teaching methods.

A *passion for literature*

My passion for literature first blazed up under the encouragement of Mr. Inaba, but I was interested in it even before then. *Boys' World*, for example, was first published in the New Year of 1895, a little over two years after my arrival at primary school. I imagine I got hold of it almost as soon as it began to appear, and came to know Kyo no Warabei's name from its pages. This, as I had learned very early on, was the pen name of Horino Yoshichi, who owned the Bunrokudo bookshop and was a graduate of our school; and I had sometimes hung about in front of his shop hoping to satisfy my curiosity with a glimpse of him.

The first time I ever tried to write something of my own was also quite early, while I was a fourth-year student in the lower level, under Mr. Nogawa. Around that time there was a boy in our class called Hashimoto Ichimatsu, the son of one of the Kabuto-cho people; and a literary-minded youth named Nomura Kotaro was in the habit of visiting Hashimoto's house frequently. Nomura was the son of a broker in Kakigara-cho and had left school without graduating, during his third year at the Middle School of Commerce and Industry in Otemachi. Now he was taking it easy, not working at any job. But he had learned something about how to write, especially in the elaborate style then in fashion, and he had attended an art school and so gained an understanding of painting. He began putting out a small group magazine called *Students' Club*, with the assistance of Hashimoto and Washio Shinsaku, another classmate of ours who lived in Kabuto-cho. The magazine came out monthly and was written in brush and ink on inexpensive Edogawa paper; approximately seventy or eighty pages were bound together to make up the single copy of each issue, which was then passed around among the members for perusal. The cover picture and other illustrations were mostly Nomura's work; and the other boys, under his direction, wrote biographical sketches, fiction, and articles on geography, natural science, painting and calligraphy, and miscellaneous subjects. In time Sasanuma, Wakita, and I all joined the group at Hashimoto's urging. Soon afterward, the "editorial office" was moved from Hashimoto's house to Sasanuma's room at the Kairakuen; at the same time both the format and the content of the magazine were greatly improved. For a while we tried hectographic printing rather than writing things by hand, but it made the magazine seem somehow dull so we reverted to brush and ink.

Almost every day we met in the "editorial office" at the Kairakuen and, under the guidance of Nomura as principal writer, debated matters of style and evaluated the strengths and weaknesses of one another's compositions. Nomura was six or seven years older than the rest of us, and as he sat at his desk in the office writing articles or drawing illustrations, we would gather around and watch with bated breath, trying to model ourselves on him. Nomura looked very pleased with himself and wielded his brush with confidence, occasionally stopping to lick its tip or glance up and give us, his audience, a sharp, penetrating look.

We all thought how splendid it would be if we could write and draw like him; there was not one of us who wasn't consumed with envy of his talents. The maids at the Kairakuen, however, disliked his habit of looking at people with an upward flick of the eyes, and secretly criticized him: "It's the most important time of life for him, and he ups and quits middle school. Then, instead of studying or going to work as an apprentice somewhere, he just wastes his time playing games with kids. What does he think he's doing? He'll never amount to anything much, that's for sure!" But to us at that time he was an irreplaceable teacher and guide to the world of literature.

Even after reaching the upper level of primary school and coming under the direction of Mr. Inaba, we continued for a time to publish the magazine, changing its name from *Students' Club* to *The Garden of Learning*. Mr. Inaba helped us with the work, writing something for each issue; and I believe his commentary on the *Shiramine* story in *Tales of Rain and Moonlight* appeared in our magazine. He also read our compositions with great care, making copious notes and comments in the margins; thus the magazine steadily improved in quality and range.

As Mr. Inaba's influence on us grew, however, Nomura Kotaro's naturally and inevitably began to wane. Nomura himself seemed to realize that he was not as brilliantly talented as we had all at first thought, and began to regret spending "the most important time of life" in a useless way. He suddenly went to Yokohama to work as a live-in apprentice, trying to learn commercial law. But he was at a difficult age, neither quite young nor quite old enough to permit things to go smoothly; both he and his employers were dissatisfied, and he soon returned to Tokyo. Then he found a job at the Fukagawa branch of the Tokyo Printers, working on block copies for lithographs, and eking out his pay by doing watercolors on the side. But Mr. Ito Shinsui would be a better source for the details of his life at that time than I. Shinsui was several years younger than either Nomura or I, and during his years of struggle to put himself through school he worked as a junior employee at the same printing company. Sometime around 1910, Nomura introduced me to him, and Shinsui was kind enough to send me a scroll of a Japanese beauty that he had painted. Unfortunately the painting, a souvenir of my friendship with Nomura as well, was lost in the fires that accompanied the Great Kanto Earthquake of 1923.

Around, I think, 1907, when I was enrolled in the First Higher School, on a night in late autumn, I was seized with a desire to see Nomura, with whom I had lost contact for a long while. I found him living in a small, shabby house beside the Tomioka Park in Fukagawa. It was the first time I had visited his home, having always met him at the Kairakuen or on the street somewhere. According to my father, Nomura's father had once been an influential owner of a rice dealership; but he had failed in business in his last years and had acquired a rather bad reputation even among the Kakigara-cho people. At the time I am describing, he had already died, and Nomura, the only son, was living alone with his mother in this dismal dwelling by the park. He was by now twenty-six or -seven, an age at which he might have been expected to have a wife; but it was no doubt out of the question for financial reasons. Besides, though he had a handsome face, he was obviously scrofulous, with a thin, unhealthy look about him; his physique looked as if it would not bear the strain of marriage.

A chill passed over me as I stood in the narrow entranceway and saw what a wretched and forlorn existence the two of them shared, mother and son. Apart from the entrance, there was only a six-mat room, where Nomura sat with a book (perhaps Shimazaki Toson's *Wakana-shu* collection of poems) open to an illustration of the priest Saigyo gazing at the moon; above the figure of Saigyo was written the first half of one of his well-known *waka*: "Does the moon make me sad, bidding me lament? . . ."

It was a very bright moonlit night and the branches of the trees in Tomioka Park had a velvety sheen. Even the shabby interior of the Nomura house had the clear, pellucid atmosphere of an aquarium about it. When Nomura's mother entered from the kitchen with the tea things, I was struck by the beauty of her face, seen against the *shoji* bathed in moonlight. I have not forgotten even now my wonder at what I saw. Given Nomura's age, his mother must have been at least forty-three or forty-four. But never were the words "a lingering beauty" more apt. The most extraordinarily beautiful persons are to be found in the most unlikely places in this strange world of ours, I thought to myself.

My own mother's complexion was exceptionally fair. But this woman was larger than my mother and her hands and feet were correspondingly long and slender. In contrast to Nomura, who was thin and undernourished-looking, her whole body was plump and full, and her skin very fair. Her face too was large, and there was about her something of the stateliness of the actors who portray women on the Kabuki stage. I had often deplored my father's irresponsibility in letting a splendid woman like my mother eke out a hard existence in poverty. Now I wanted to attack Nomura too on the same grounds.

Yet in reality what drew me to her was precisely the fact that she was no longer young, and was poor, and wore such old, faded clothes. Her rather dull, slack skin had nonetheless a strange charm: she possessed a kind of weary beauty which no young woman has. And, above all, she was quite unaware of this. Nomura too seemed not to realize his mother's true worth. If he had, surely he would have mentioned her before, yet he had never breathed a word to me that he had someone like this hidden away. Could it have been that, remembering her as she was in her younger days, he was embarrassed to let others see her now, in such shabby circumstances?

Perhaps it was the sorcery of that strange moonlit night that made me feel as I did. At any rate, it seemed to me that with a mother like this there was no need for Nomura to take a wife: with his income it would be all he could do to care for her alone; to protect and cherish her should be enough for him. He need have no other purpose in life apart from that.

It was some years later that I learned after the event from Maruyama Kin'ichiro, the son of a thread merchant in Kayaba-cho, that Nomura and his mother spent their last weeks lying side by side on their sickbeds in that wretched house in Fukagawa, the one preceding the other in death by only a little. This Maruyama was another classmate of mine from primary-school days; his father was a kindhearted man and had been trying to look after Nomura for some time past. When both he and his mother became ill enough to be confined to their beds, the Maruyamas, father and son, took turns nursing them. Nomura was dying of consumption; I do not know what the mother died of, but she was probably of a delicate constitution and had become infected with his illness. Nomura survived his mother by a few days, which at least was a blessing both for the unhappy mother and her unfortunate son.

If I have devoted too much space to this account of Nomura Kotaro's end, it is because I am convinced that the debt I owe him for his help during my formative years is a heavy one.

Looking at Kimura Shoshu's *History of Children's Literature*, I see that Iwaya Sazanami's *New Hakkenden* began to appear in serialized form in *Boys' World* in January 1898, when I was thirteen. It was the work that gave me my first real taste of the pleasures of fiction—the creation of an imaginary world, and the joys of entering into it and wandering freely there. Up to then I had read, and even written, some fictional pieces; but I had never encountered anything that unfolded before me a realm as bold, unfettered, and free as Sazanami's romance. I could hardly wait for *Boys' World* to appear each month, and as soon as I got it my eyes flew to the first pages, where the *New Hakkenden* was to be found. I knew that the story of the papier-mâché dog that gives birth to eight living, moving, papier-mâché puppies was an impossibility; but far from finding it unnatural, I even wished it could come true. And when I saw Takeuchi Keishu's illustrations, in which the papier-mâché dogs walked and ran about, I felt so even more strongly. I yearned for that world of the *New Hakkenden* the way an adolescent going through puberty yearns for love.

It was just around this time that I happened to see Sazanami at the Kairakuen. I had heard from O-ito that he sometimes came to the restaurant with Ozaki Koyo and other writers. Then one day, when I was visiting Sasanuma in his room, a message came from O-ito: "Iwaya Sazanami and Ozaki Koyo are in the private dining room on the second floor. Why don't you try to get a look at them from the garden?"

Sasanuma and I rushed outside. There were one or two other guests besides the famous pair of authors; but, as luck would have it, the others were seated on the far side of the room, while Sazanami and Koyo were leaning against a round Nagasaki-style table near the veranda facing the garden. Sasanuma and I stood on tiptoe and craned our necks but at first managed to see only the celebrities' heads. Then both of them leaned forward and turned their faces toward the garden—had they perhaps noticed us? Sazanami had an empty glass in his hand and, as he turned it this way and that, his gaze met mine for a moment. Even though my friend assured me that it was in fact the famous Iwaya Sazanami, I had my doubts at the time. But when I was first introduced to him around 1910 (in the lobby of the Yurakuza theater, at a preview by the Free Theater Company), I recognized the face I had seen some ten years earlier, and memories of my boyhood came flooding back. As for Ozaki Koyo, that distant glimpse of him at the Kairakuen was all I had; I never actually met him.

Commenting on the *New Hakkenden* in his *History of Children's Literature*, the author wrote: "It is very grand in conception and full of wondrous transformations. With each issue and each installment, there are events that almost defy the imagination. Keishu's illustrations also endow the inanimate papier-mâché dogs with a kind of soul, giving them the appearance of the utmost liveliness."

Certainly the *New Hakkenden* was a particularly ingenious, elaborate, and painstaking work, among all Iwaya Sazanami's numerous stories of wonder and romance. I do not know whether my extraordinary affection for it was due to a desire to create the same kind of fictional world myself one day, or simply to a more casual attraction to the kind of realm Sazanami depicted so well. Probably in those days I did not yet make a distinction between the pleasures of reading and of writing fiction. Even so, it was around that time that I began to feel the stirrings of the creative urge within me, to know the joys of letting the mind wander at will in an imaginary world, and to acquire the habit of yielding to those joys. At the same time, oddly enough, I was benefiting from an elitist education at Mr. Inaba's hands and becoming familiar with works that were far too difficult for a boy of my age. Thus, the realm of the romances coexisted with a more adult one in my mind and heart. While dreaming of a land in which papier-mâché dogs go through all sorts of adventures, I also studied the *Historical Tales, Old and New* in classical Chinese and learned the *Tales of Rain and Moonlight* in the language of Edo Japan.

My second-favorite novel in *Boys' World* was *The Beggar Prince*, a translation of Mark Twain's *The Prince and the Pauper* done by Kawa Sanjin and revised by Iwaya Sazanami, with the assistance of Kuroda Kosanjin. This did not weave the strange fantasies of the *New Hakkenden*, but had rather the charm of a story that might actually have happened. Yoda Gakkai's *Lord Toyotomi* was another novel that was serialized over a long period in the same magazine, and it marked the beginning of my interest in historical fiction. Apart from these, the stories from *Boys' World* that remain in my memory are Koda Rohan's *The Storehouse of Civilization* and *Holiday Tales* and Morita Shiken's *Fifteen Boys*. Rohan in particular was recognized from about this period, even by us children, as an outstanding figure, of a quite different caliber from ordinary writers.

I must not omit the name of Owada Tateki, the author of *Tales from Japanese History*. He later became famous throughout the country for his *Song of the Railroads*, but *Tales from Japanese History* was published several years before that long poem. It consisted of a series of twenty-four volumes, beginning with "The Foundation of Japan," with illustrations by Yamada Keichu, and ending with "Weihaiwei," illustrated by Koyama Mitsukata. I read most of the series, and found it hard to put aside some volumes, reading them over and over again: "Lord Sugawara" (illustrated by Kajita Hanko), "The Soga Brothers" (Ogata Gekko), "Sagami Taro" (Yamanaka Koto), "Kuro Hangan Yoshitsune" (Tsutsui Toshimine), "Akushichibyoe Kagekiyo" (Mizuno Toshikata), "Lord Kusunoki" (Kobayashi Eiko), "Prince Morinaga" (Utagawa Kunimatsu), and a number of others. According to the *History of Children's Literature*, only the first volume in the series was actually written by Owada Tateki; the rest were done by his most talented disciple, Fukushima Shiro (later the president of the *Ladies News*). But of course I knew nothing of that. I was not especially drawn to the literary style of these historical tales but rather to the subjects themselves, as well as by the fact that they were presented in a clear, straightforward way, easy for a child to understand. "Kuro Hangan" and "Akushichibyoe" reminded me once again of the dramas about Yoshitsune and Kagekiyo performed by Danjuro or Kikugoro, which I had seen when I was a little boy. "Lord Kusunoki" and "Prince Morinaga" were excellent preparation for the *Taiheiki* which I was soon to begin to read in the original version. I am not sure how much of the content of these stories was based on historical fact, in the strict sense, or how much of an admixture there was of fiction and legend; at any rate, at that age I did not feel much of a gap between historical fact, traditional legend, and fiction. Plays like *Yoshitsune and the Thousand Cherry Trees* and *Kagekiyo Victorious* were like bridges spanning events that actually happened in the past and purely fictive stories. I crossed those bridges freely, moving from one shore to the other, at play in the realms of the imagination.

I daresay I was not alone in my confusion: all the children of that period probably went through a stage when they made no distinction between history and fiction in their reading. I recall that it was just after passing through that phase that I began to read the *Taiheiki*. Mr. Inaba always gave as examples of its most beautiful or impressive passages "Lord Toshimoto Returns to the Kanto Again" in the second chapter; "Prince Morinaga Flees to Kumano" in the fifth; "A Superb Horse Is Presented to the Emperor" in the thirteenth; and "The Demise of the Former Emperor" in the twenty-first. And truly for a long time I was charmed by the way the seven-syllable, five-syllable alternating rhythms felt on the tongue in such lines as "The fallen flowers lie beneath his feet like snow, as he wanders the spring paths of Katano when cherries bloom..." from the description of Lord Toshimoto's return to the Eastlands; or "He gazed across the harbor at Yura, where in the offing a boat drifted, its rudder useless, over wave upon wave, as numerous as the flowers in bloom along the shore..." from the section on Prince Morinaga's flight to Kumano. Still finer, I thought, was the description in classical Chinese style of the death of the former Emperor Go-Daigo in chapter twenty-one. Even after I had begun to realize the vulgarity of the seven-syllable, five-syllable form and try to free myself from its influence, I still admired this classical Chinese mode for its combination of melodic beauty and depth of meaning.

Let me give two examples:

How sad, that though the Emperor's state is as lofty as the North Star and he is attended by the Hundred Officials, ranged like constellations in the heavens, there is none to attend him on the road that leads to the Underworld's Nine Springs. What can be done? Though a myriad troops are gathered like clouds around the distant Southern Hills, there is no warrior to stop the advance of the foe known as Impermanence. The officials feel as if their boat had capsized in midstream, and they were being buffeted by the waves; as if the only light in the darkness of night were quenched, and they must go on into the deep night rains....

and

In the depths of the desolate, lonely hills, a bird cries: the sun has set. The grass grows high upon the earthen mound; their tears are spent, but not their grief. The former officials and the Empress weep and gaze with longing at the clouds, like those above Lake Ting; they vent their grief upon the moon above, and, feeling the sharpness of the winds that blow across the grave, think back upon their parting from their lord; they long for him like flowers glimpsed within a dream.

In such passages, the most important thing is the combination of Japanese and Sino-Japanese sounds and the fascination that comes from the very forms of the ideograms themselves. The contents are quite meager; yet at the time passages like these were generally regarded as examples of excellent style. One reason was that, during the Meiji period, the Mito School's advocacy of reverence for the Southern Court in the fourteenth century was still very influential. Thus, just as the youth of today sing the praises of democracy and peace and oppose war and fascism, so we in those days hated the injustice of the Ashikaga clan, who had usurped power from the imperial family, and naturally felt pain, sorrow, and indignation at the sad end of the Emperor of the Southern, or Yoshino, Court and his champion, Kusunoki Masashige. As a result, we were all the more stirred by the kind of writing I have quoted above.

It was in January of 1890 that Koda Rohan wrote his work *To a Skull*, and in May of 1892 that he wrote "This Day," the first part of *A Tale of Two Days*. One notices a strong tendency toward elaboration of style in his works of this period, a reflection of contemporary literary trends:

Ah, short is the faithless night, and when dawn comes our brief love ends. You are a flower that floats upon the Katashina River, its fragrance borne by the swiftly flowing stream, ten leagues in an instant. I am the willow that stands immovable on the riverbank, its shadow sinking to the river's depths. . . .

Abandoned by the world, and abandoning it, he repeated the words, now roughly, now in forlorn tones, until he had no breath. Glaring into space, he brandished his bamboo staff and beat the trees and stones by the roadside like one insane. Wildly leaping, he beat them. Inflamed with rage and gone quite mad, he disappeared, no one knew where.

These passages from *To a Skull* have a rhythm all their own, and to read them with our contemporary sensibility is unquestionably to risk many misunderstandings. Still, we can recognize that the work as a whole represents a world that only Rohan could have created. It is one of the treasures of Japanese literature, and one can easily imagine the amazement that must have greeted its publication. I first came to know it around the age of fourteen or fifteen, and the phrase "You are a flower that floats upon the Katashina River" has stayed with me to this day.

The solitary pine gazes at me with a consoling look because my life seems chill and friendless: like the pure waters of a mountain stream, I will not go out into the dusty world. O pine, you do not change your color throughout the three long months of winter, and I too shall never change my resolve. If, when a strong wind blows, you cast your green shadows on the book upon my table, I shall entrust the smoke of incense to the wind, till it wreathes the flowers on your branches. . . .

What folly, to preach the Law of Deliverance to me, now that the very Buddha is my enemy. . . . The fireflies in the marshes rise to the heavens, and dark and evil thoughts rage like flames upon the earth. It is in darkness that I move and work, in darkness that I laugh and take my rest—I am the Great Lord of the Land of Eternal Night, deep within this massy earth! . . . The Buddha is Wisdom, I am passion. If the waters of His Wisdom fill a thousand-league lake, then the flames of my passion will shoot up a thousand leagues. Where my foot treads, the willows will turn crimson and the flowers green; where I point my finger, crows will turn white and herons black. I shall make the heavens stand still and cause the earth to dance; I shall darken the sun and moon, and dry up rivers and seas. Great rocks and stones will laugh and sing, withered grasses bloom and be fragrant. Lions will nuzzle at Beauty's knees, and great serpents disport themselves where infants sit. The north wind will be warm, and snowfalls scented; pebbles will sparkle like gems and dry wells spout forth fine wine. Butterflies will sing songs of love in the depths of night. The deaf will hear, and the blind see. Swords and spears will be turned into ploughshares, and the torture vats made into warm baths for the weary. . . .

"This Day," from Rohan's A *Tale of Two Days*, borrows its central idea from the Edo-period writer Ueda Akinari, so the author cannot lay claim to much originality: in that sense it is inferior to his *To a Skull*. Yet I think one can argue that "This Day" is clearly superior, for example, to Takizawa Bakin's treatment of the Shiramine section of his *Yumiharizuki* romance. One assumes that Rohan, who had great confidence in his own talent, wished to test himself against his two great literary predecessors of the Edo period. His gorgeous style in this work may seem too flowery in comparison with the elegant simplicity of Ueda Akinari's *Tales of Rain and Moonlight*; but only he could have achieved such consummate beauty in the mixed Sino-Japanese style, employing to the full the richness of diction and rhetoric found in both Japanese literature and the Chinese Buddhist scriptures.

In time, our group magazine, *Students' Club* and later *The Garden of Learning*, stopped coming out, and nobody seemed interested in planning another one. So I worked at polishing my writing by myself; and when I happened to produce something I liked, I would take it to Mr. Inaba for evaluation. The idea of "polishing" or "elaborating" one's writing is either forgotten or disregarded by most people nowadays, but in the past it was one method of "doing literature." For a time, as one means of improving my style, I excerpted the best passages from a variety of classical works and then tried to incorporate them in a new work of my own. And with Rohan's "This Day" I carefully copied out the last half and committed it to memory, as I did also with certain passages in Owada's *Tales from Japanese History*.

There may be some who would say that the great amount of energy earlier writers expended on developing a rich, highly ornamented style was wasted effort; but until my childhood years at least, anyone who wanted to enter the gates of literature had to pass along that road, and I for one do not think that kind of effort went unrewarded.

The author and his wife, Matsuko, in 1936.

Tanizaki in his seventies.